and they don't appeal to me."

—GRAHAM PARKER

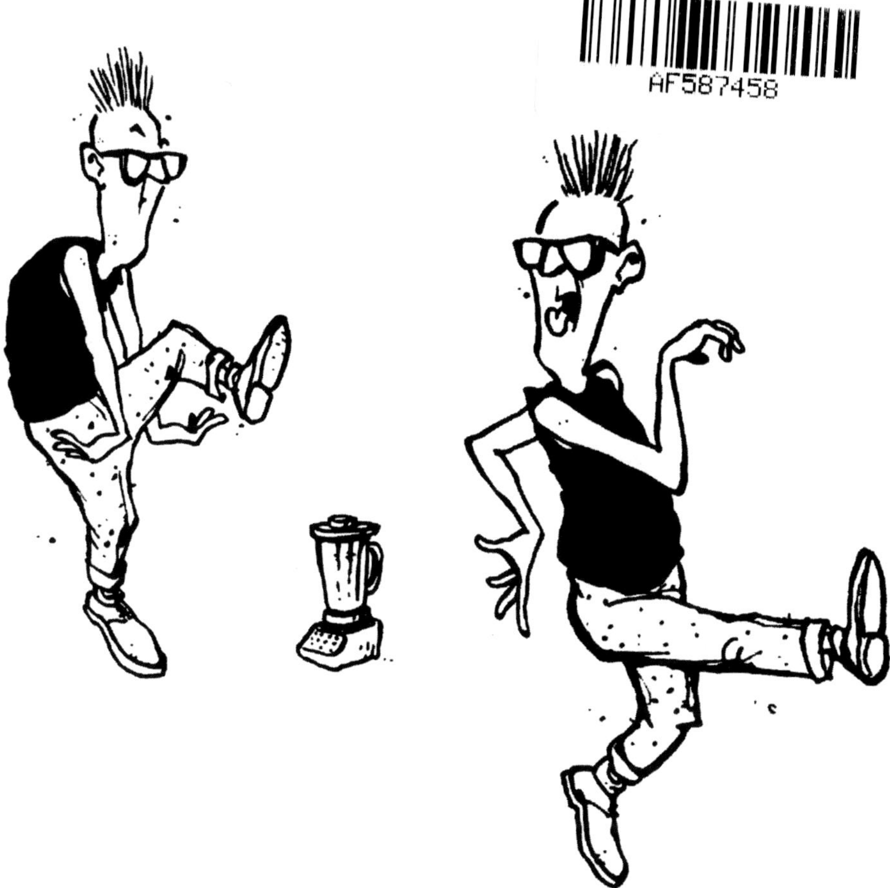

Also by Rod Filbrandt

Dry Shave: (a comic strip)

Rod Filbrandt

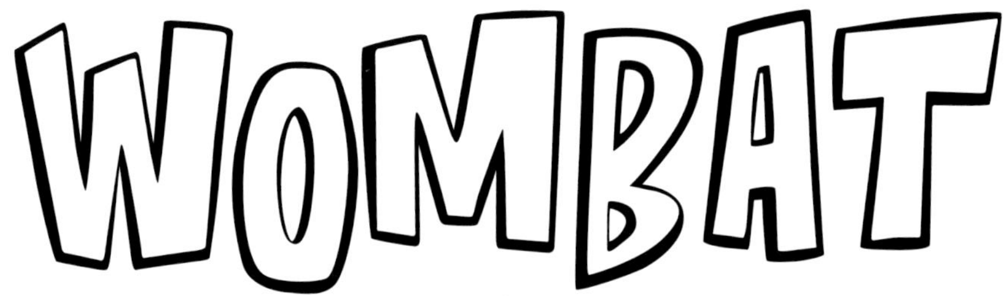

The Collected Comic Strip

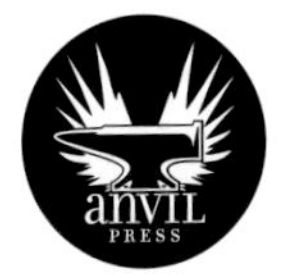

Anvil Press Publishers Inc.
P.O. Box 3008, Main Post Office
Vancouver, B.C. V6B 3X5 CANADA
www.anvilpress.com

Library and Archives Canada Cataloguing in Publication

Filbrandt, Rod
Wombat : the collected comic strip / art by Rod Filbrandt ; foreword by John Armstrong.

ISBN 978-1-897535-30-1

I. Title.

PN6734.W64F56 2010 741.5'971 C2010-901067-1

Printed and bound in Canada
Book design by Derek von Essen

Represented in Canada by the Literary Press Group
Distributed by the University of Toronto Press

The publisher gratefully acknowledges the financial assistance of the Canada Council for the Arts, the Book Publishing Industry Development Program (BPIDP), and the Province of British Columbia through the B.C. Arts Council and the Book Publishing Tax Credit.

For Lynda

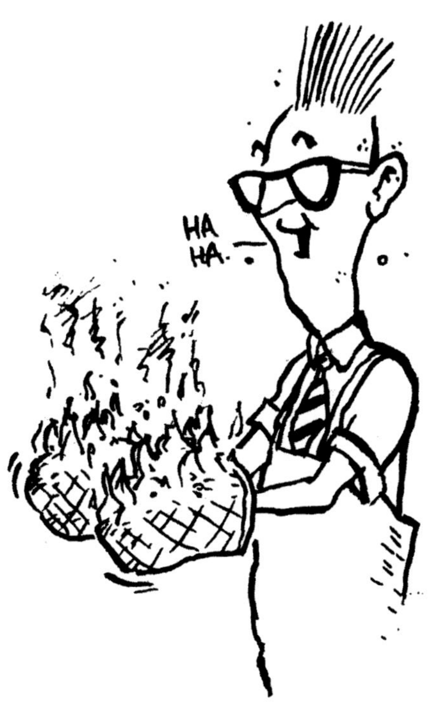

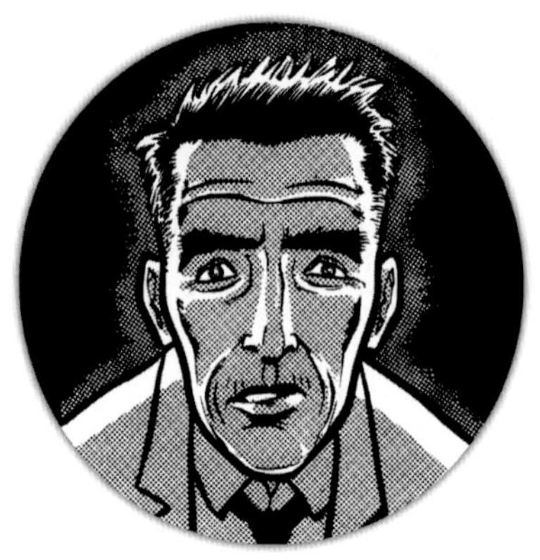

"Down these mean streets a man must go who ... talks as the man of his age talks, that is, with rude wit, a lively sense of the grotesque, a disgust for sham, and a contempt for pettiness."

—Raymond Chandler
The Simple Art of Murder

Foreword

Down those rain-slick, neon-lighted streets Chandler sent Philip Marlowe; meanwhile, a few blocks over, several decades later, Rod Filbrandt sent his own knight errant and holy fool—a man in a porkpie hat, a sportshirt and pants that can only be described as trousers. A man known by a single name only: Wombat.

If that was his name. We never knew—he was both strong and silent, and generally either drunk or hungover. It could be either and you would be hard put to tell the difference. If the eyes are the windows of the soul, the rollerblinds on these peepers were permanently drawn and the only clues were the muffled sounds issuing from within ... Robert Mitchum singing calypso, or Miles blowing Birth of the Cool and the tell-tale, pneumatic inhalation and sickly sweet odour of what the hepcats call "tea."

Was there ever a character such as this? If every generation gets the comic strip they deserve, what did we do to merit this? Dick Tracy upheld the law, Charlie Brown played out the existential quandaries of contemporary life, Heathcliff frankly sucked balls—but none showed the one quality which separates great art from mere entertainment. We're talking about Personal Growth.

In the earliest strips our man was a disaffected youth of indeterminate age with a "pineapple" hairdo, evidently a member of the punk rock generation. But within two brief years of that landmark first appearance he had undergone a metamorphosis and reappeared as the now-iconic hipster *manque* we know so well. Cast into a black, white and grey universe whose angular buildings and off-kilter signage both threaten and mock, our hero trudges towards the horizon under a sunless sky and a starless night, seeking the faint light that blinks its semaphore message "cocktails."

Cicero nailed it: *"O tempora, o mores"* or put another way: *An refert, ubi et in qua arrigas?* Indeed. The Latins had a word or three for it.

Wombat was never afraid to ask the Big Questions, slurred and garbled though they might be, and the answers much the same. Who was he, really, and where has he gone? Who knows, and who can say? Like a phone number written on a wet bar napkin, the truth is hard to discern.

Truly, we can only sigh at the memory and say: "Now he belongs to the ages."

Put that in your pipe and smoke it, bub.

—John Armstrong (aka "Buck Cherry")

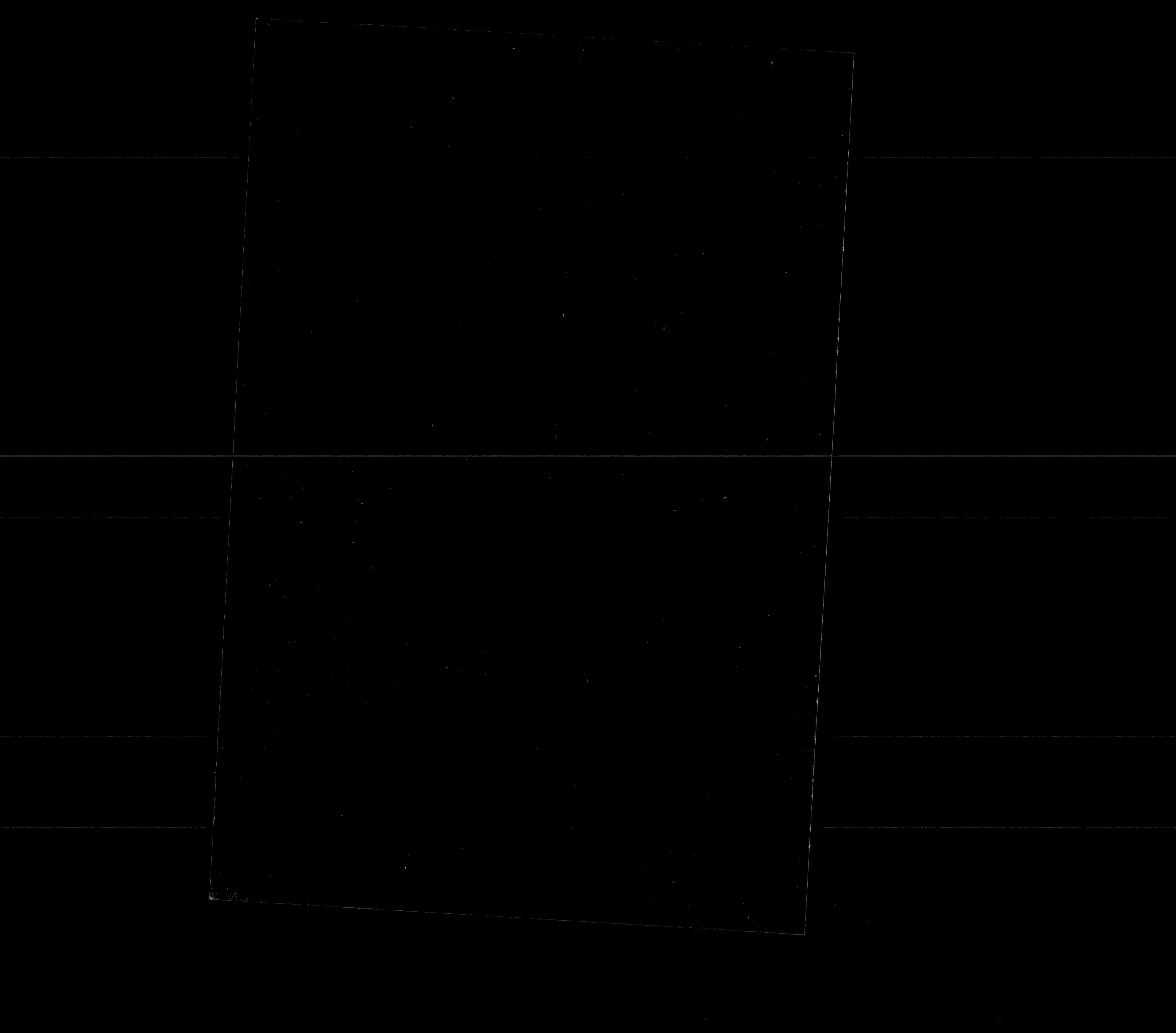

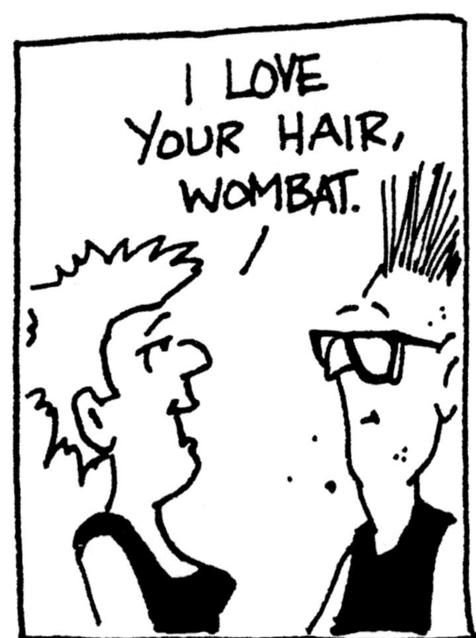
I LOVE YOUR HAIR, WOMBAT.

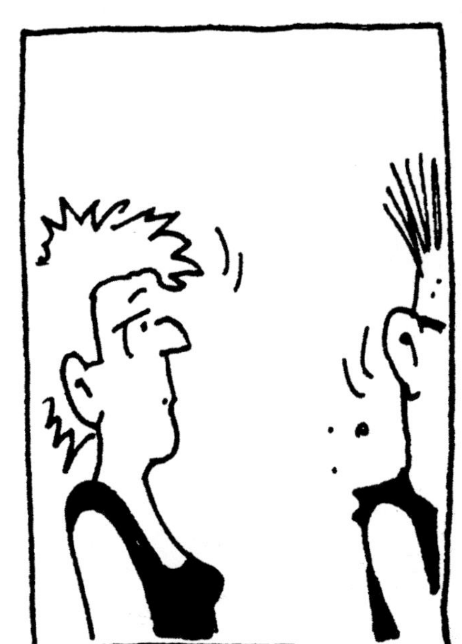

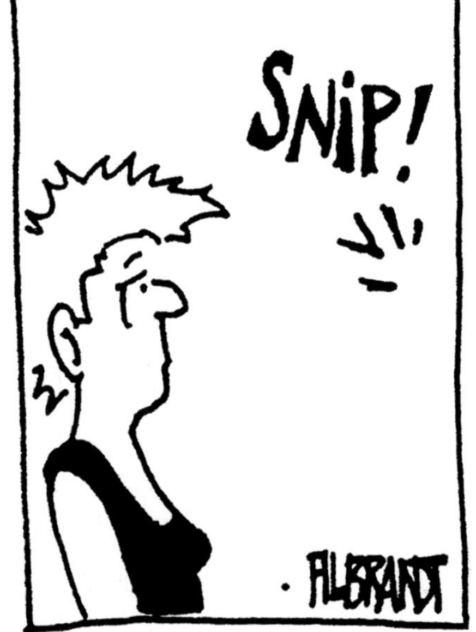
SNIP!
FILBRANDT

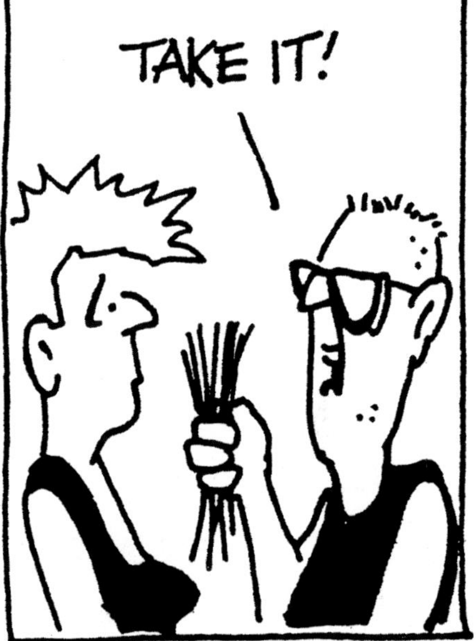
TAKE IT!

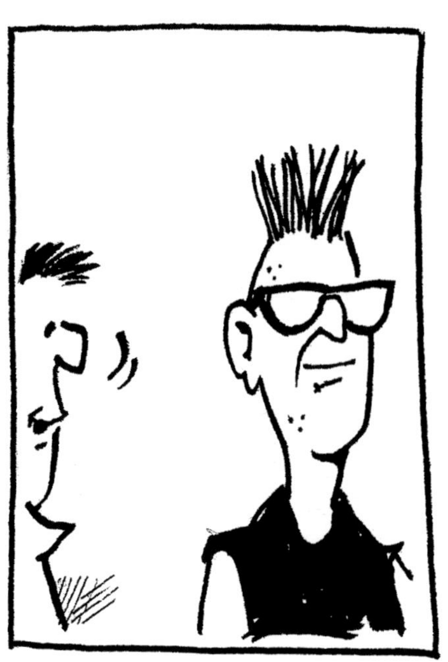

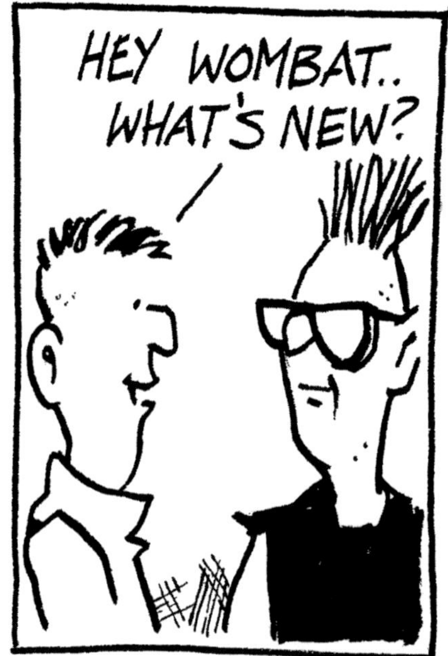
HEY WOMBAT..
WHAT'S NEW?

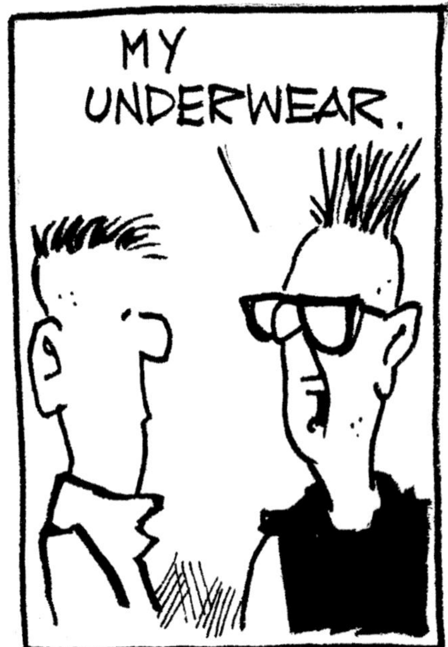
MY
UNDERWEAR.

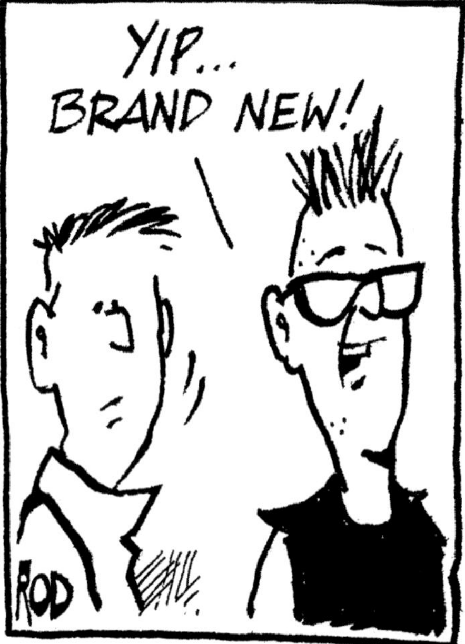
YIP...
BRAND NEW!
ROD

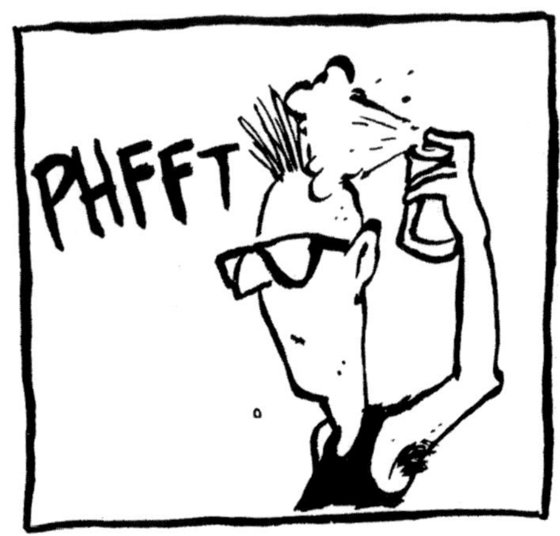
PHFFT

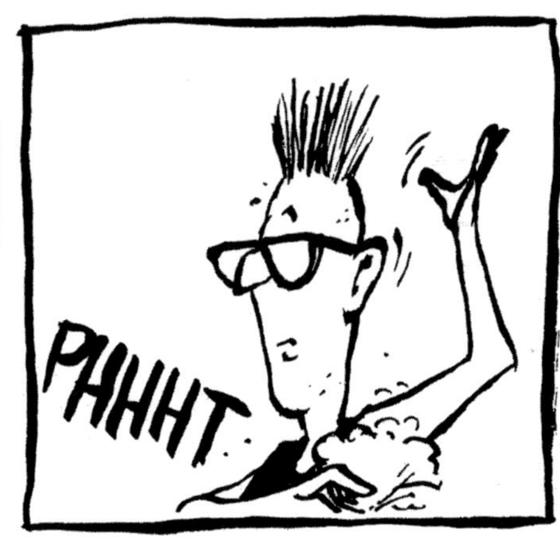
PHHHT

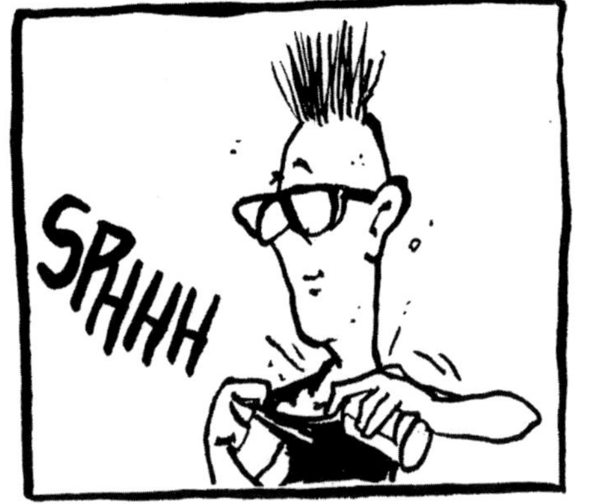
SRHHH

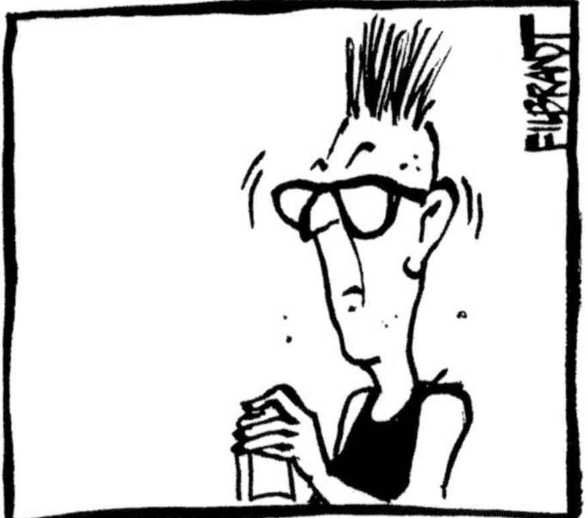

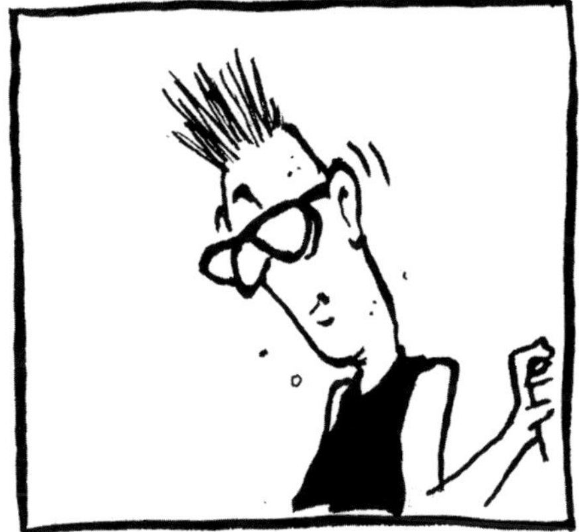

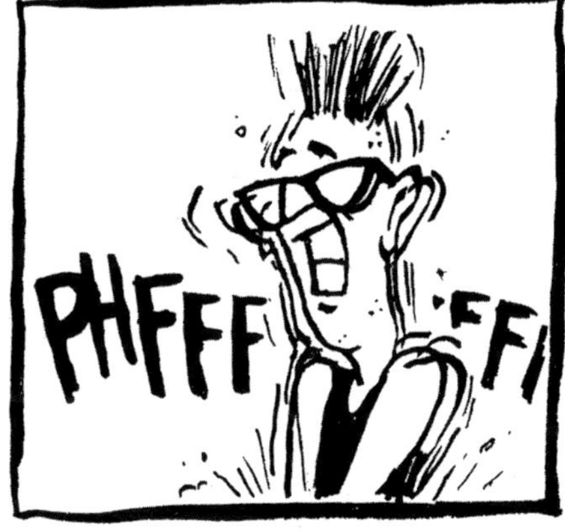
PHFFF
FFI

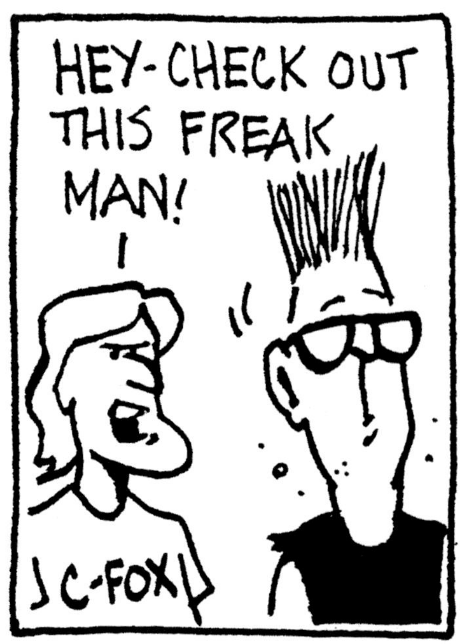
HEY-CHECK OUT THIS FREAK MAN!
J C-FOX

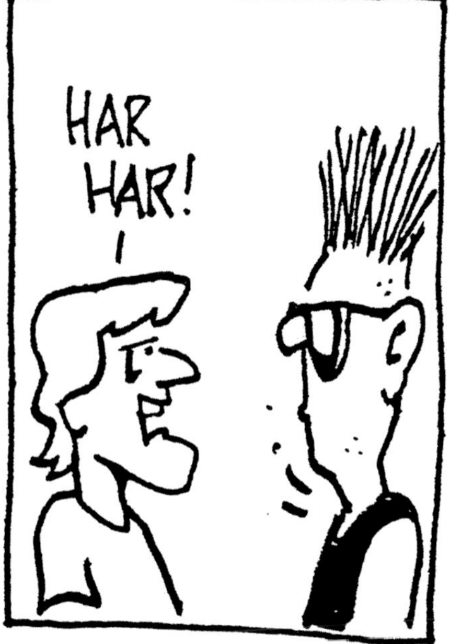
HAR HAR!

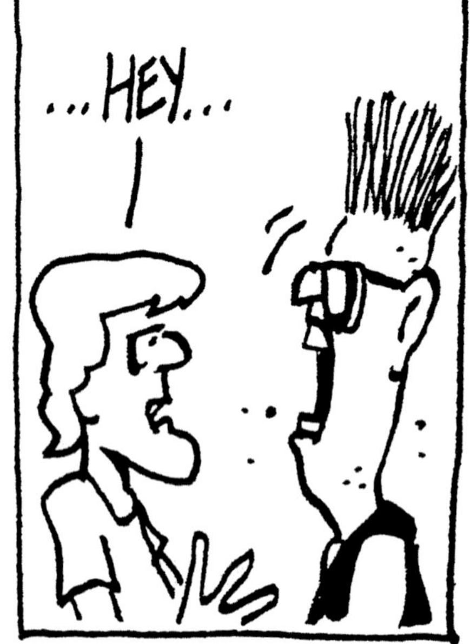
...HEY...

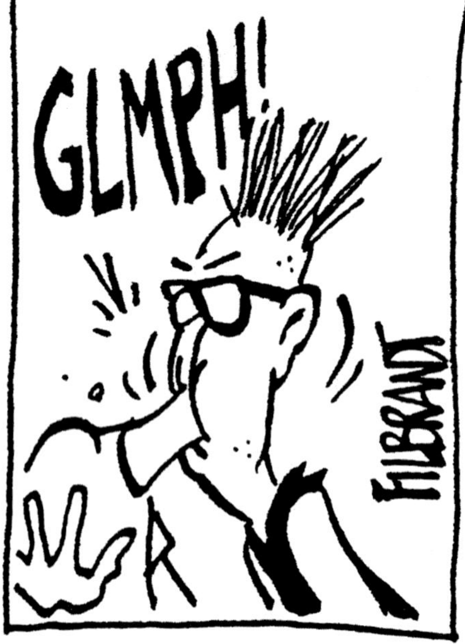
GLMPH!
FILLBRANDT

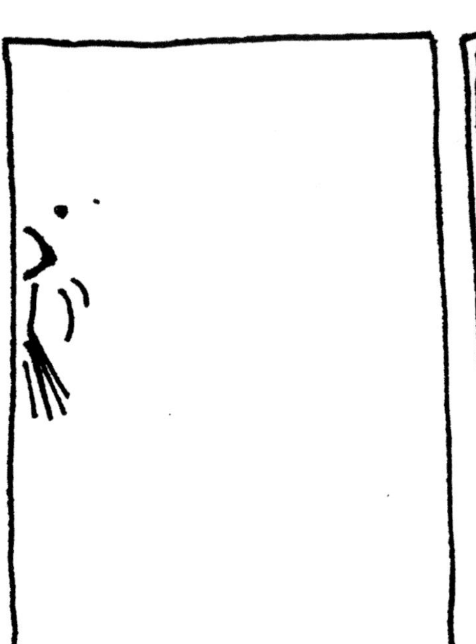

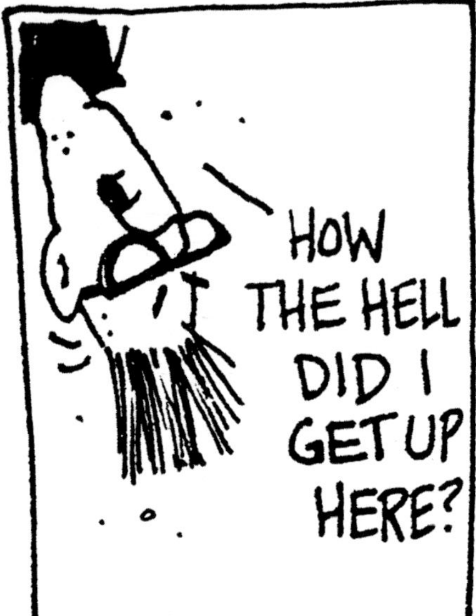
HOW THE HELL DID I GET UP HERE?

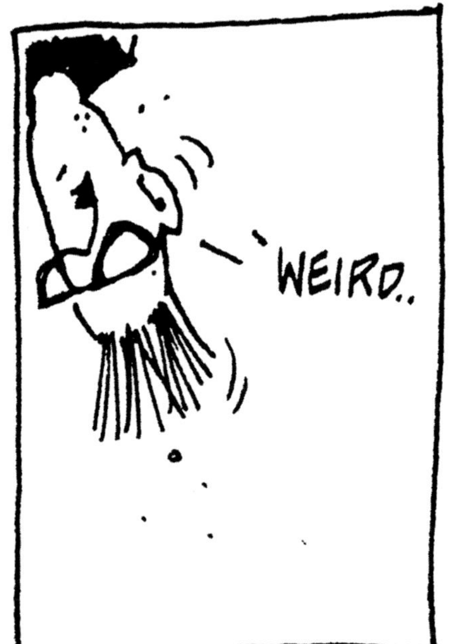
WEIRD..

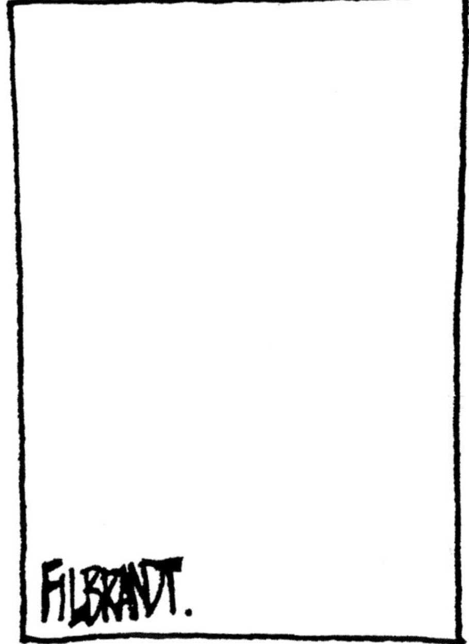
FILBRANDT.

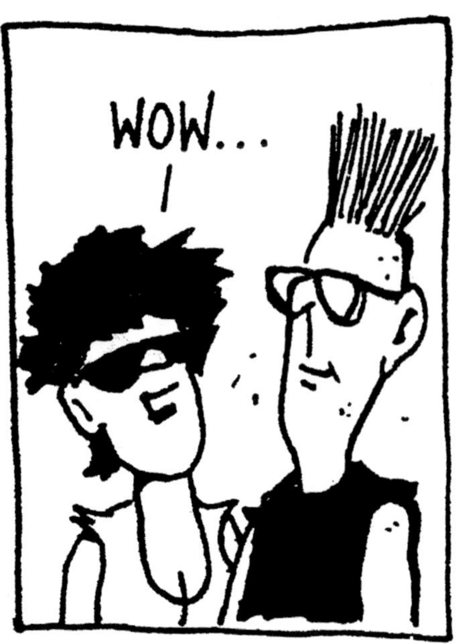
WOW...

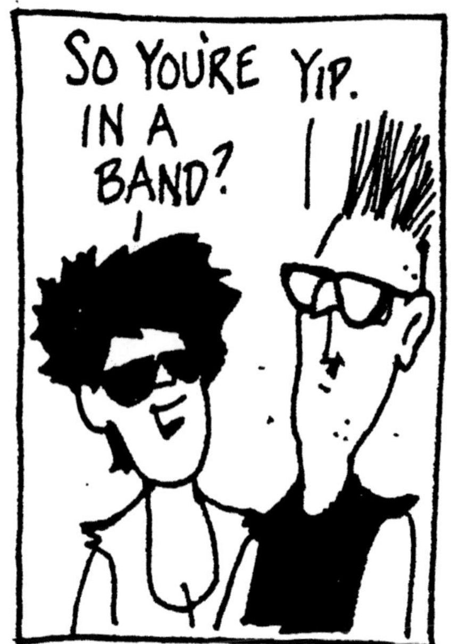
SO YOU'RE IN A BAND?
YIP.

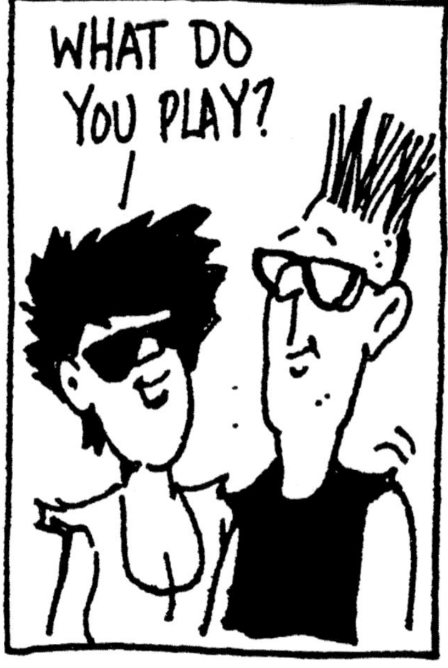
WHAT DO YOU PLAY?

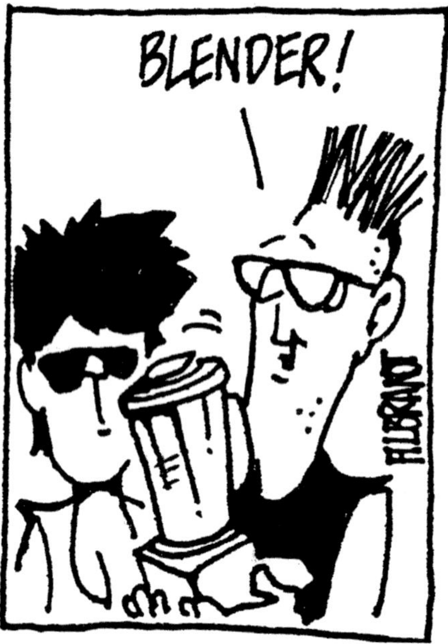
BLENDER!

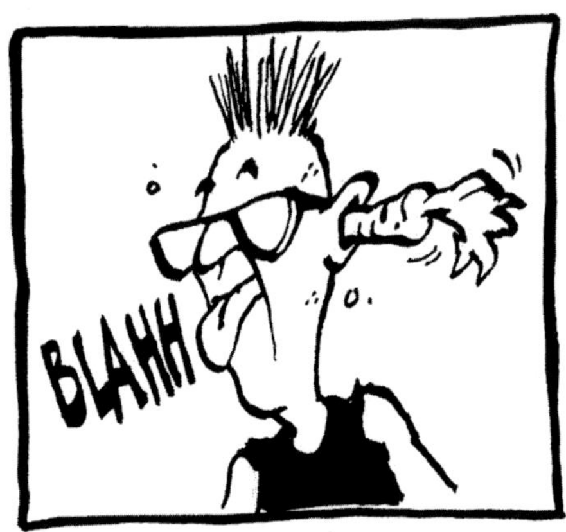
BLAHH

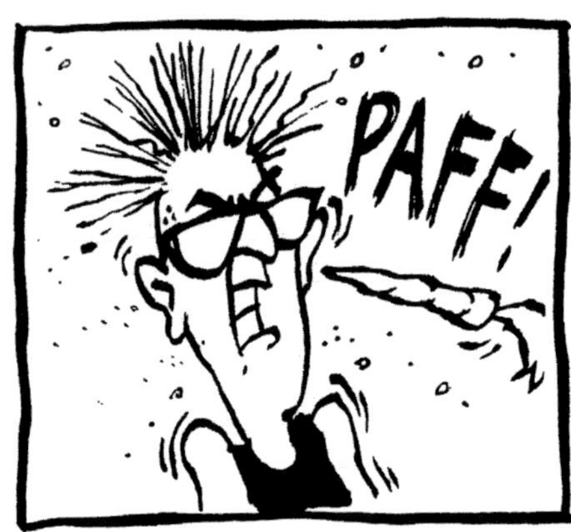
PAFF!

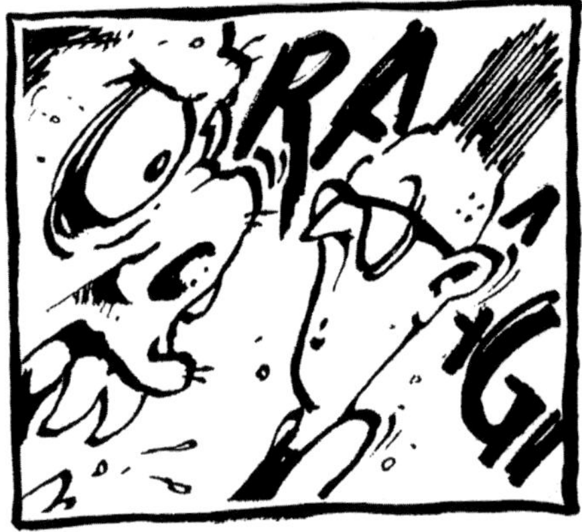
RA

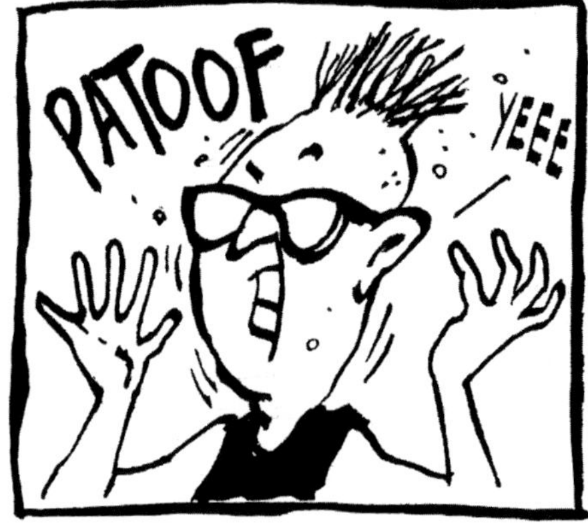
PATOOF
YEEE

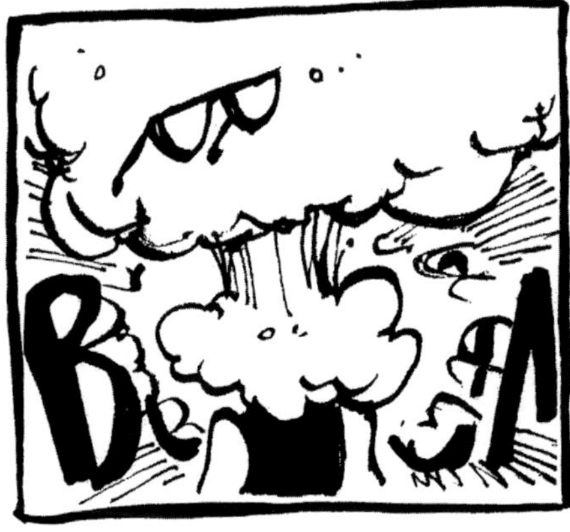

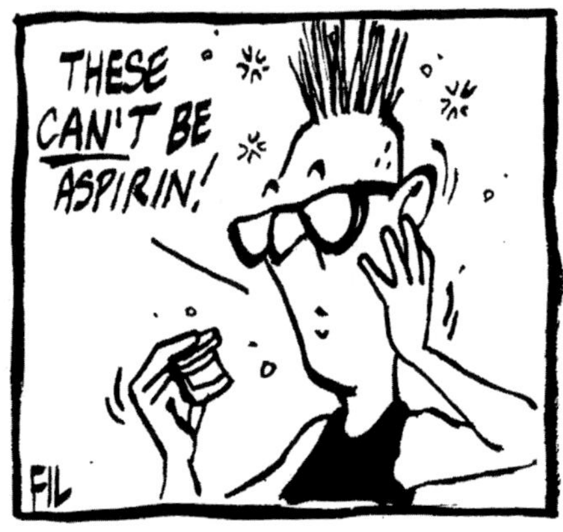
THESE CAN'T BE ASPIRIN!
FIL

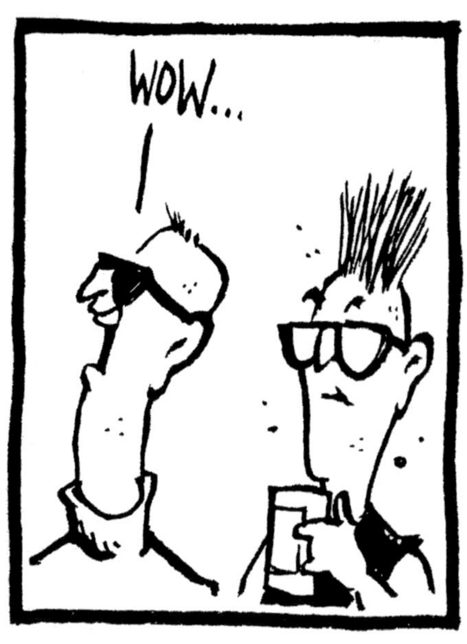
WOW...

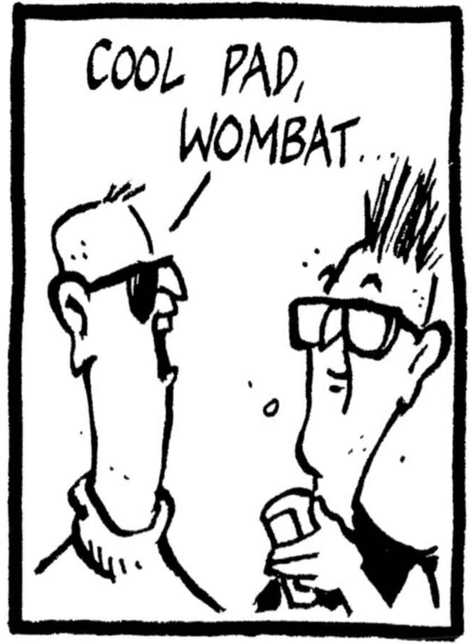
COOL PAD,
WOMBAT...

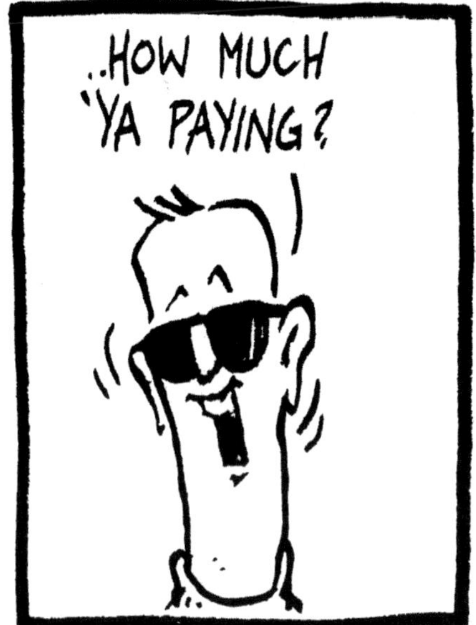
..HOW MUCH
'YA PAYING?

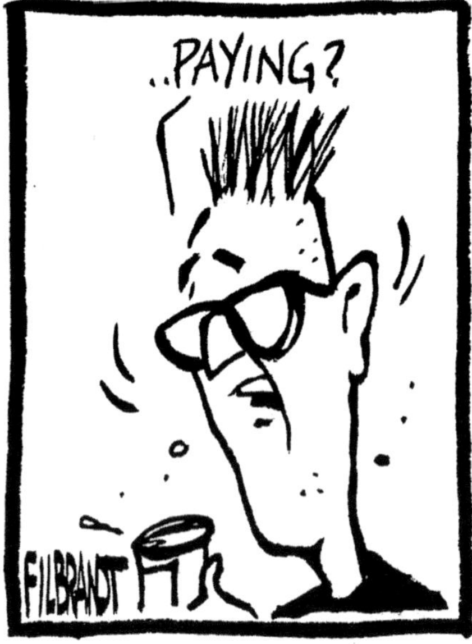
..PAYING?
FILBRANDT

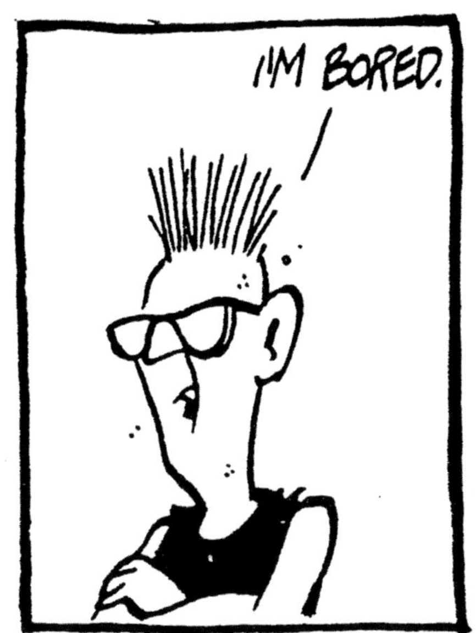
I'M BORED.

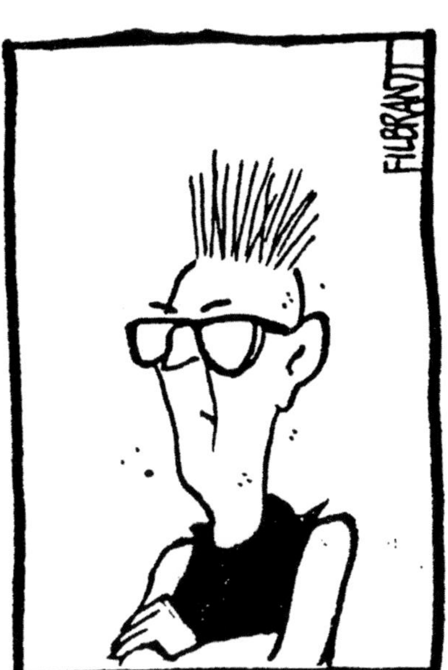

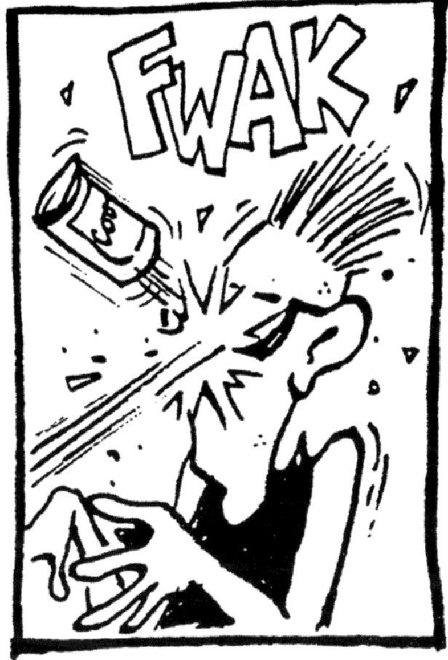
FWAK

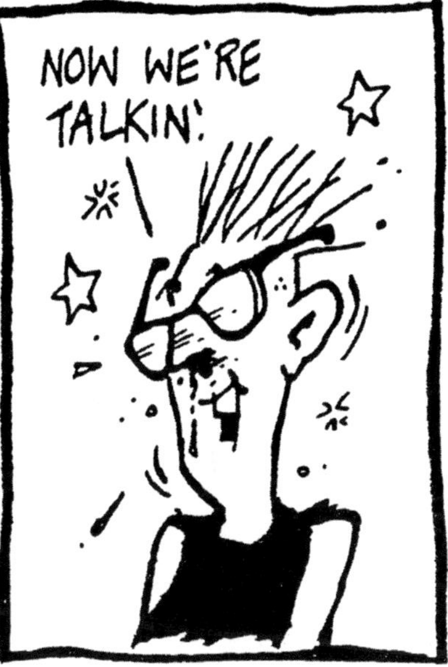
NOW WE'RE TALKIN'.

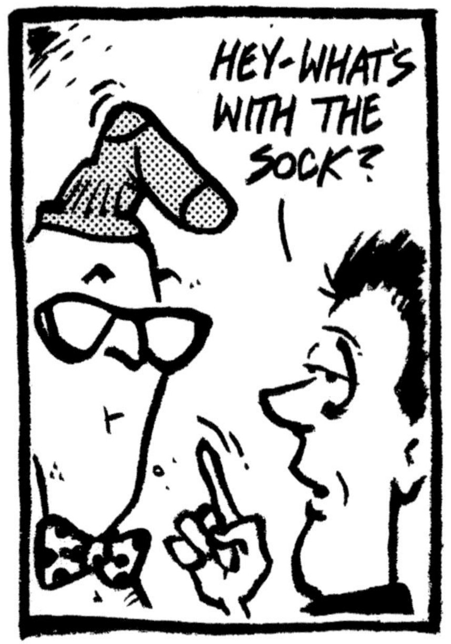
HEY-WHAT'S WITH THE SOCK?

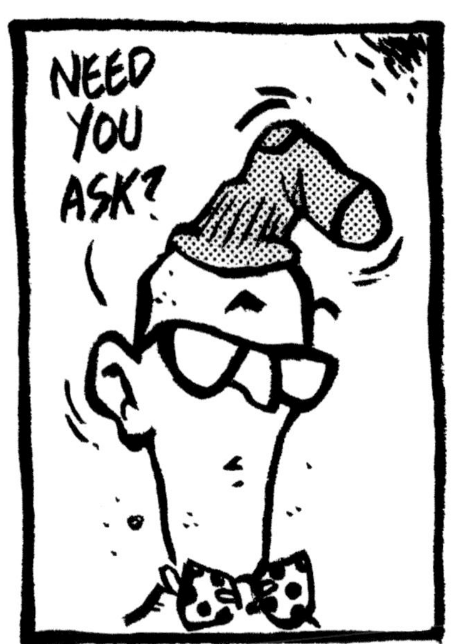
NEED YOU ASK?

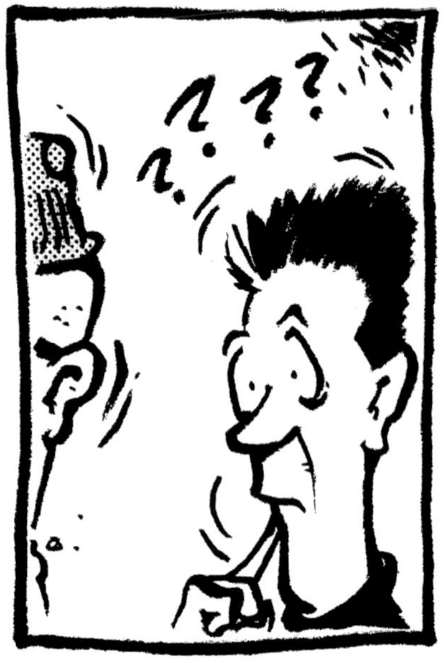
???

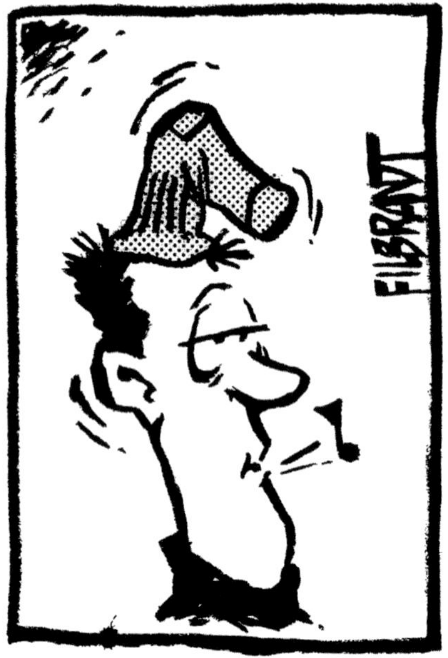
FILLBRANDT

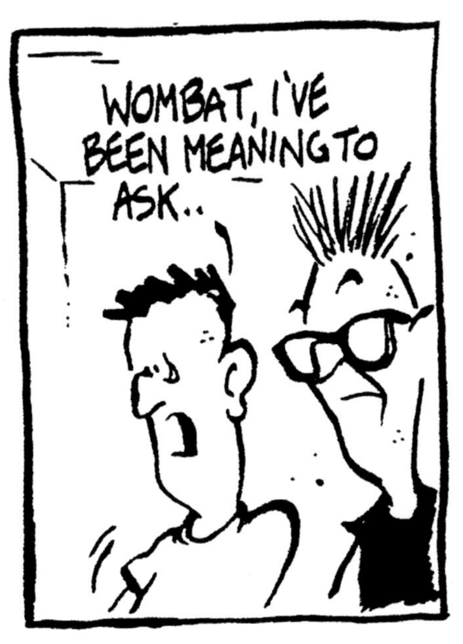
WOMBAT, I'VE BEEN MEANING TO ASK..

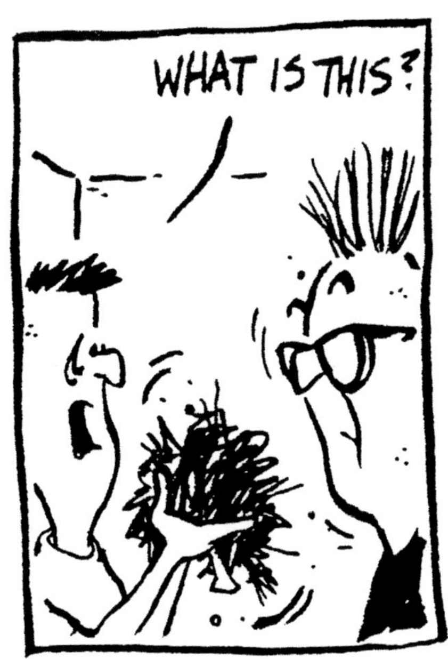
WHAT IS THIS?

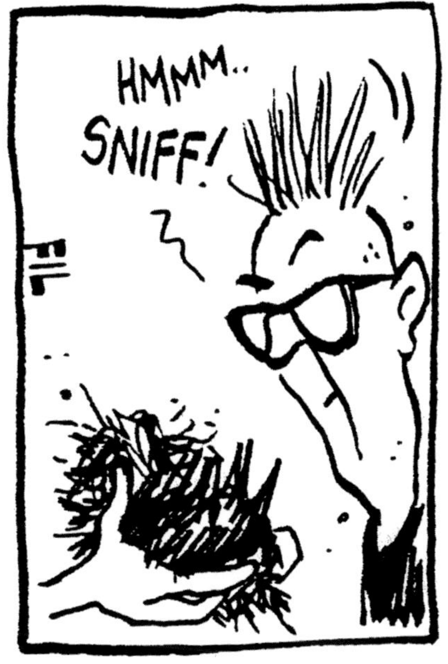
HMMM..
SNIFF!
FIL

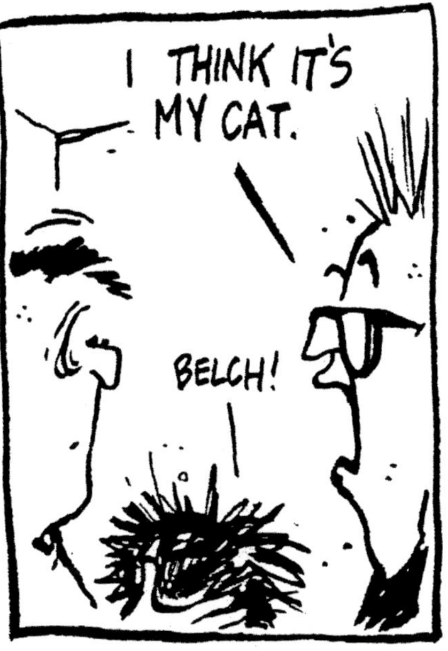
I THINK IT'S MY CAT.
BELCH!

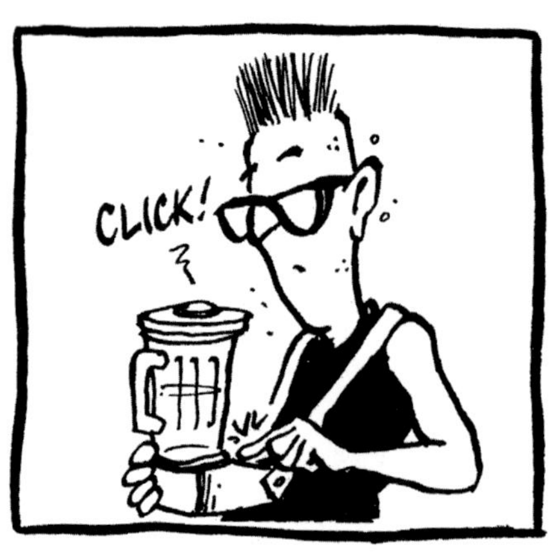
CLICK!

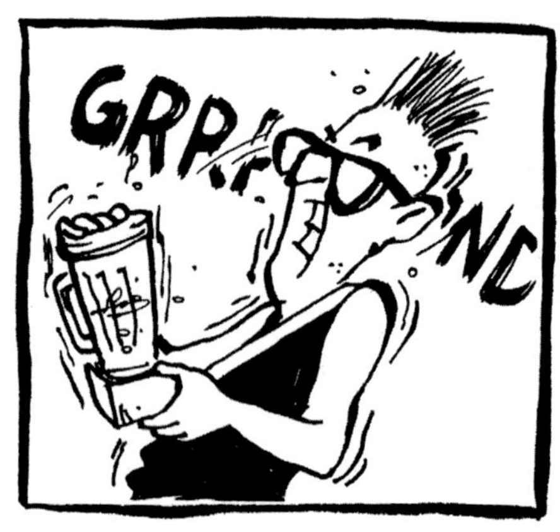

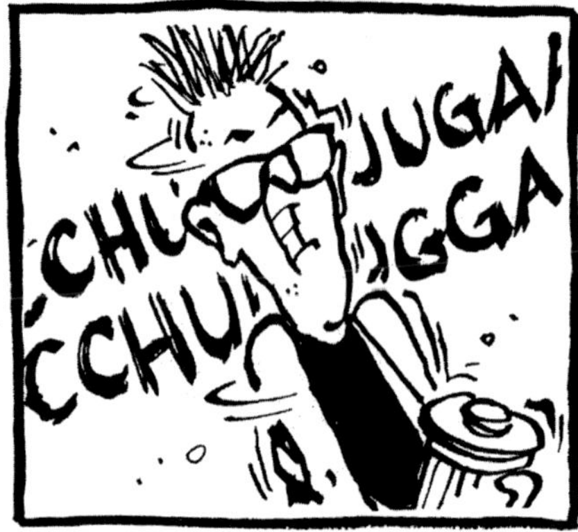

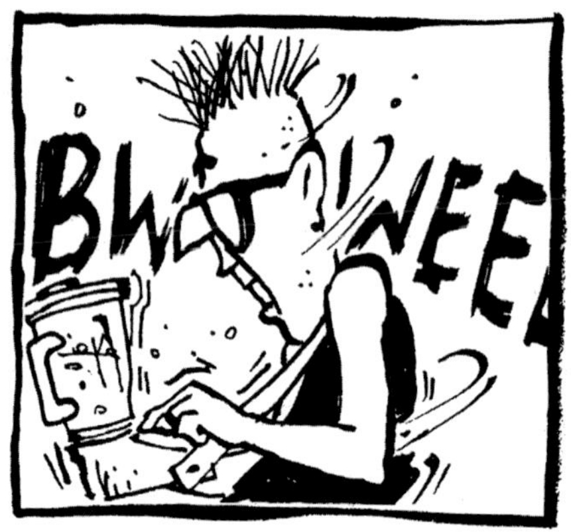

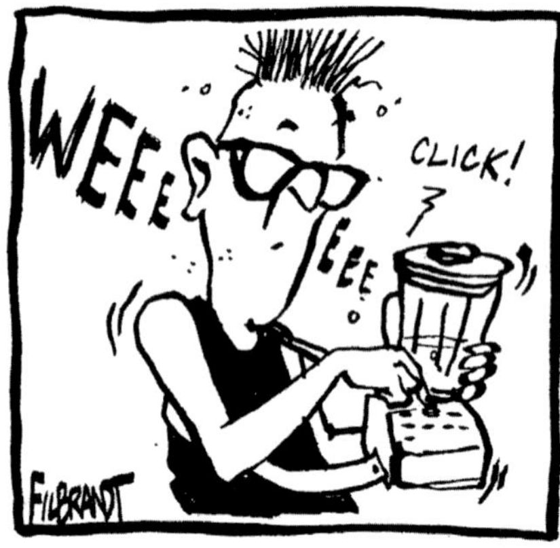
WEEEE
EEE
CLICK!
FILBRANDT

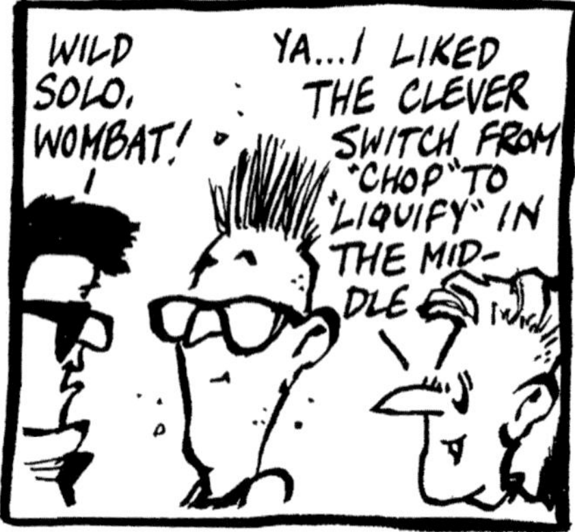
WILD SOLO, WOMBAT!
YA...I LIKED THE CLEVER SWITCH FROM "CHOP" TO "LIQUIFY" IN THE MID-DLE

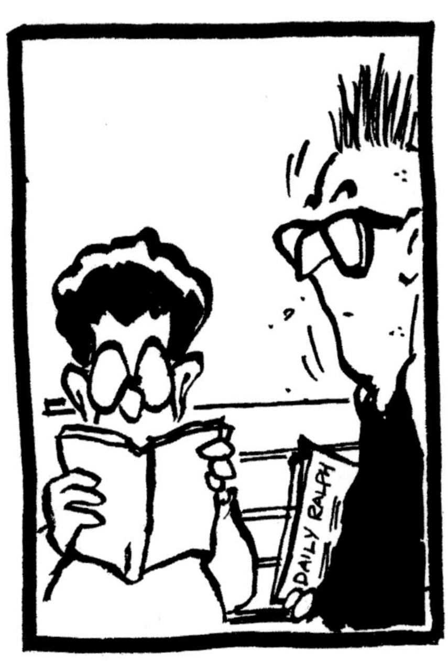
DAILY RALPH

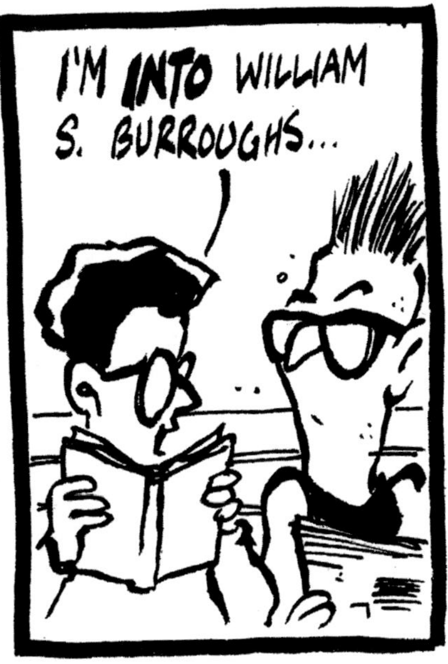
I'M INTO WILLIAM S. BURROUGHS...

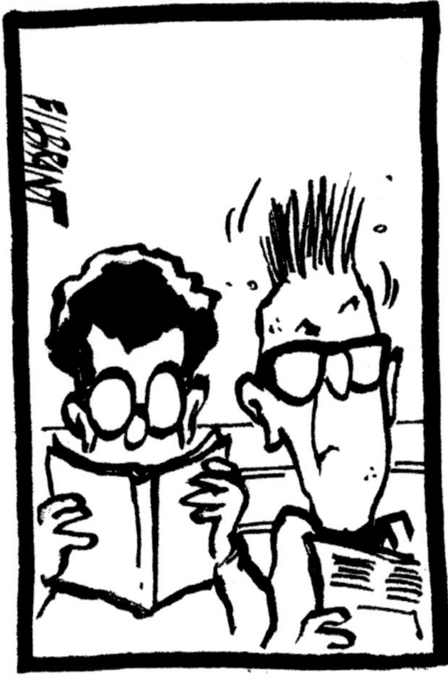

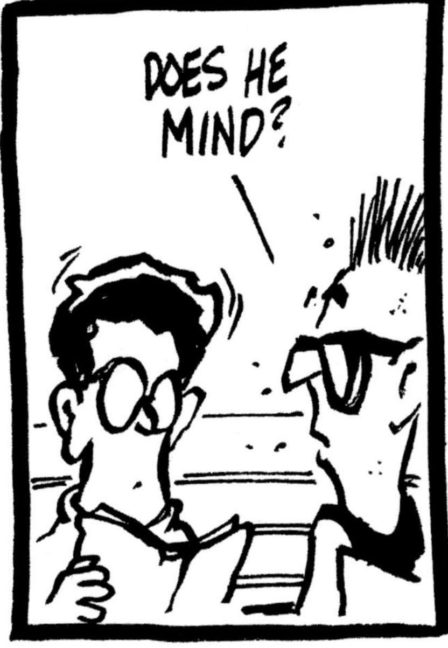
DOES HE MIND?

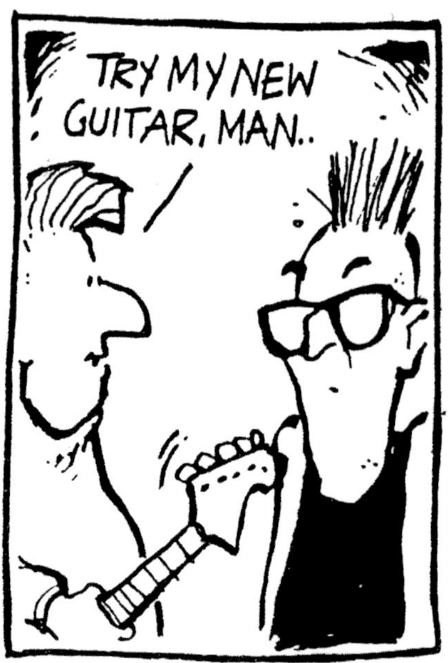
TRY MY NEW GUITAR, MAN..

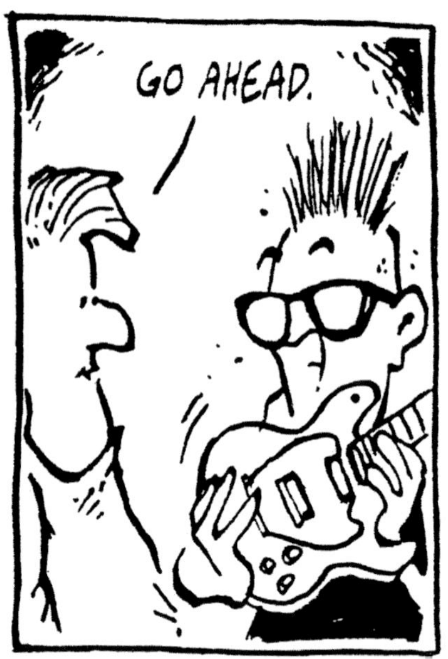
GO AHEAD.

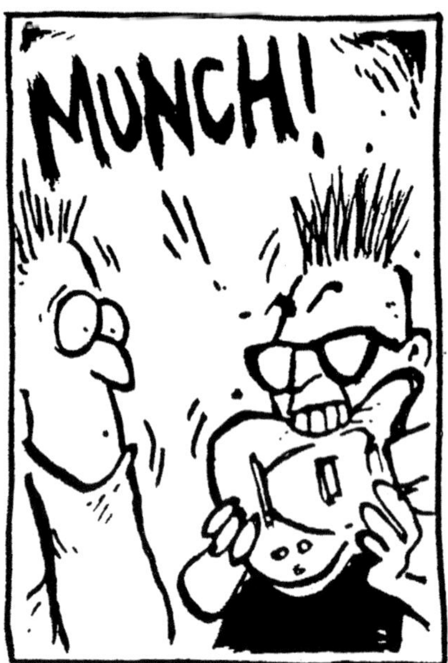
MUNCH!

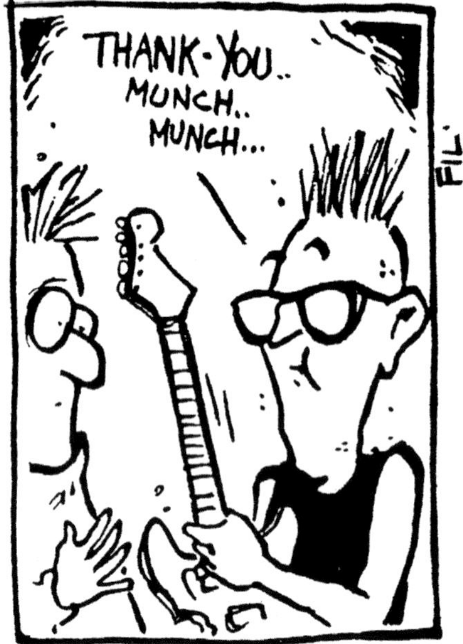
THANK-YOU.. MUNCH.. MUNCH...
FIL

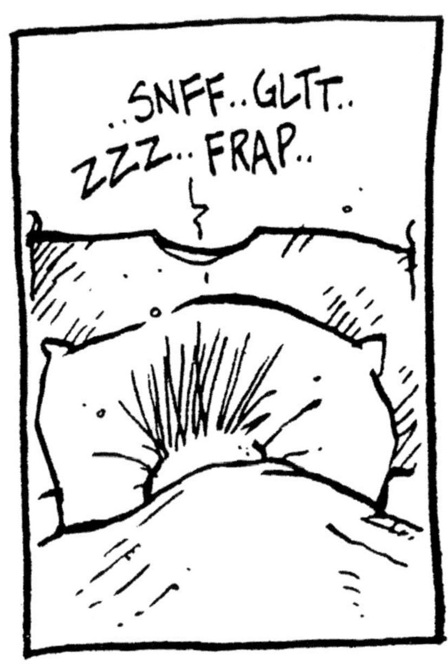
..SNFF..GLTT..
ZZZ.. FRAP..

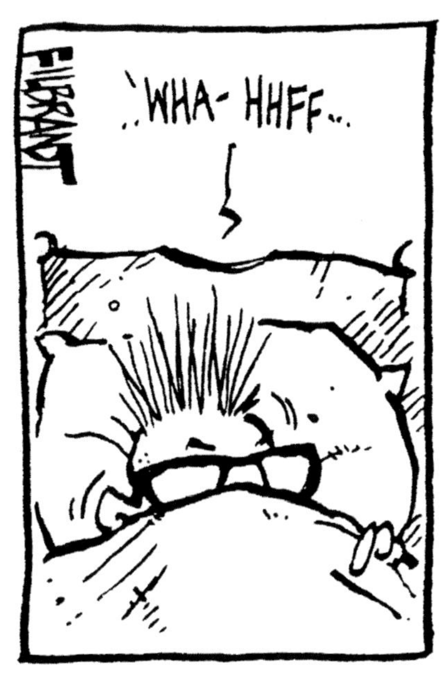
..WHA- HHFF..

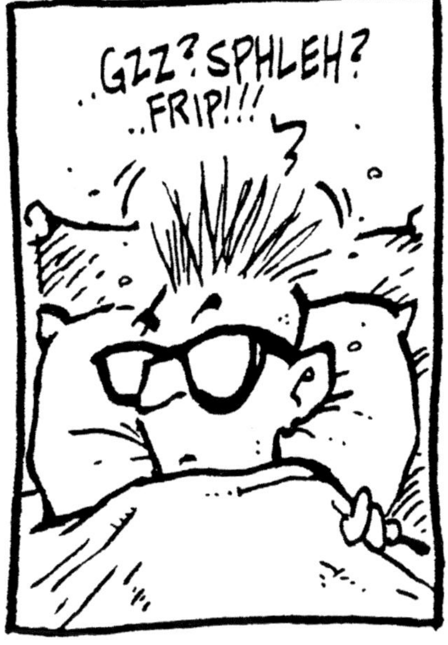
..GZZ? SPHLEH?
..FRIP!!!

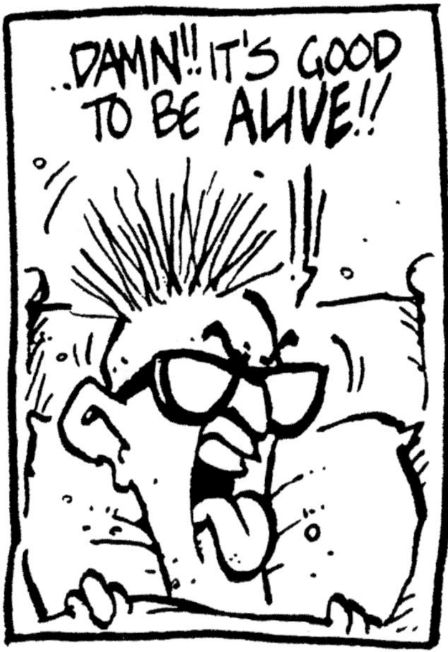
..DAMN!! IT'S GOOD TO BE ALIVE!!
!!

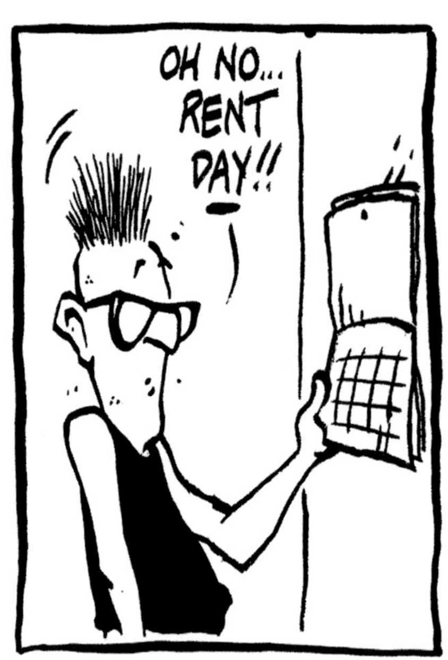
OH NO... RENT DAY!!

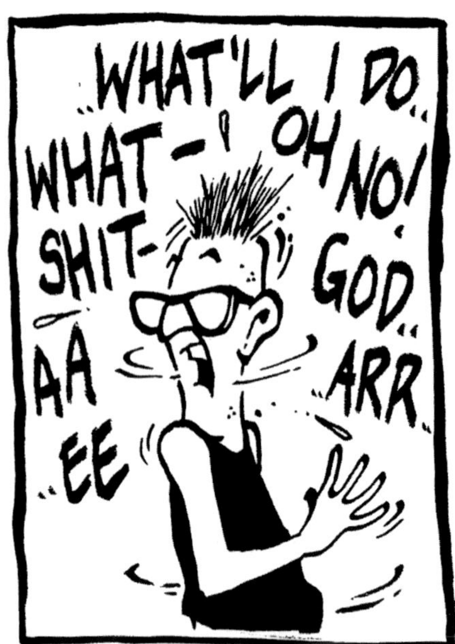
...WHAT'LL I DO...
WHAT-! OH NO!
SHIT-
GOD...
AA
ARR...
..EE

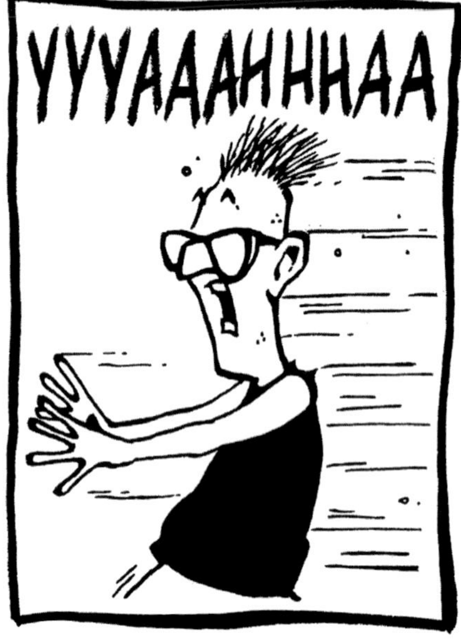
YYYAAAHHHAA

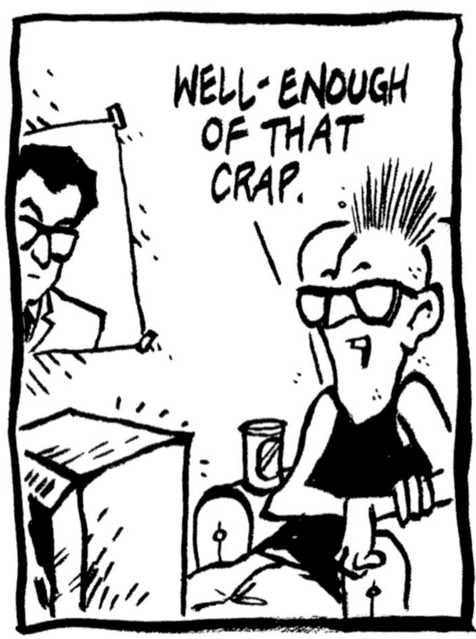
WELL-ENOUGH OF THAT CRAP.

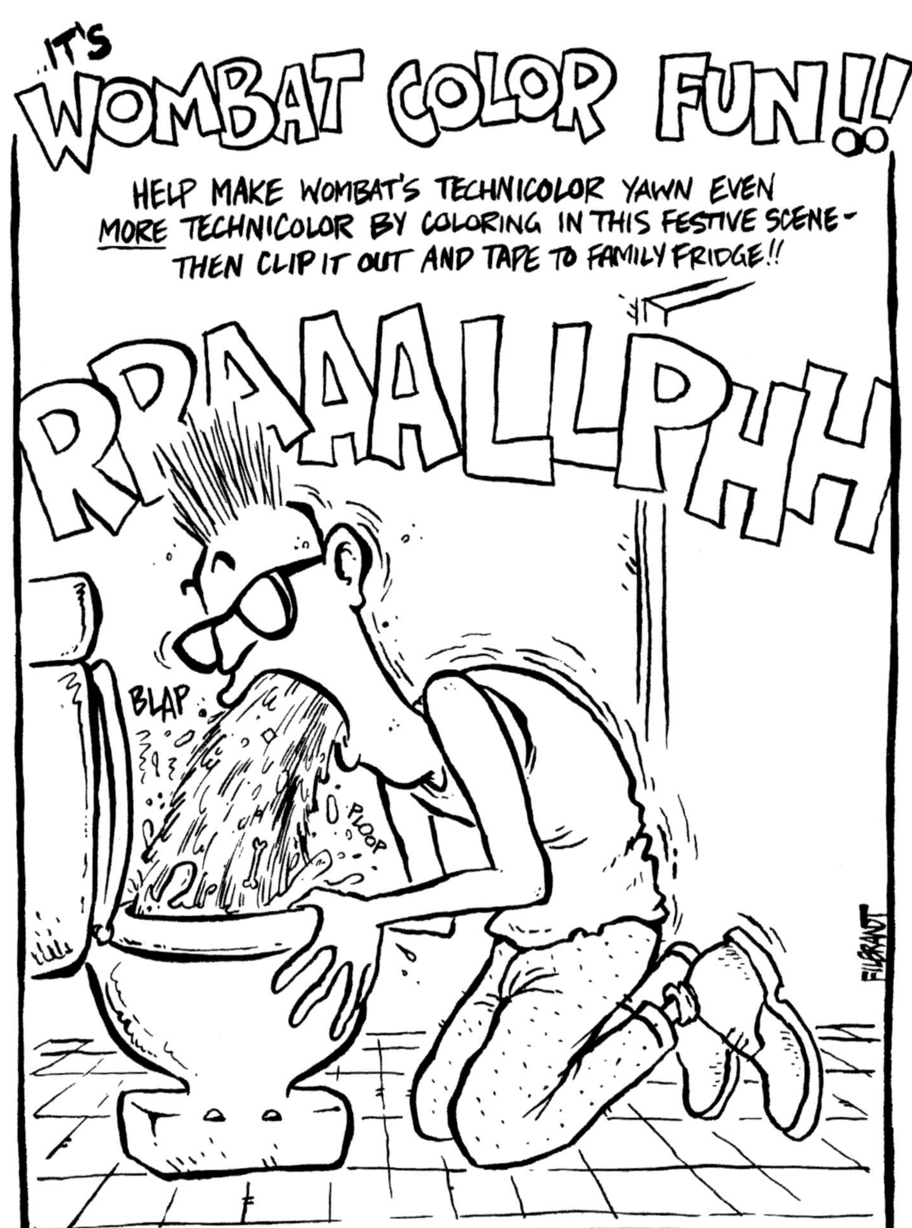
IT'S WOMBAT COLOR FUN!!
HELP MAKE WOMBAT'S TECHNICOLOR YAWN EVEN MORE TECHNICOLOR BY COLORING IN THIS FESTIVE SCENE - THEN CLIP IT OUT AND TAPE TO FAMILY FRIDGE!!
RRAAALLPHH
BLAP
PLOOP

WOMBAT'S DATING TIPS

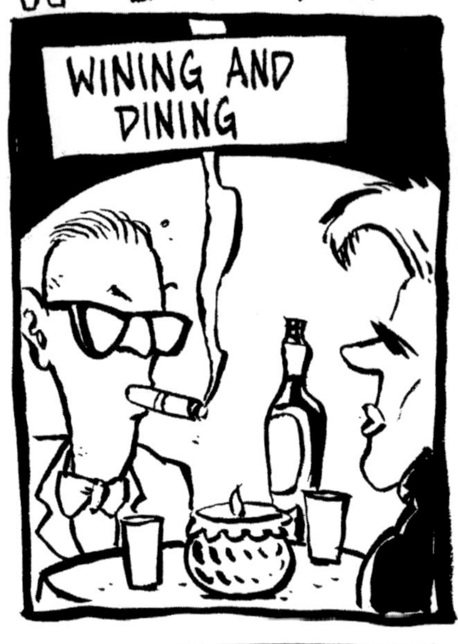

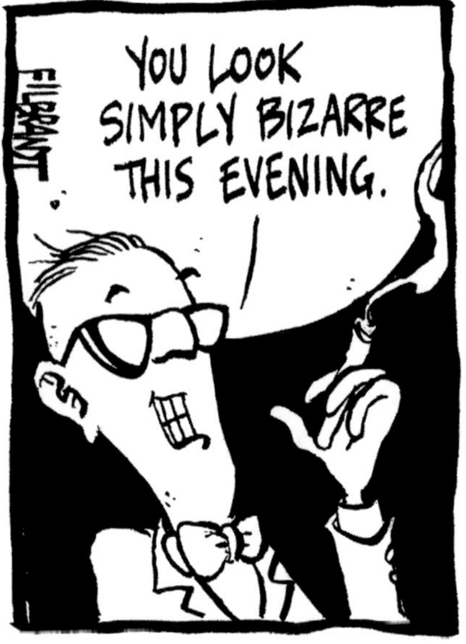

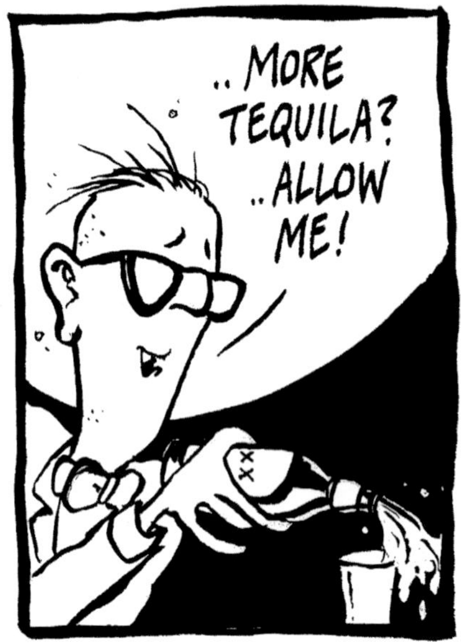

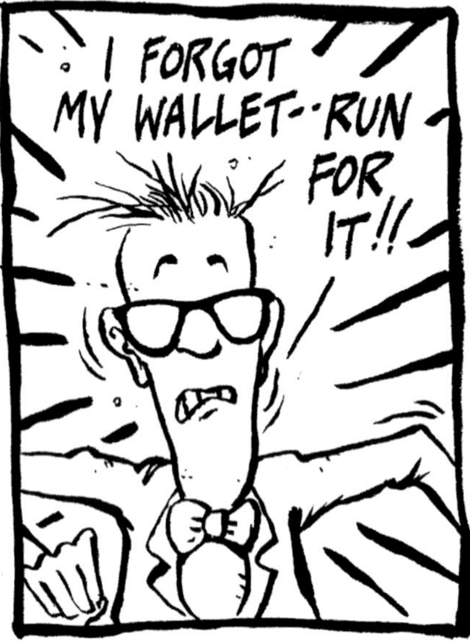

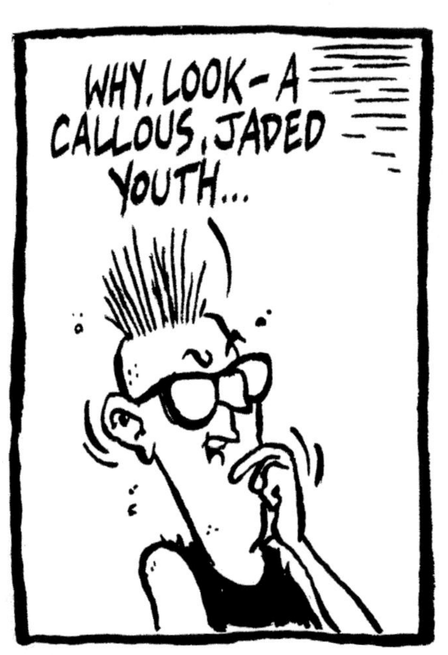
WHY, LOOK- A CALLOUS, JADED YOUTH...

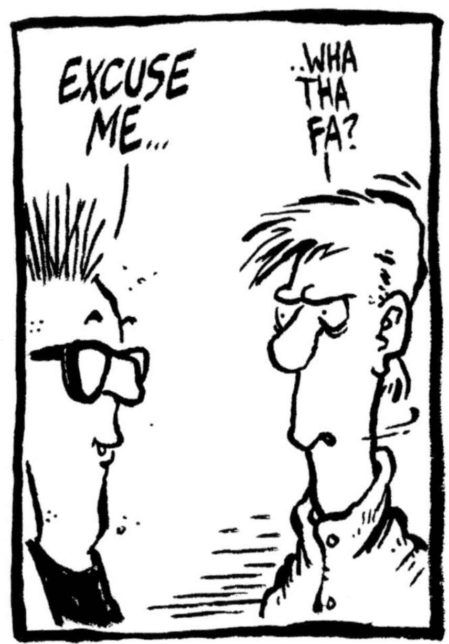
EXCUSE ME...
..WHA THA FA?

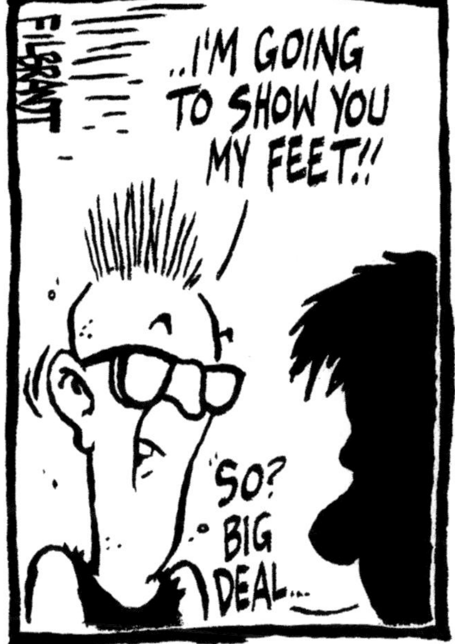
FILBRANT
..I'M GOING TO SHOW YOU MY FEET!!
SO? BIG DEAL...

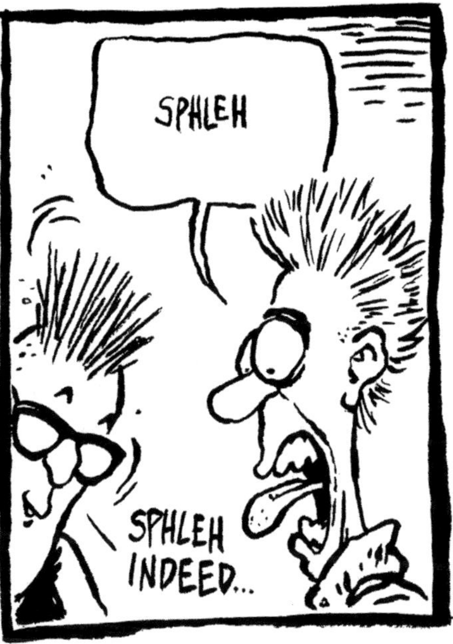
SPHLEH
SPHLEH INDEED...

WOMBAT'S UNDERWEAR GUIDE:

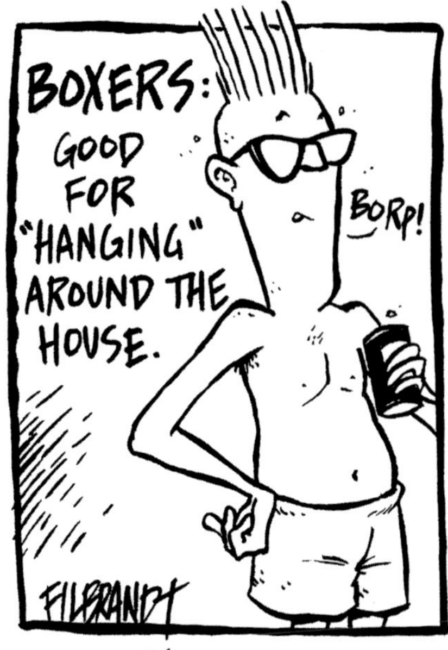

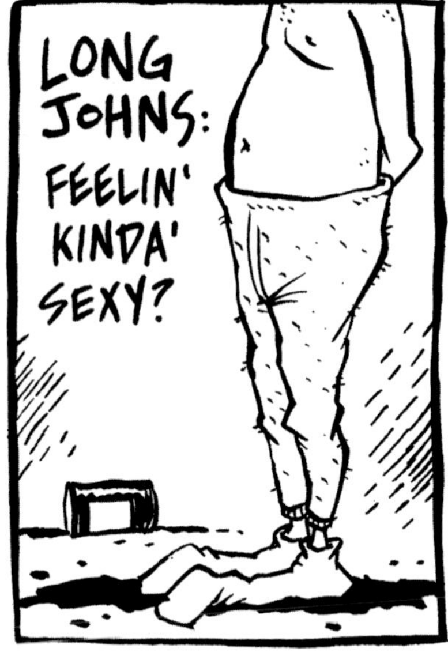

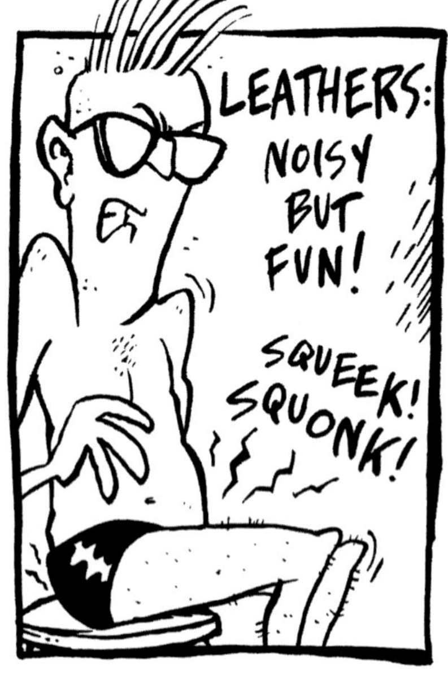

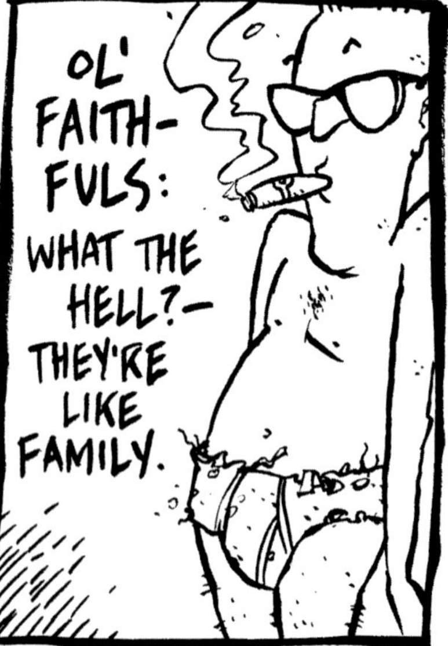

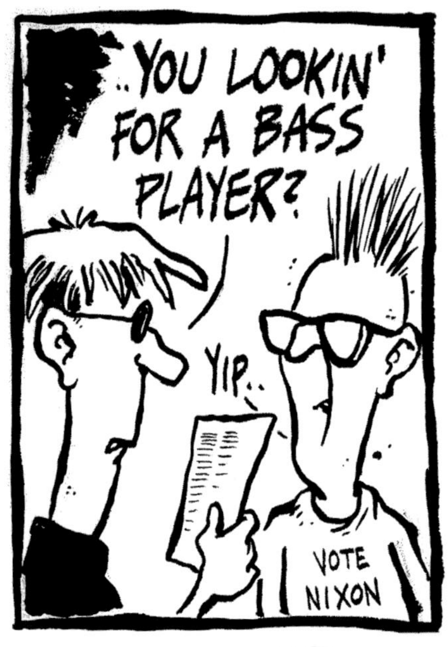
..YOU LOOKIN' FOR A BASS PLAYER?
YIP..
VOTE NIXON

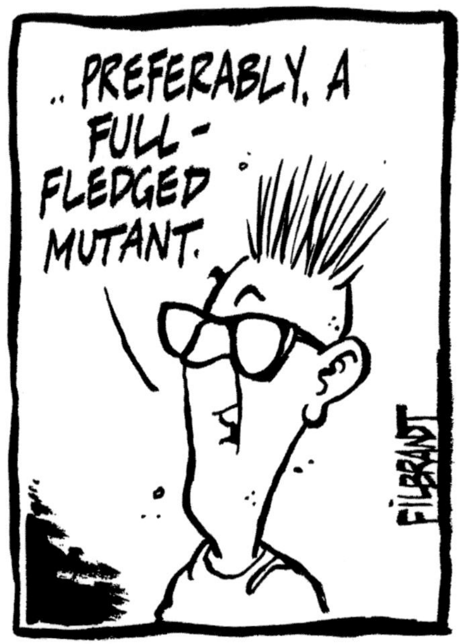
.. PREFERABLY, A FULL-FLEDGED MUTANT.
FILBRANDT

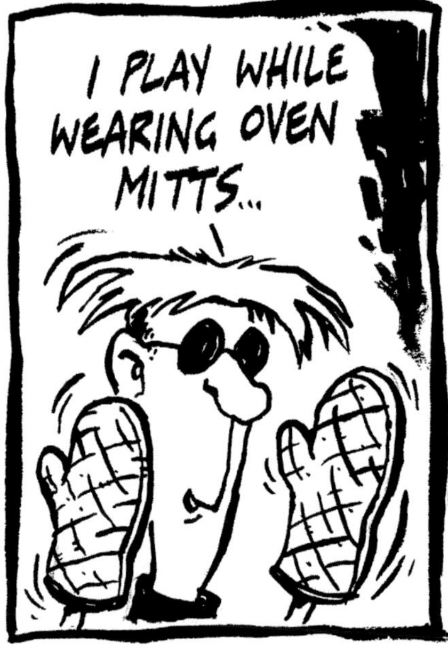
I PLAY WHILE WEARING OVEN MITTS...

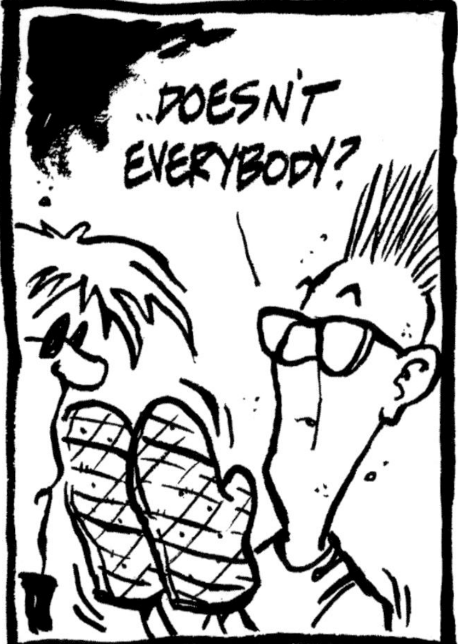
..DOESN'T EVERYBODY?

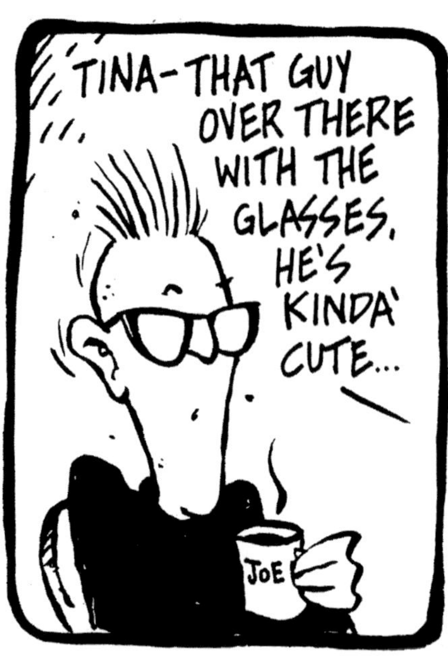
TINA-THAT GUY OVER THERE WITH THE GLASSES. HE'S KINDA' CUTE...
JOE

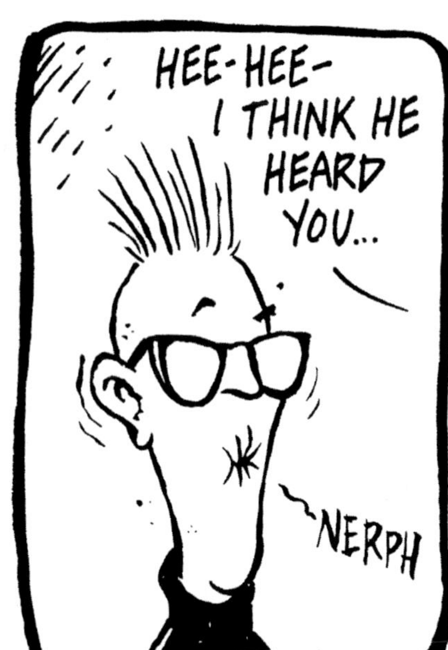
HEE-HEE- I THINK HE HEARD YOU...
NERPH

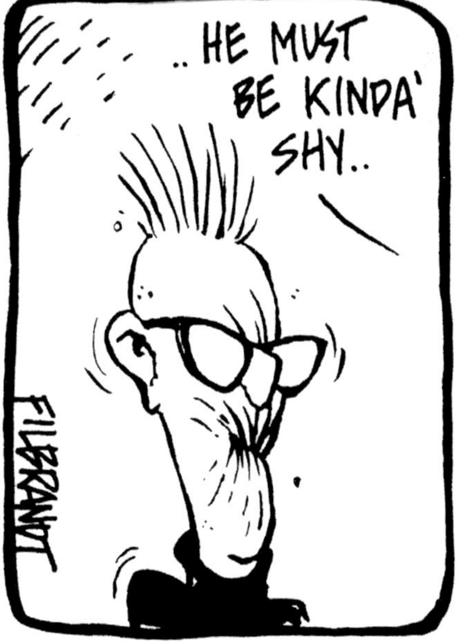
..HE MUST BE KINDA' SHY..
FILBRANDT

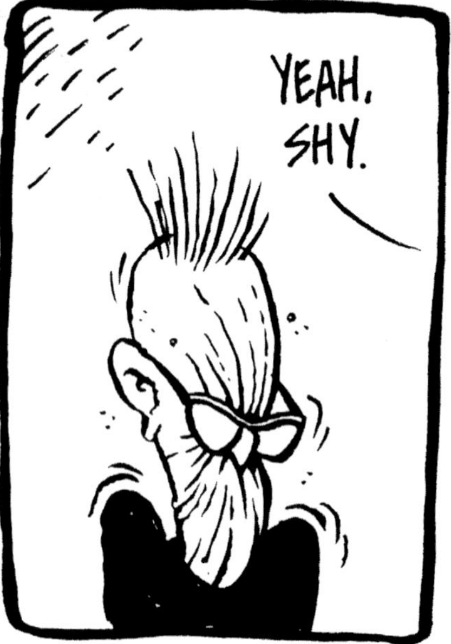
YEAH. SHY.

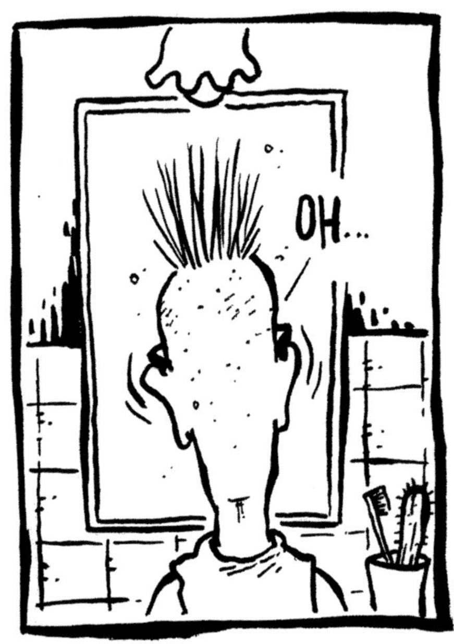
OH...

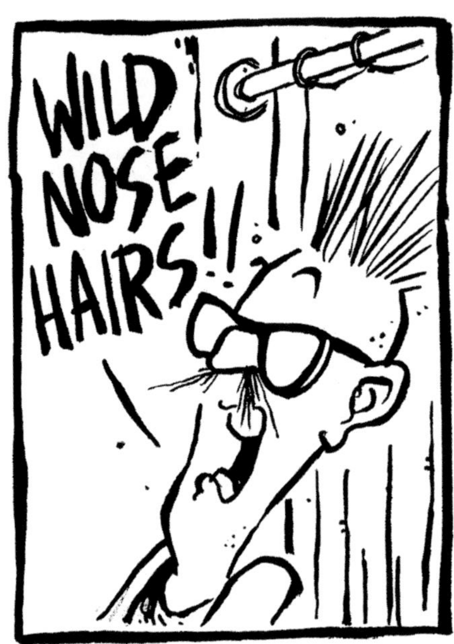
WILD NOSE HAIRS!!

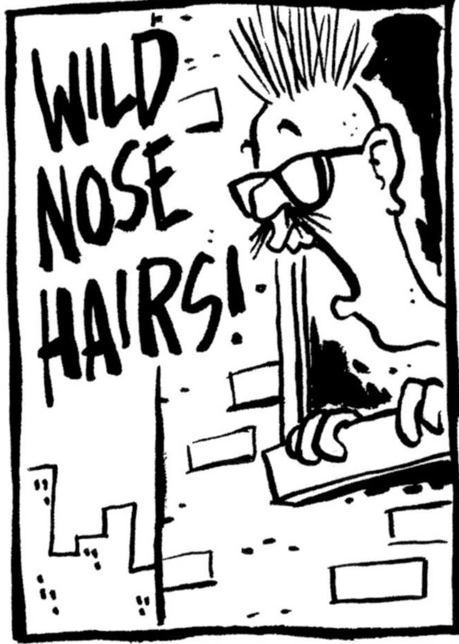
WILD NOSE HAIRS!

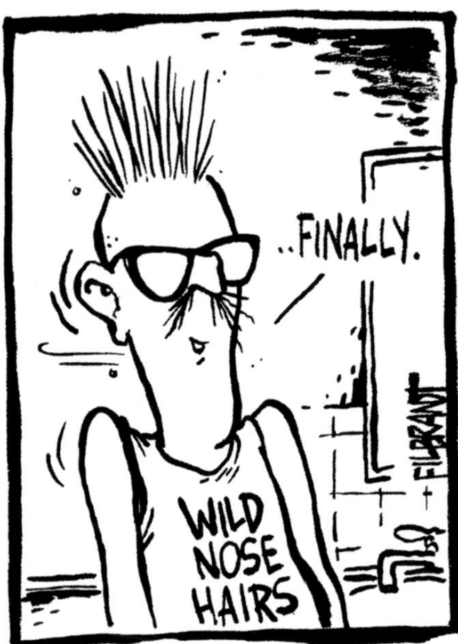
...FINALLY.
WILD NOSE HAIRS
FILLBRANDT

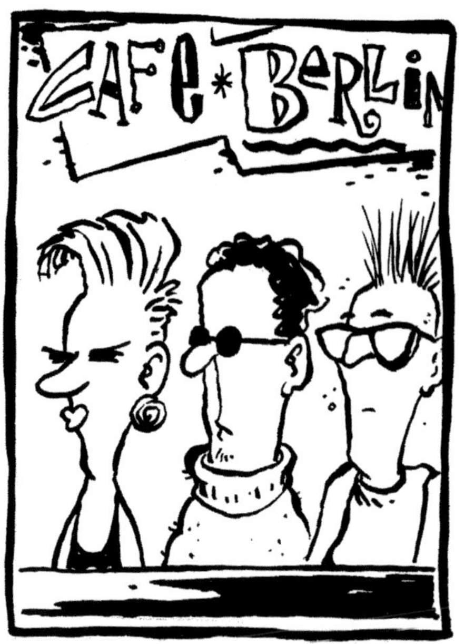
CAFE * BERLIN

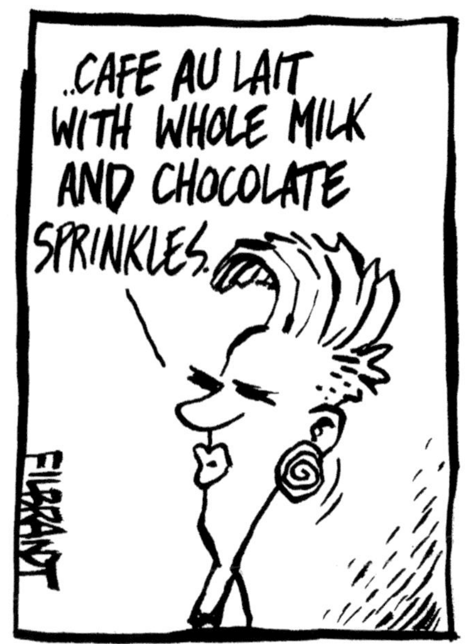
..CAFE AU LAIT WITH WHOLE MILK AND CHOCOLATE SPRINKLES.

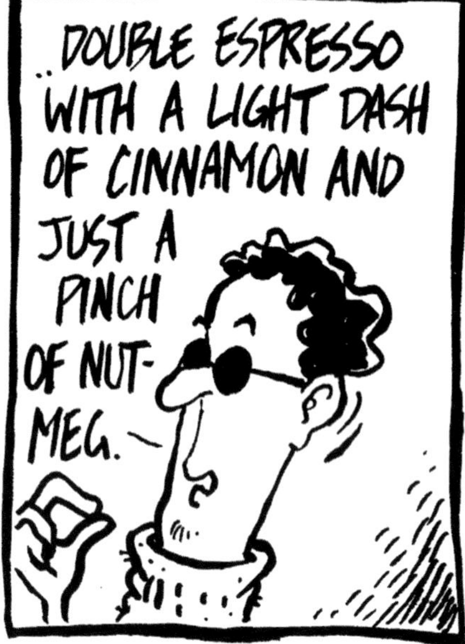
..DOUBLE ESPRESSO WITH A LIGHT DASH OF CINNAMON AND JUST A PINCH OF NUT-MEG.

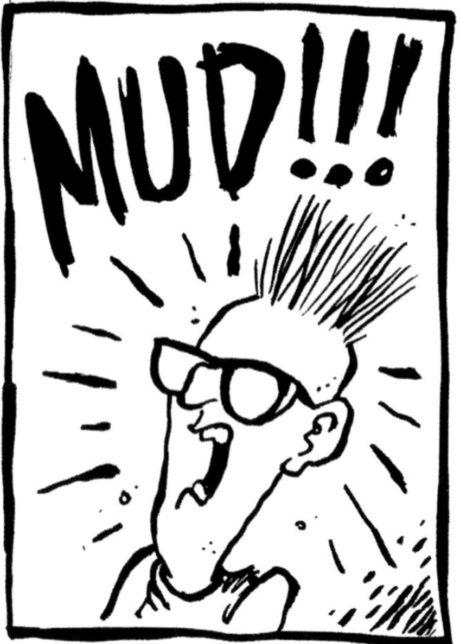
MUD!!!...

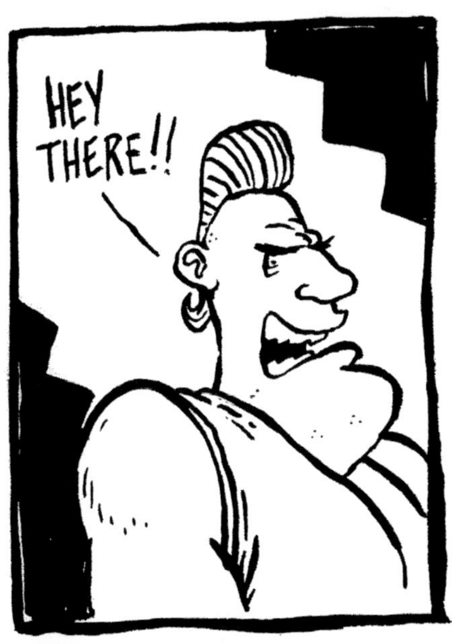
HEY THERE!!

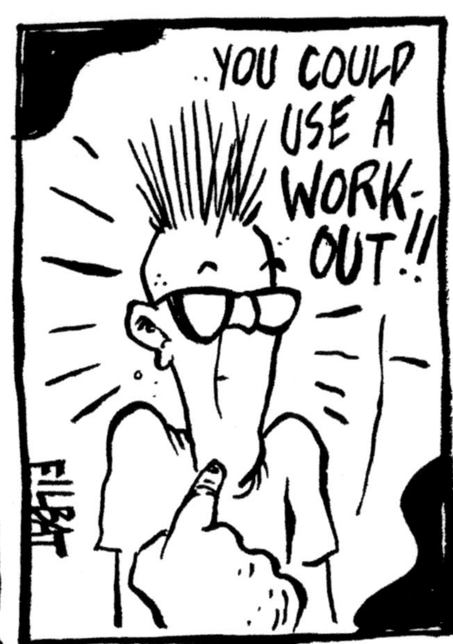
..YOU COULD USE A WORK-OUT!!

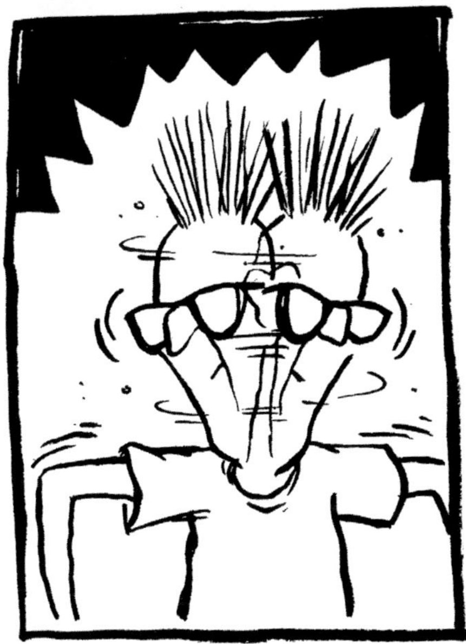

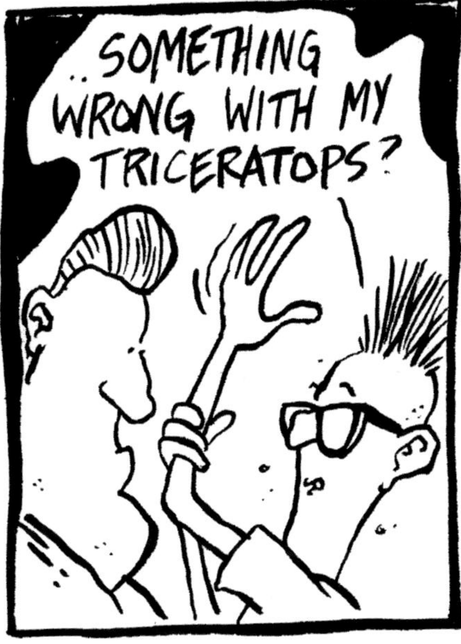
..SOMETHING WRONG WITH MY TRICERATOPS?

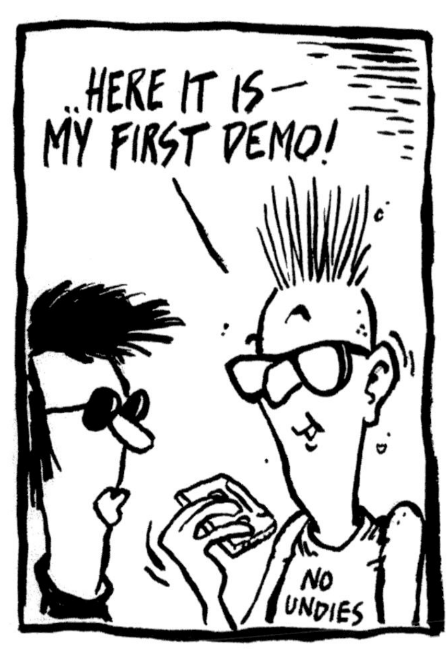
..HERE IT IS—
MY FIRST DEMO!
NO
UNDIES

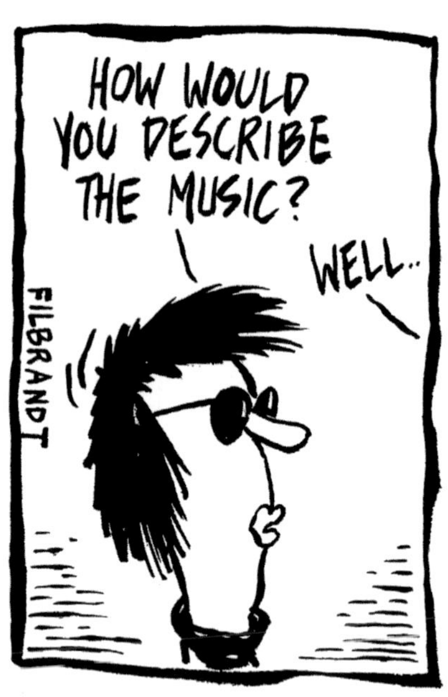
HOW WOULD
YOU DESCRIBE
THE MUSIC?
WELL..
FILBRANDT

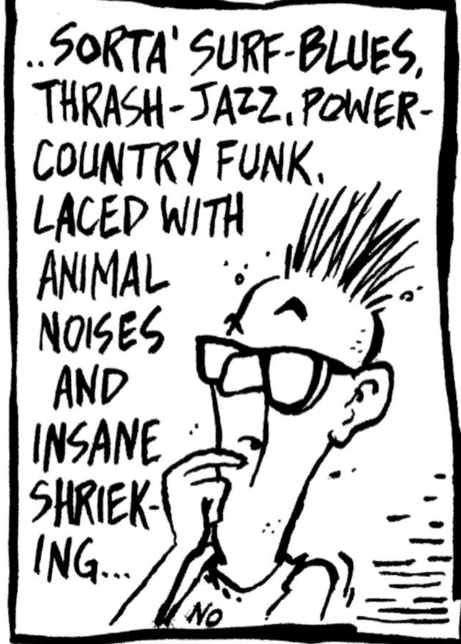
..SORTA' SURF-BLUES,
THRASH-JAZZ, POWER-
COUNTRY FUNK,
LACED WITH
ANIMAL
NOISES
AND
INSANE
SHRIEK-
ING...
NO

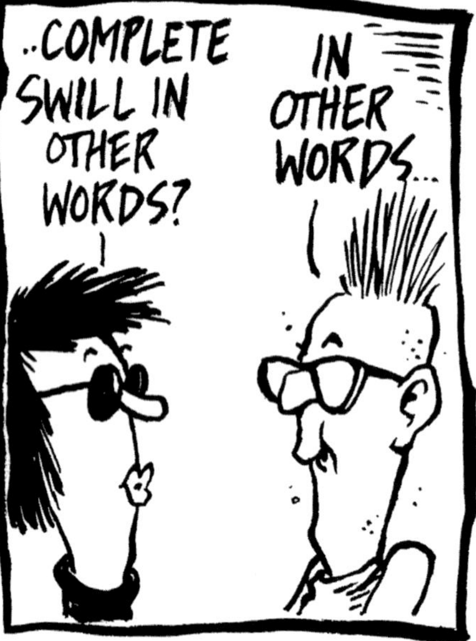
..COMPLETE
SWILL IN
OTHER
WORDS?
IN
OTHER
WORDS...

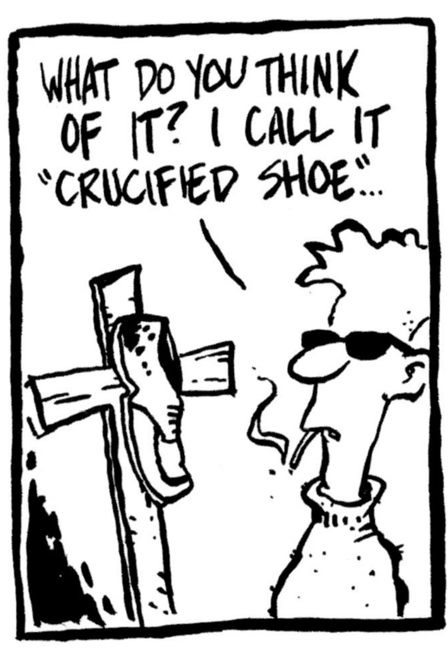
WHAT DO YOU THINK OF IT? I CALL IT "CRUCIFIED SHOE"...

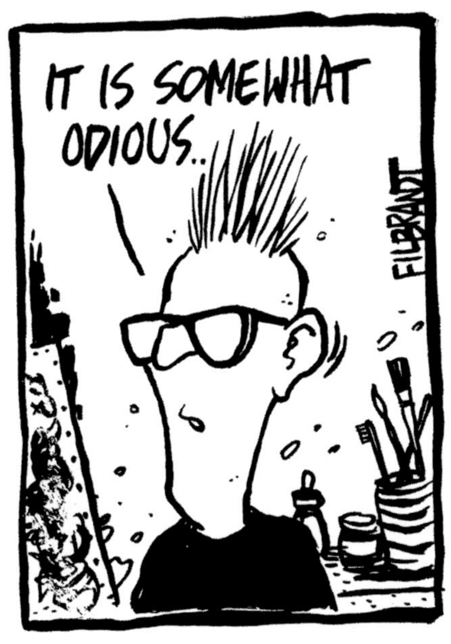
IT IS SOMEWHAT ODIOUS..
FILBRANDT

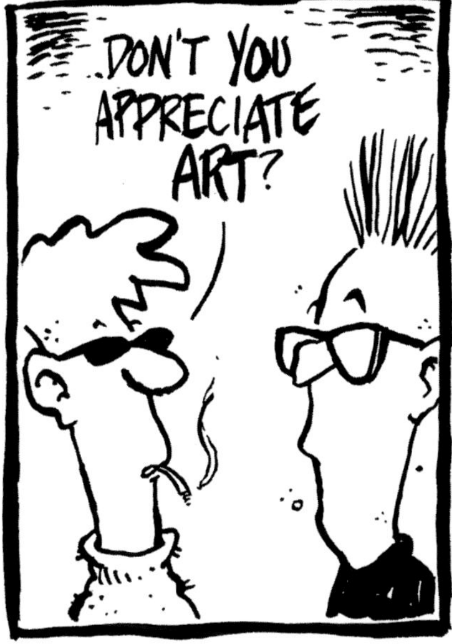
..DON'T YOU APPRECIATE ART?

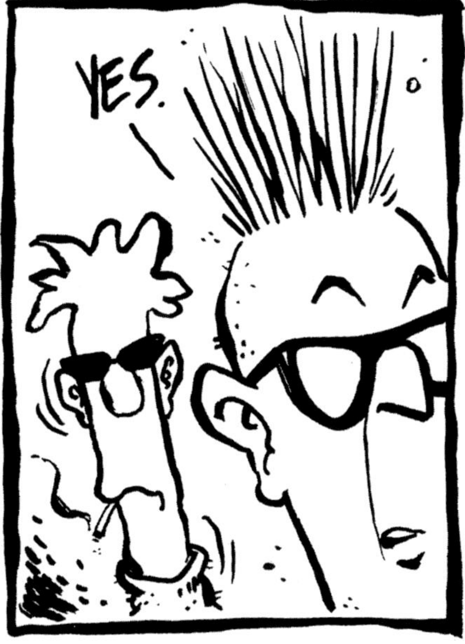
YES.

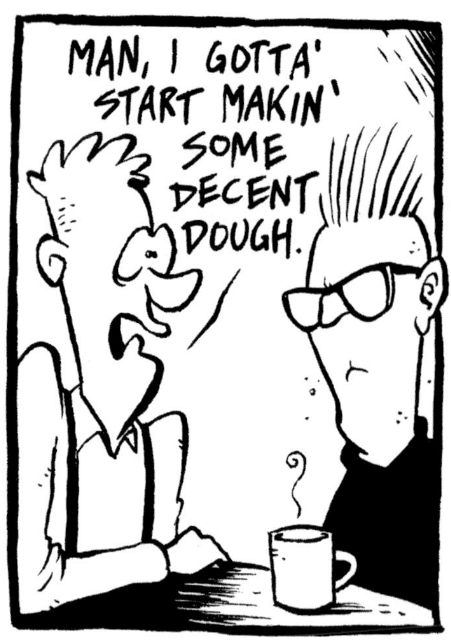
MAN, I GOTTA' START MAKIN' SOME DECENT DOUGH.

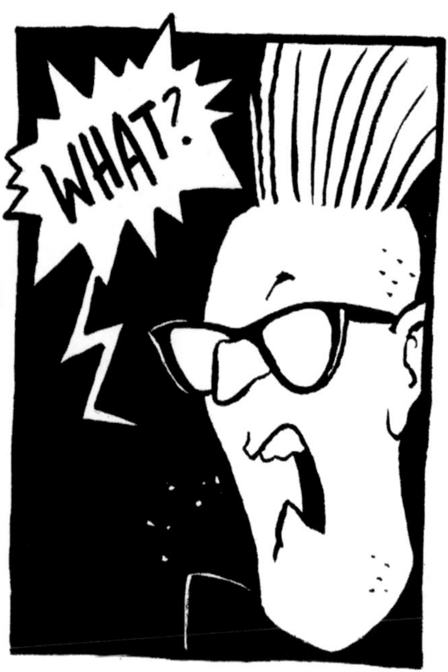
WHAT?

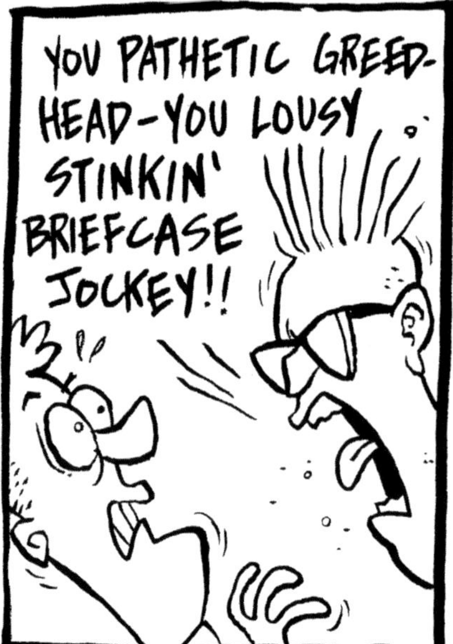
YOU PATHETIC GREED-HEAD-YOU LOUSY STINKIN' BRIEFCASE JOCKEY!!

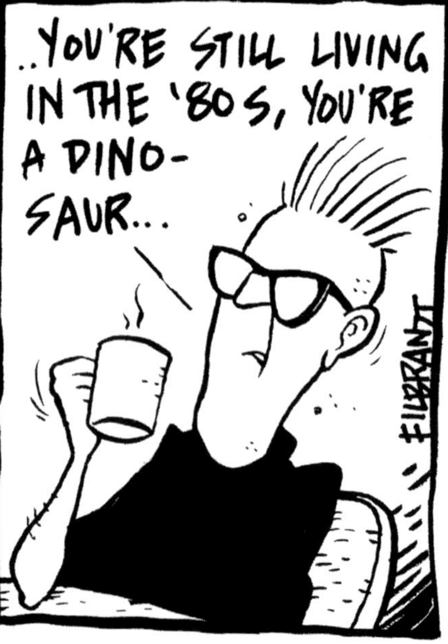
..YOU'RE STILL LIVING IN THE '80S, YOU'RE A DINO-SAUR...
FILLBRANDT

WOMBAT ~ HARDCORE BACHELORING:

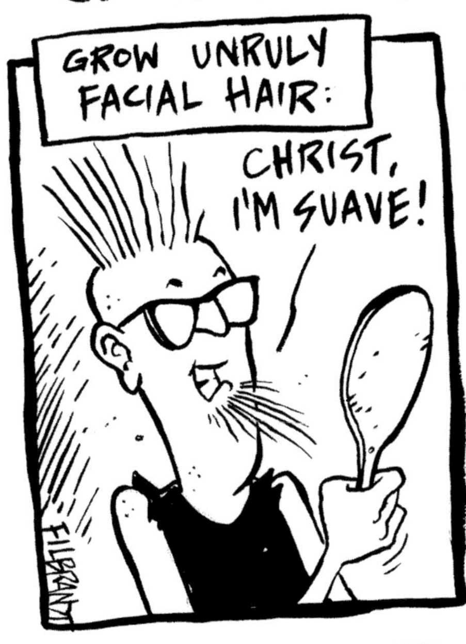

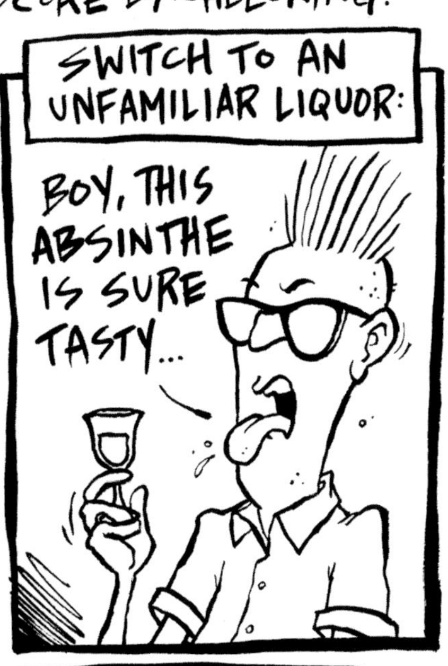

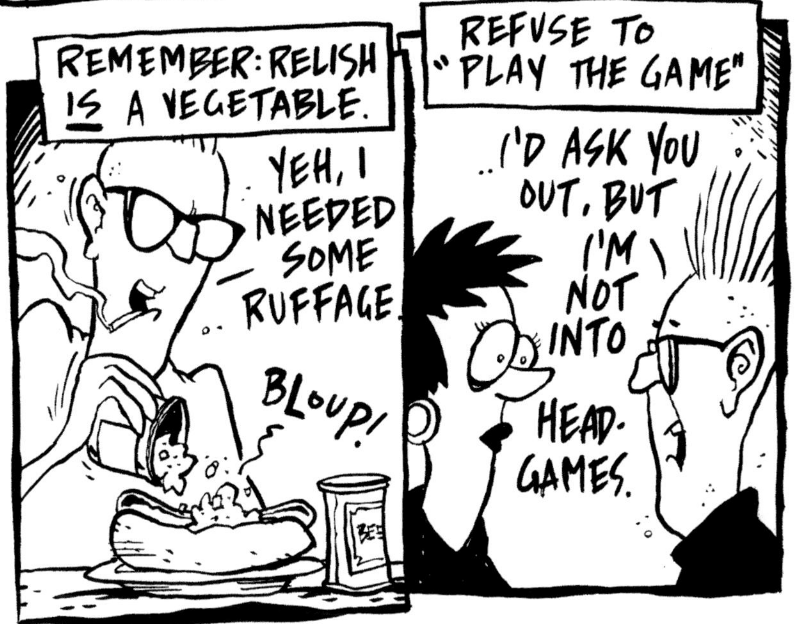

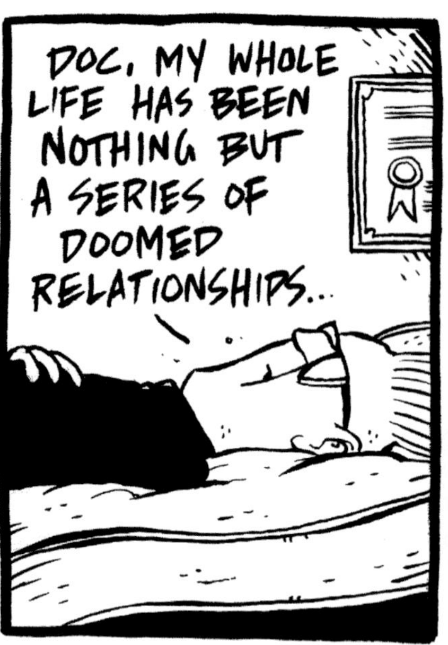
DOC, MY WHOLE LIFE HAS BEEN NOTHING BUT A SERIES OF DOOMED RELATIONSHIPS...

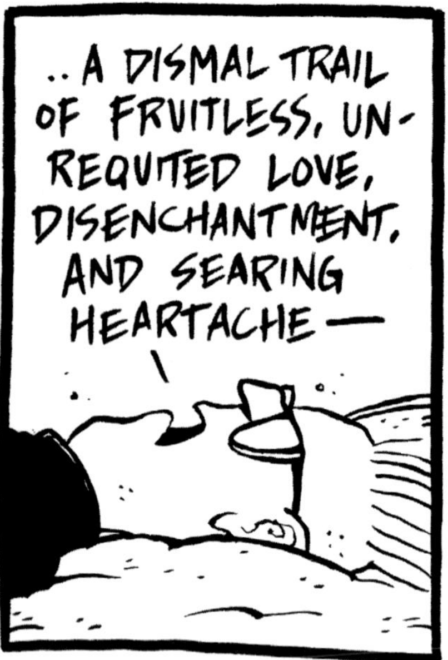
..A DISMAL TRAIL OF FRUITLESS, UN-REQUITED LOVE, DISENCHANTMENT, AND SEARING HEARTACHE—

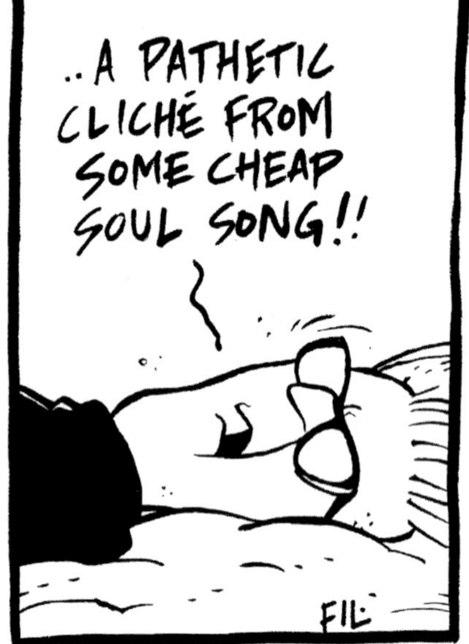
..A PATHETIC CLICHÉ FROM SOME CHEAP SOUL SONG!!
FIL

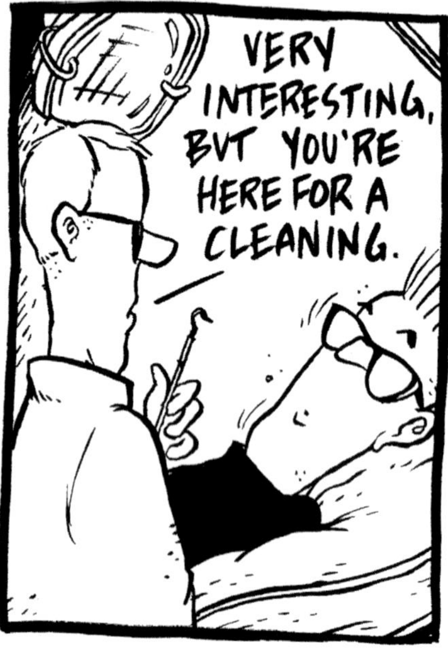
VERY INTERESTING, BUT YOU'RE HERE FOR A CLEANING.

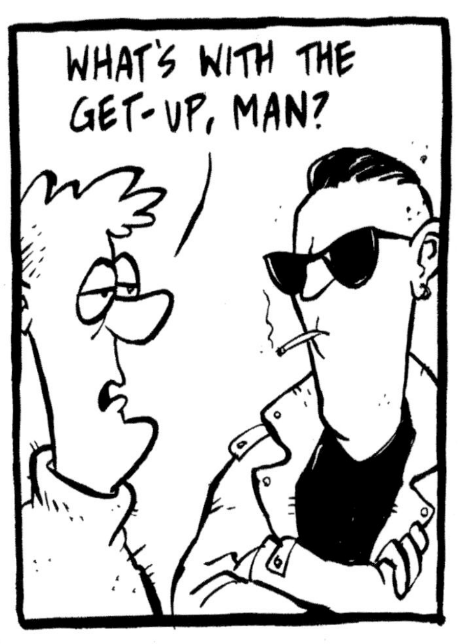
WHAT'S WITH THE GET-UP, MAN?

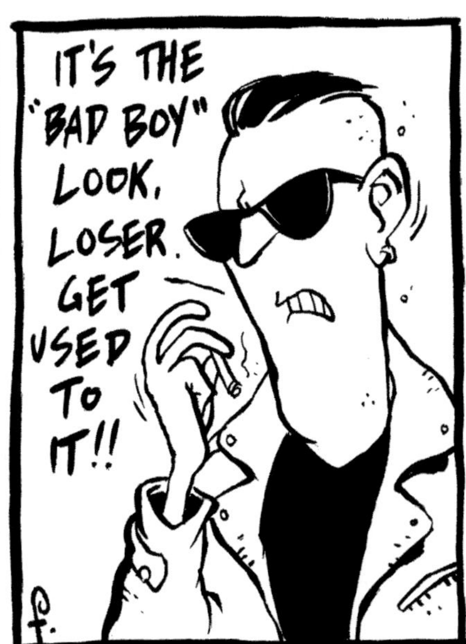
IT'S THE "BAD BOY" LOOK, LOSER. GET USED TO IT!!

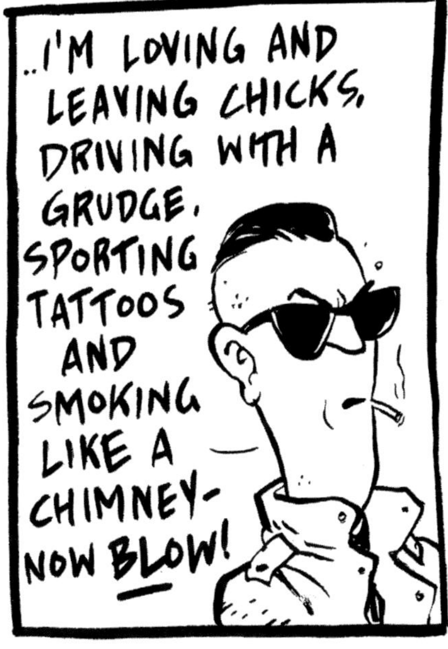
..I'M LOVING AND LEAVING CHICKS, DRIVING WITH A GRUDGE, SPORTING TATTOOS AND SMOKING LIKE A CHIMNEY- NOW BLOW!

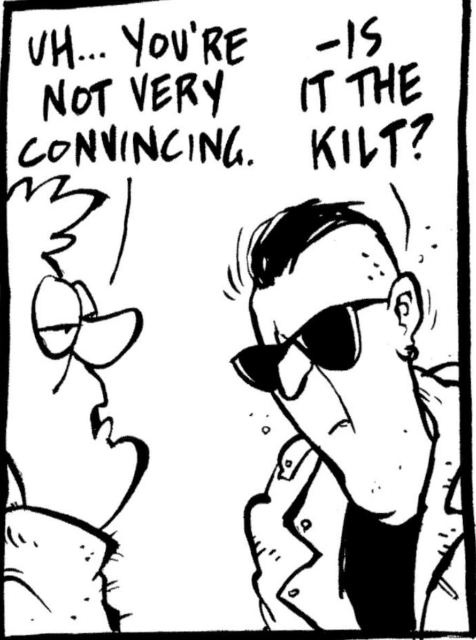
UH... YOU'RE NOT VERY CONVINCING.
-IS IT THE KILT?

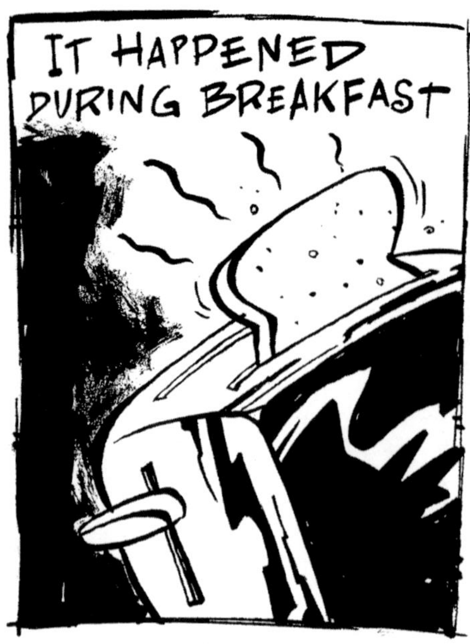
IT HAPPENED DURING BREAKFAST

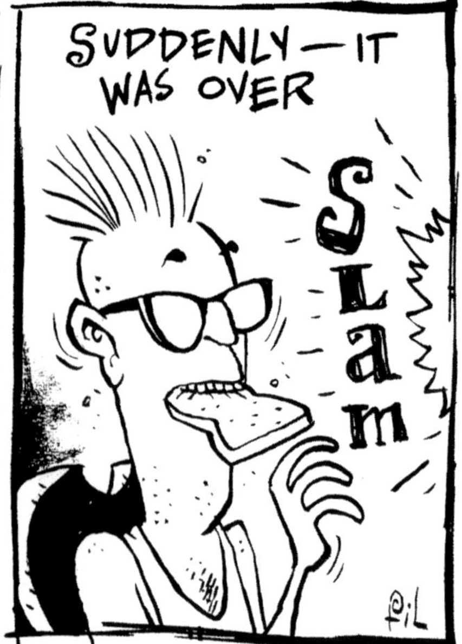
SUDDENLY—IT WAS OVER
SLAM
fil

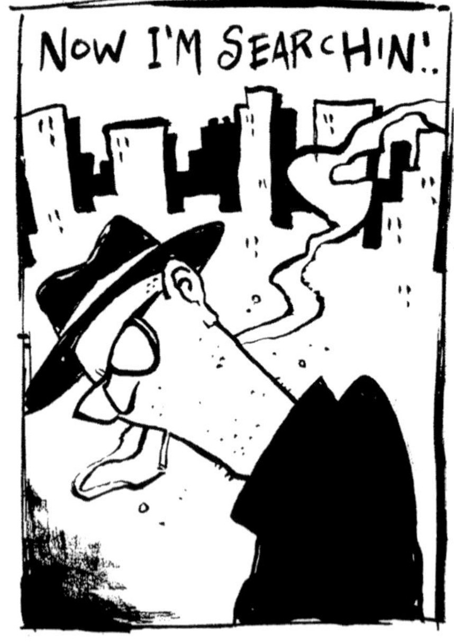
NOW I'M SEARCHIN'..

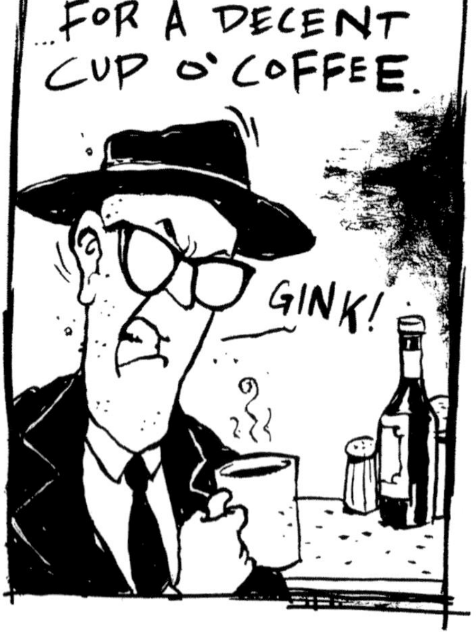
...FOR A DECENT CUP O' COFFEE.
GINK!

MARKETING MANIA CLUB!

(A DIVISION OF MEGACORPS INTERNATIONAL)

W3501-"POP-TART" COOKBOOK
LEARN THE 325 WAYS TO PREPARE THESE FUN-SNACKS.

W720-"FLAMIN-FISTS-O-FIRE"
JOKE OVEN MITTS (HIGHLY FLAMMABLE)

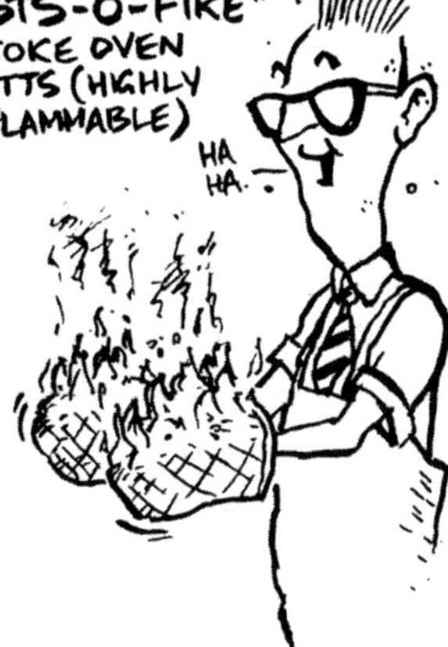

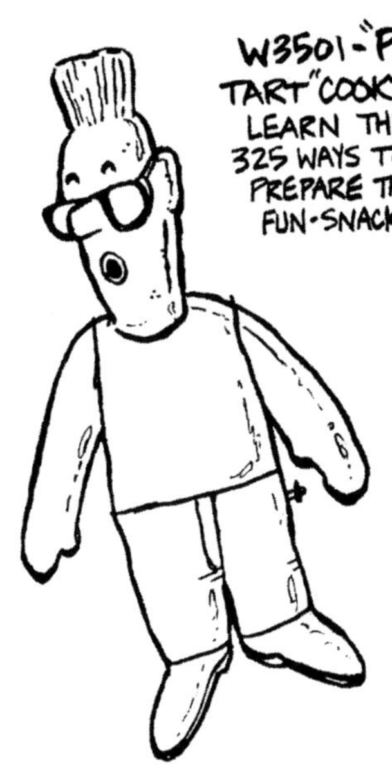

W2205- LOVE DOLL
WITH DETACHABLE PANTS FOR QUICK ACTION.

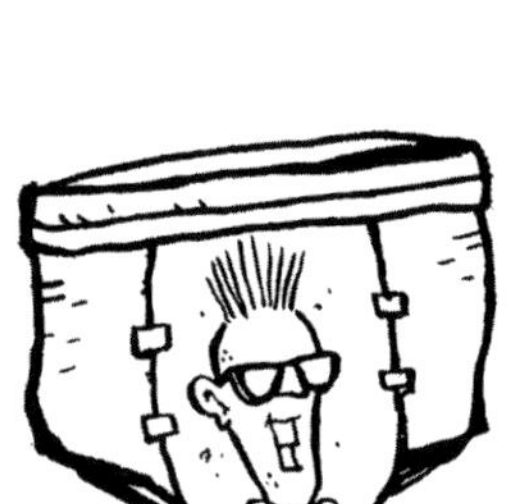

W2212-PLASTIC BLADDER CONTROL BRIEFS
ONE SIZE FITS ALL.

W521-"PACK-O-LINT"
LINT FUN FOR EVERYONE.

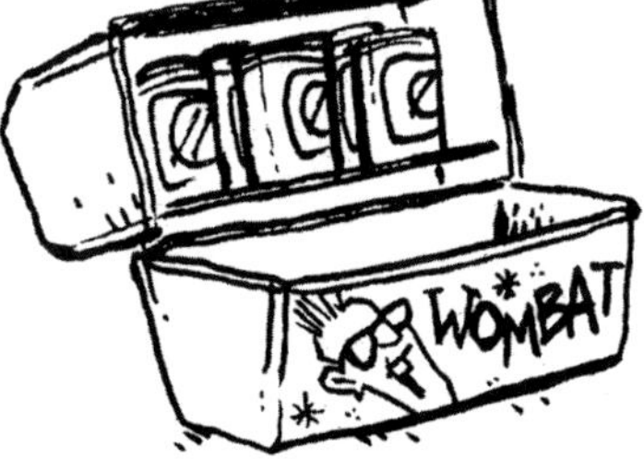

W339A-JUMBO LUNCH KIT
WITH BUILT-IN "SIXPACK-RACK." GREAT FOR THE BUDDING ALCOHOLIC.

YES! YES! SEND ME EVERYTHING-C.O.D!

Mr./Mrs.
Miss/Ms: ______________________
(please print clearly)

Address: ______________________ Apt. No: ________

City & Province: ______________________ Postal Code: ________

Signature: ______________________
(If under 18, parent must sign here)

For your convenience you may charge club purchases to your VISA or MasterCard account. Ask for details.

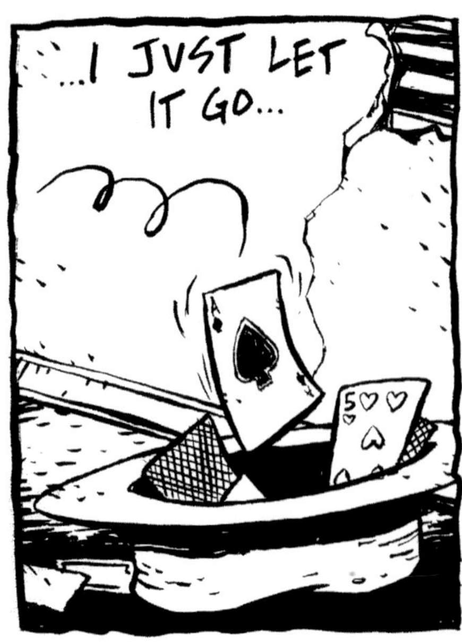
...I JUST LET IT GO...

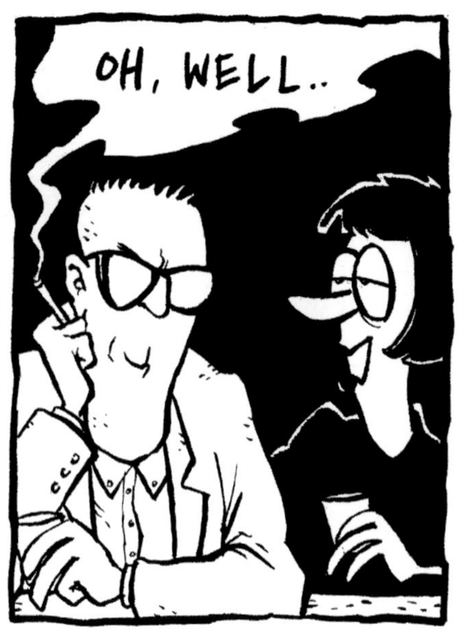
OH, WELL..

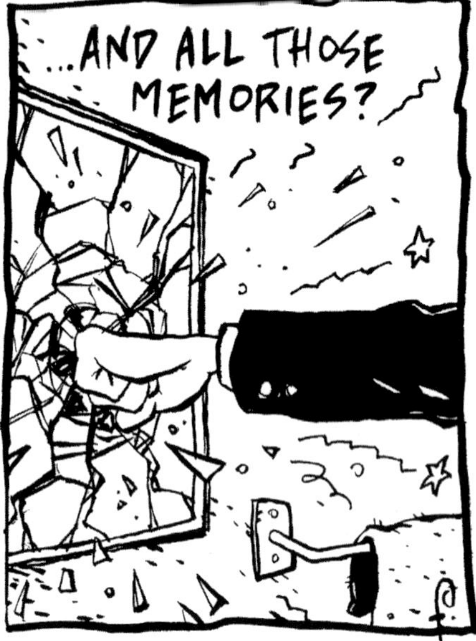
...AND ALL THOSE MEMORIES?

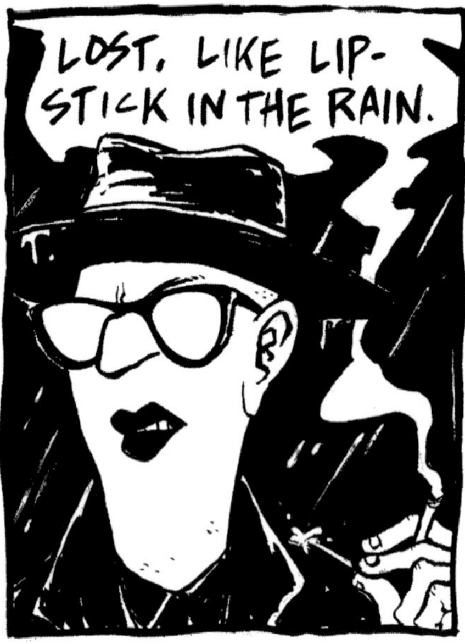
LOST, LIKE LIP-STICK IN THE RAIN.

WOMBAT — FIL..

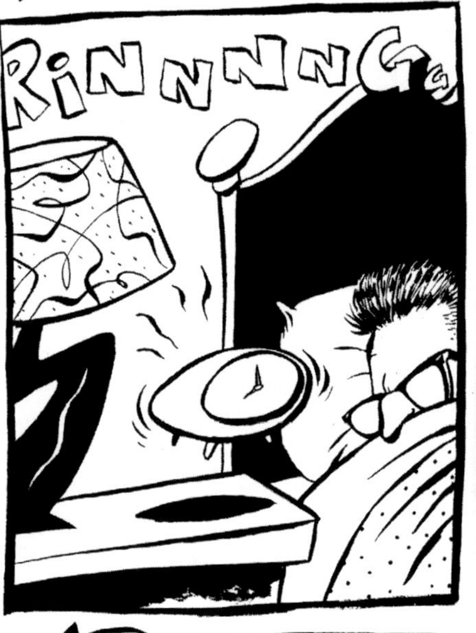
RINNNNNG

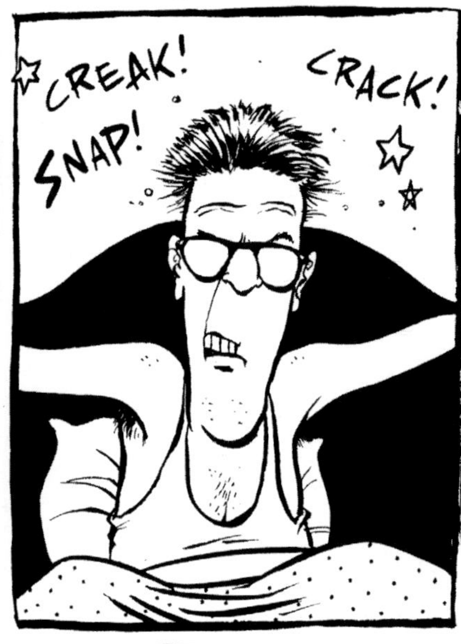
CREAK!
SNAP!
CRACK!

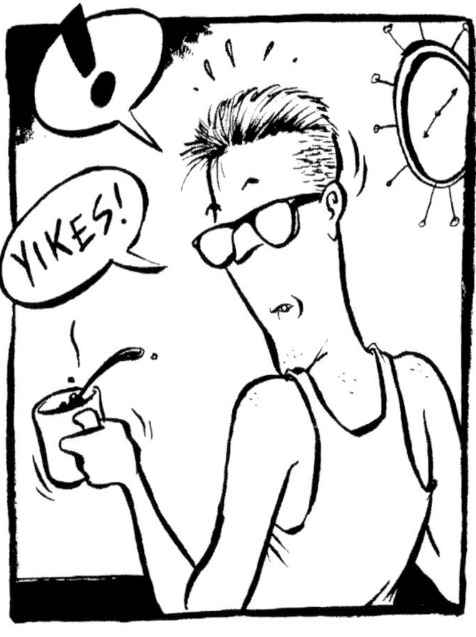
!
YIKES!

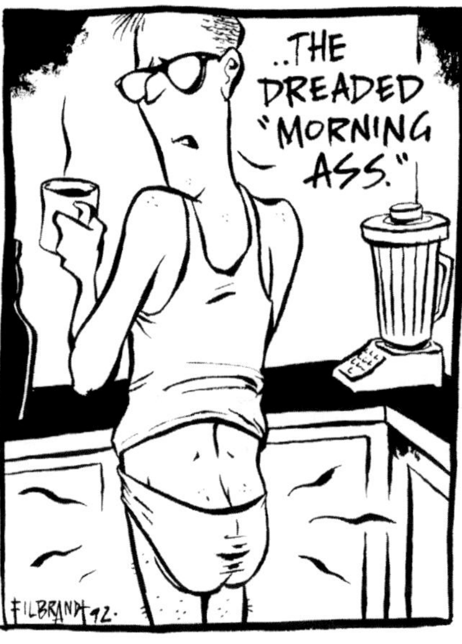
..THE DREADED "MORNING ASS."
FILBRANDT '92.

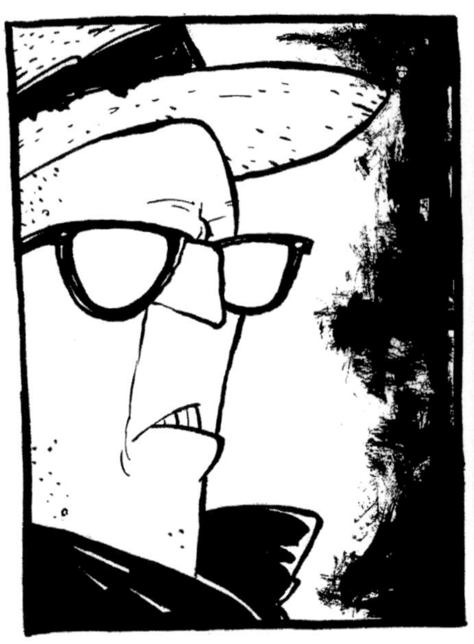

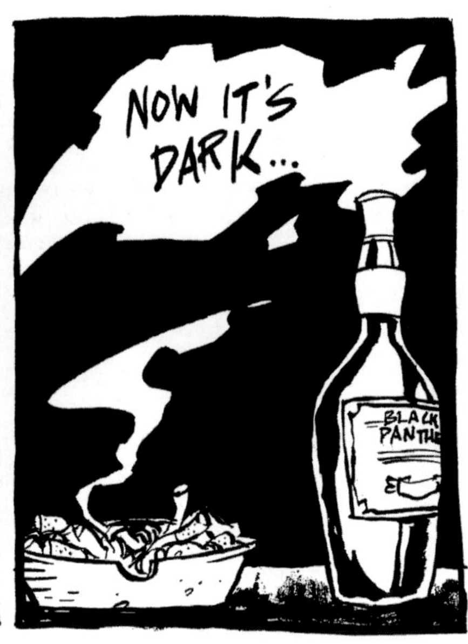

NOW IT'S DARK...
BLACK PANTH

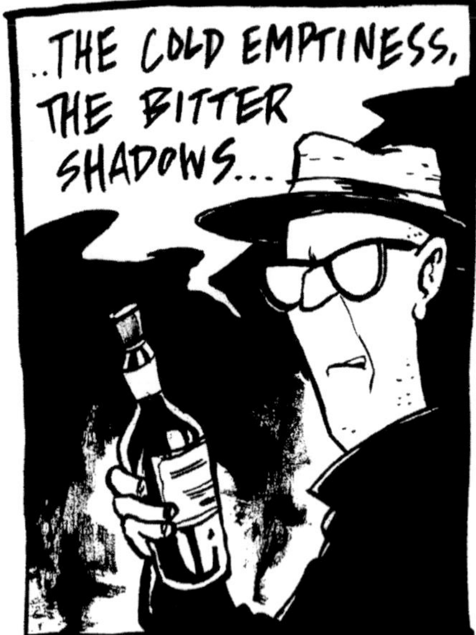

..THE COLD EMPTINESS, THE BITTER SHADOWS...

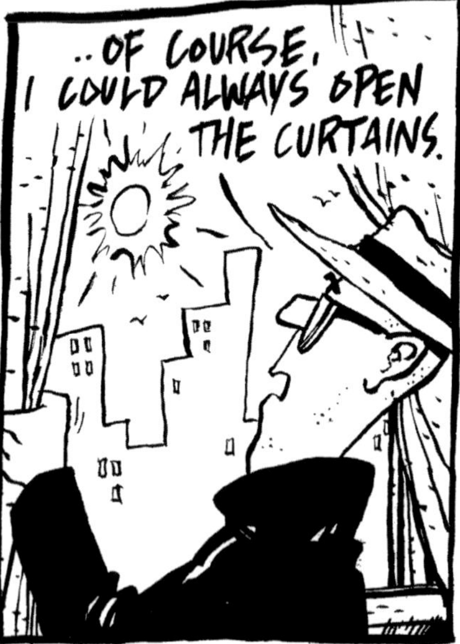

..OF COURSE, I COULD ALWAYS OPEN THE CURTAINS.

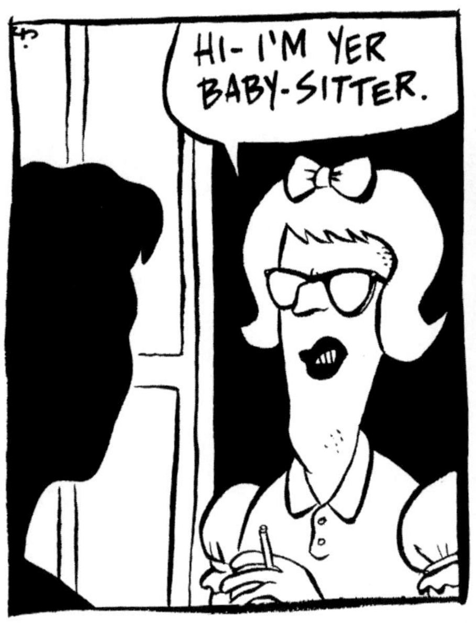
HI- I'M YER BABY-SITTER.

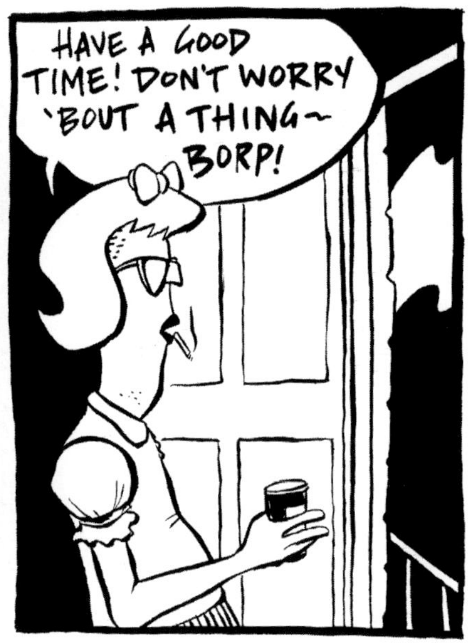
HAVE A GOOD TIME! DON'T WORRY 'BOUT A THING~ BORP!

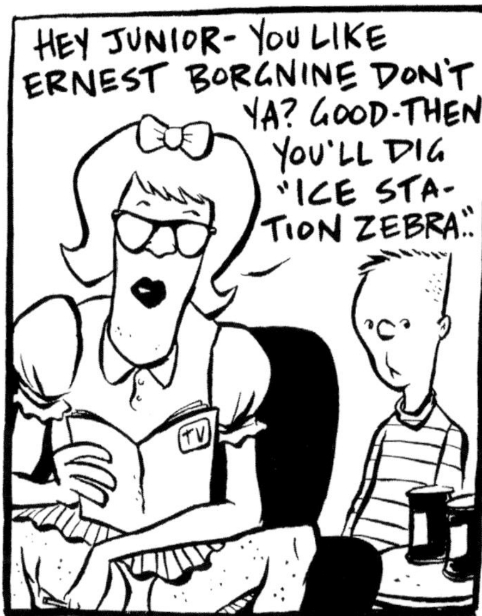
HEY JUNIOR- YOU LIKE ERNEST BORGNINE DON'T YA? GOOD-THEN YOU'LL DIG "ICE STATION ZEBRA"..
TV

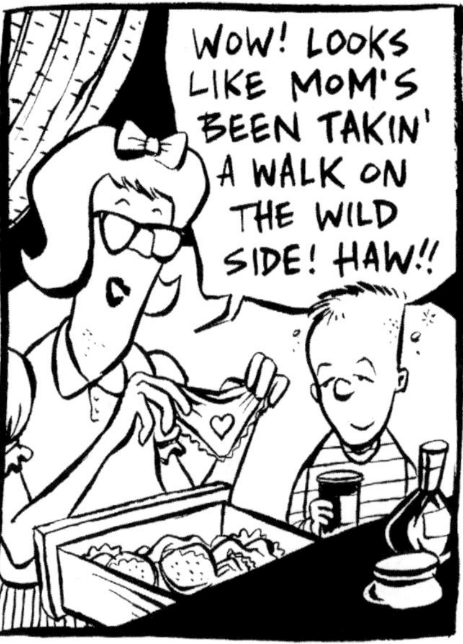
WOW! LOOKS LIKE MOM'S BEEN TAKIN' A WALK ON THE WILD SIDE! HAW!!

WOMBAT

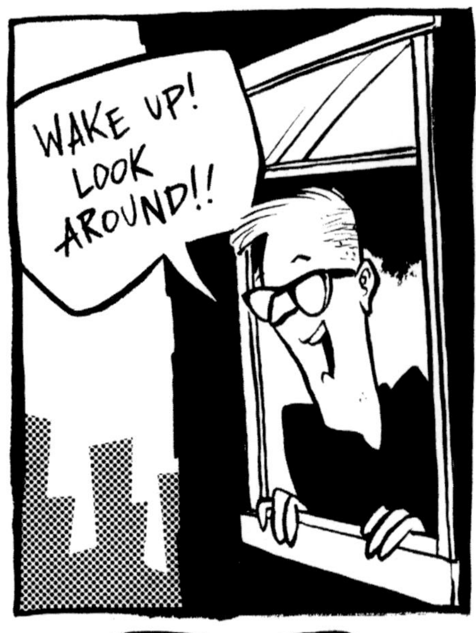
WAKE UP! LOOK AROUND!!

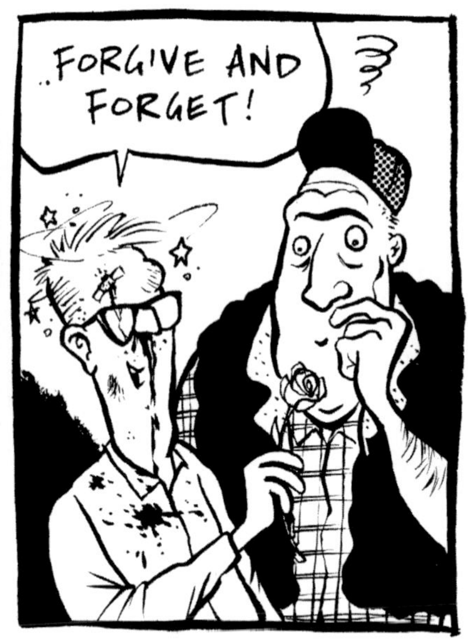
..FORGIVE AND FORGET!

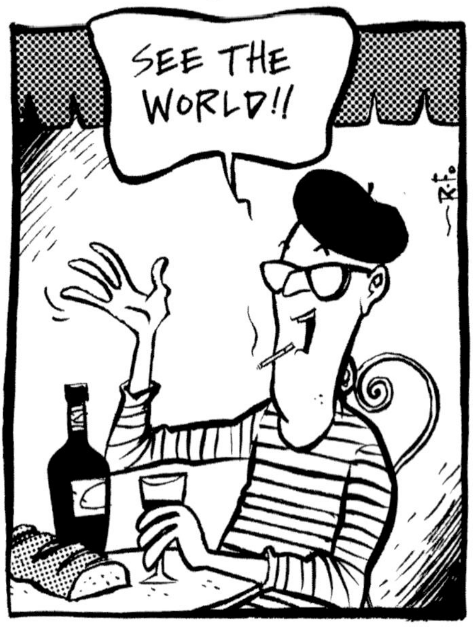
SEE THE WORLD!!

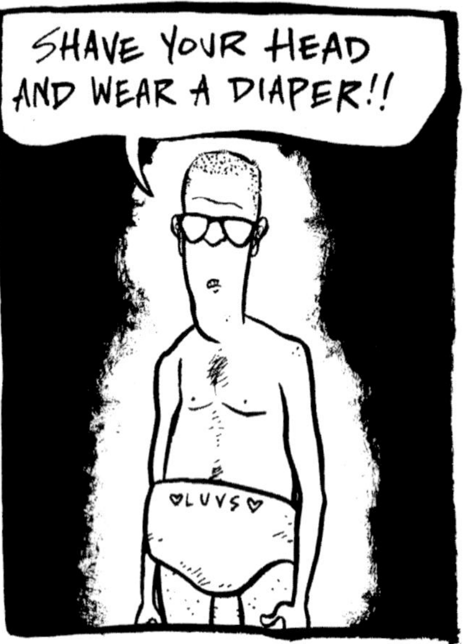
SHAVE YOUR HEAD AND WEAR A DIAPER!!
LUVS

WOMBAT R. FILBRANDT

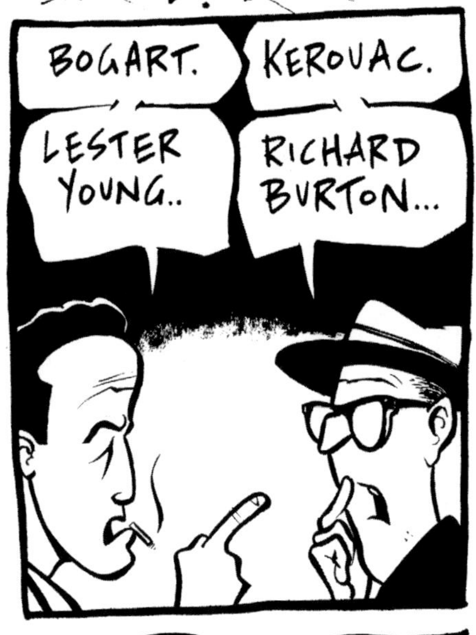

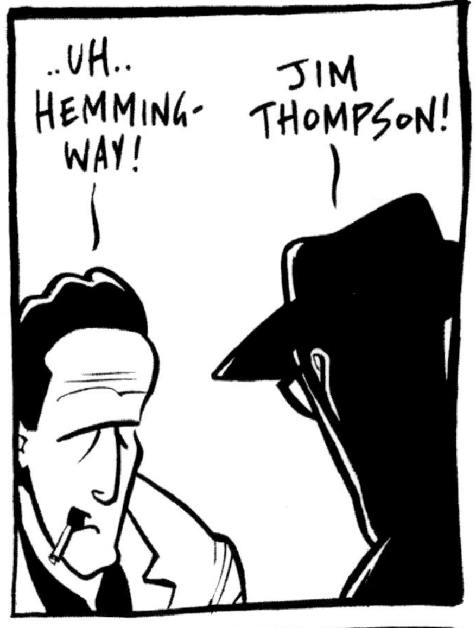

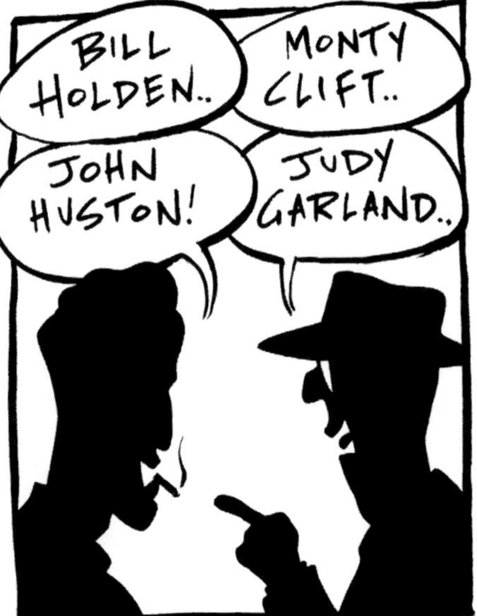

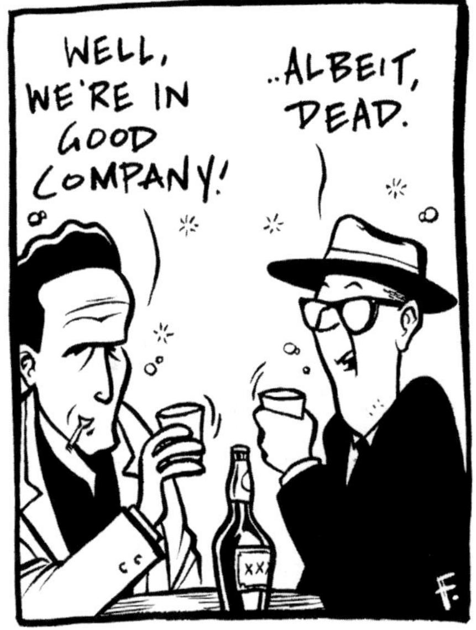

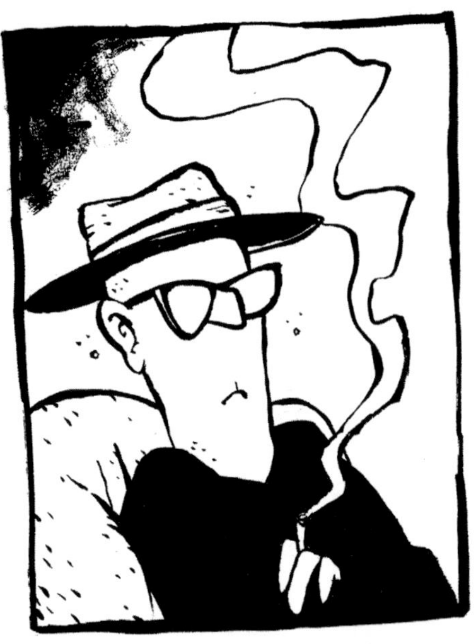

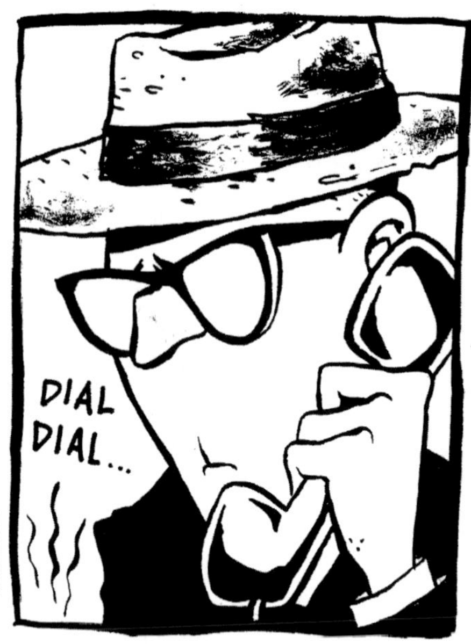
DIAL
DIAL...

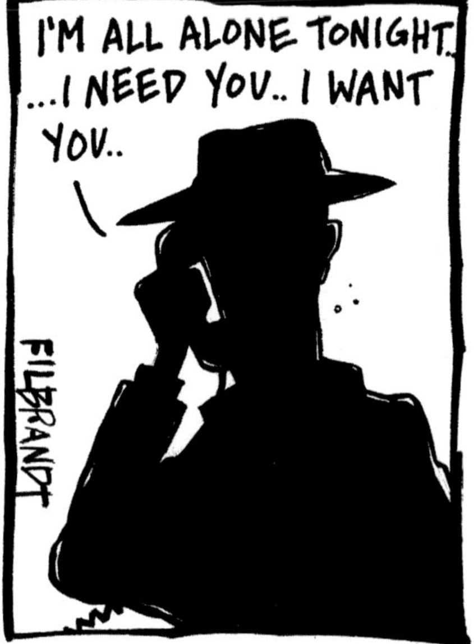
I'M ALL ALONE TONIGHT.. ...I NEED YOU.. I WANT YOU..
FILLBRANDT

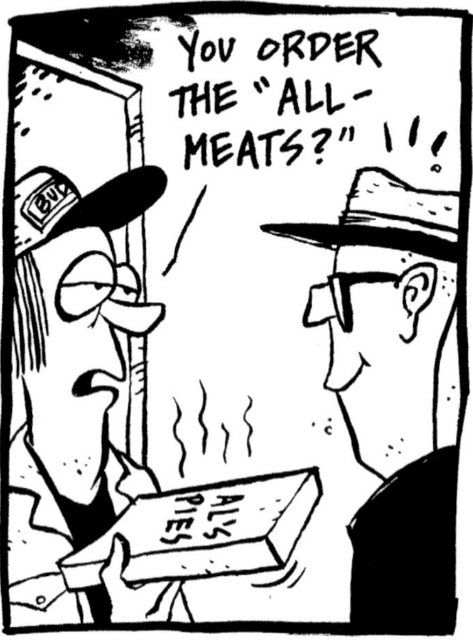
YOU ORDER THE "ALL-MEATS?"
BUD
AL'S PIES

WOMBAT * SORRY, ERNIE...

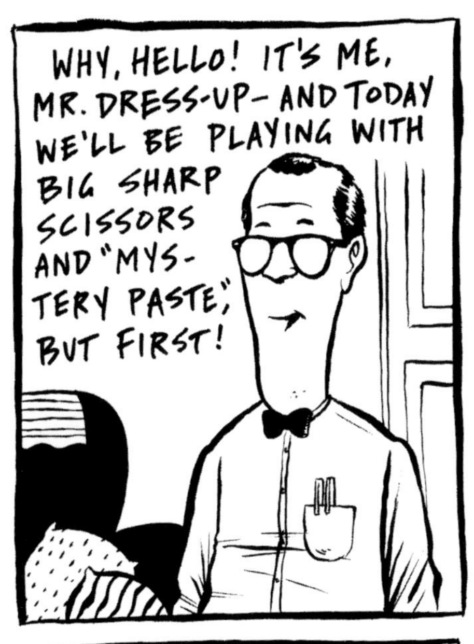

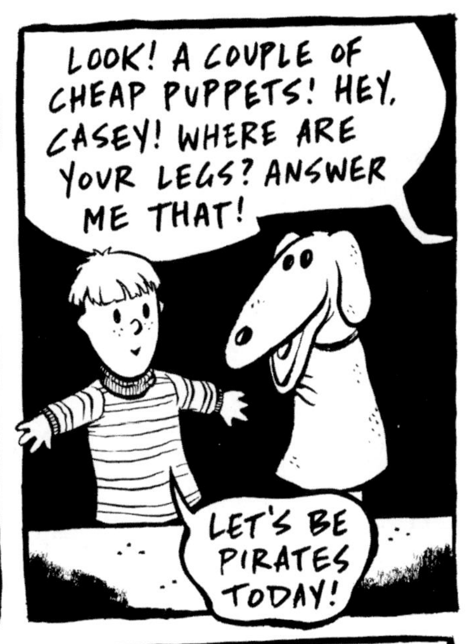

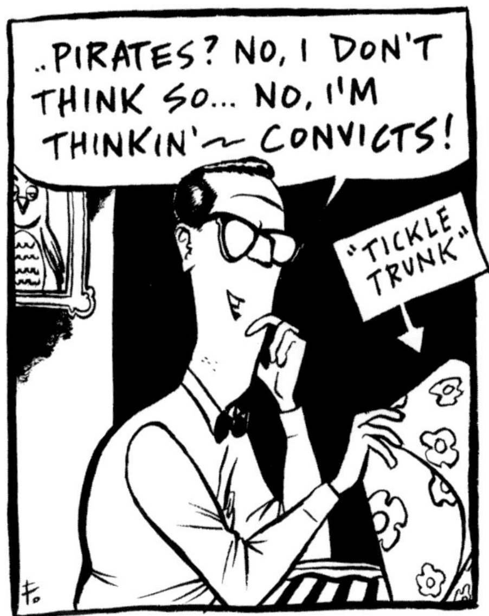

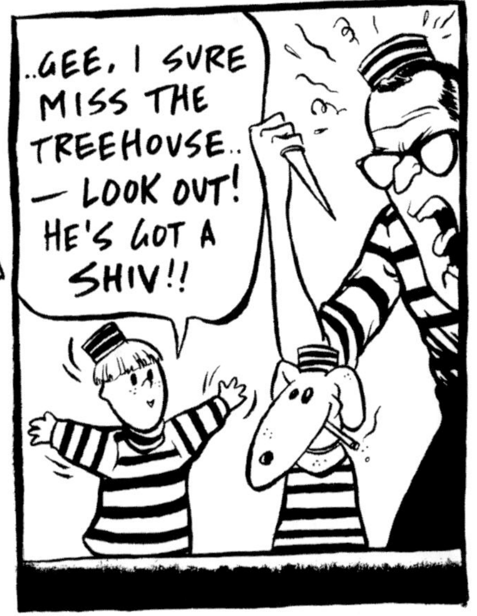

WOMBAT by Fillbrandt

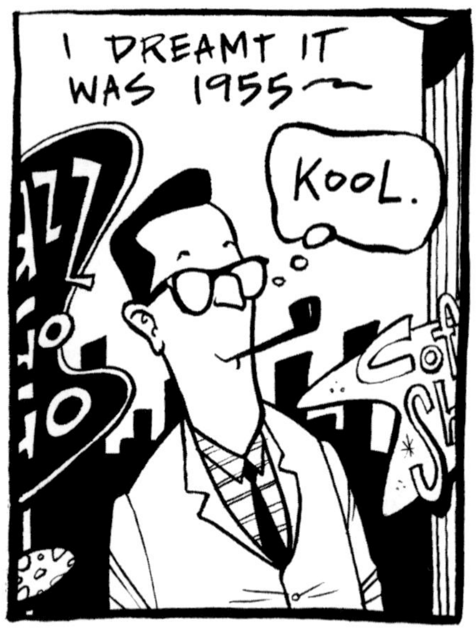

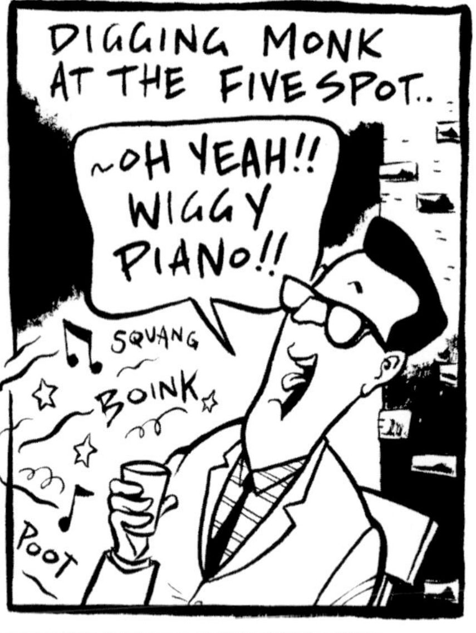

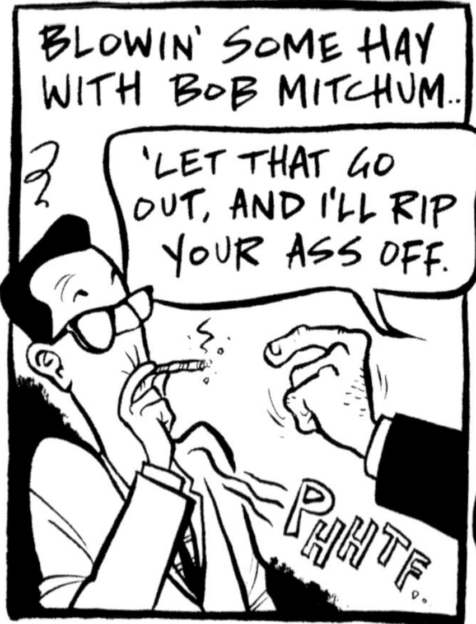

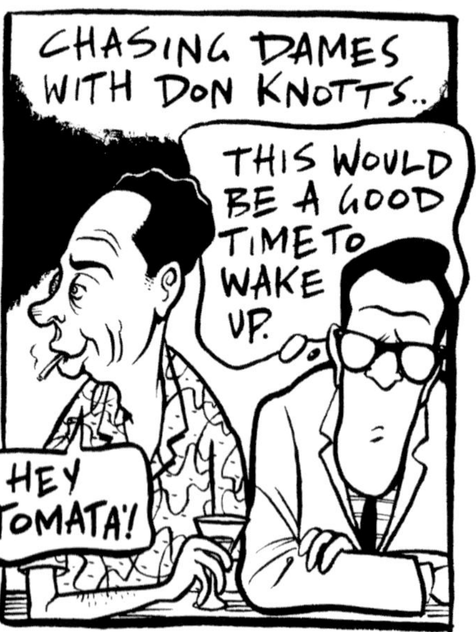

"WOMBAT" — FILBRANDT

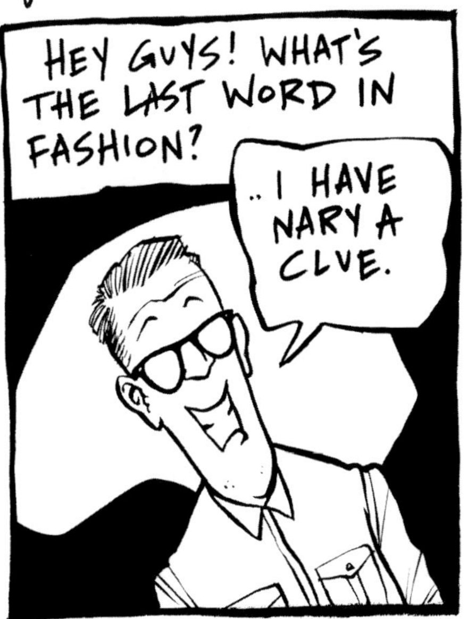

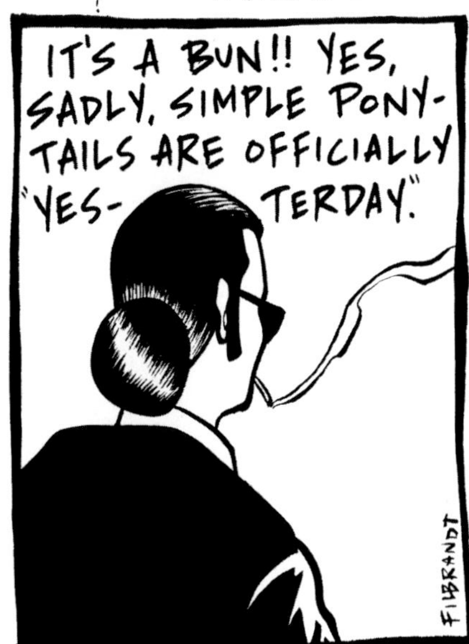

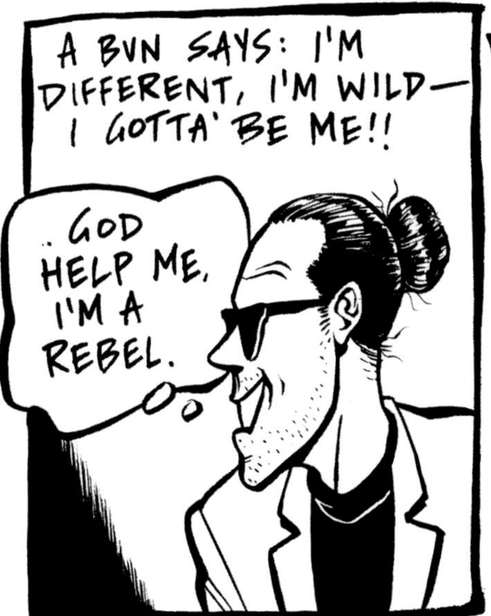

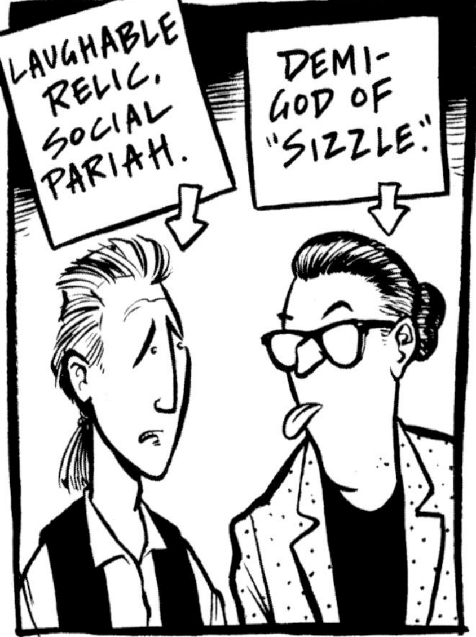

Wombat

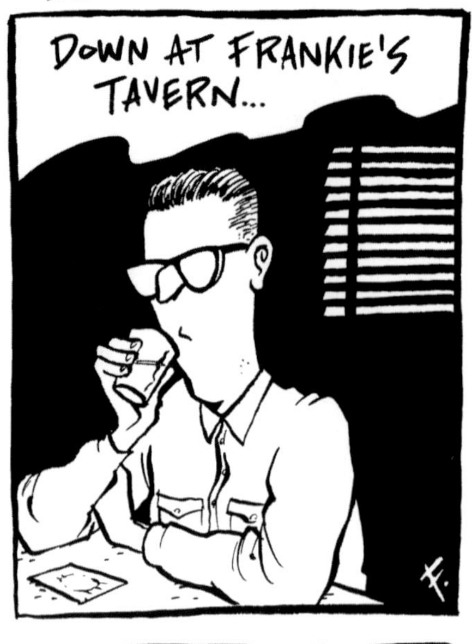
DOWN AT FRANKIE'S TAVERN...

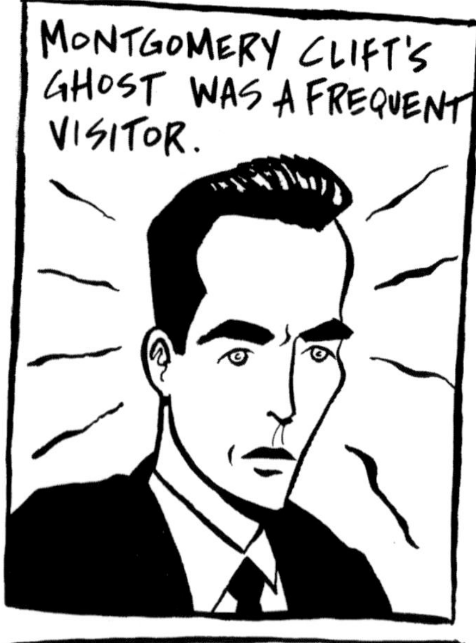
MONTGOMERY CLIFT'S GHOST WAS A FREQUENT VISITOR.

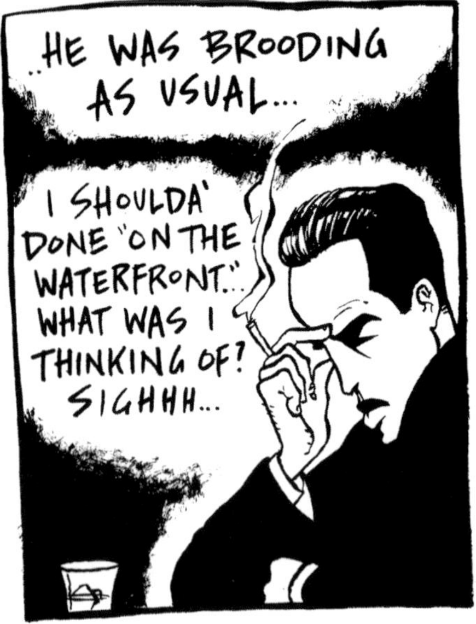
..HE WAS BROODING AS USUAL...
I SHOULDA' DONE "ON THE WATERFRONT." WHAT WAS I THINKING OF? SIGHHH...

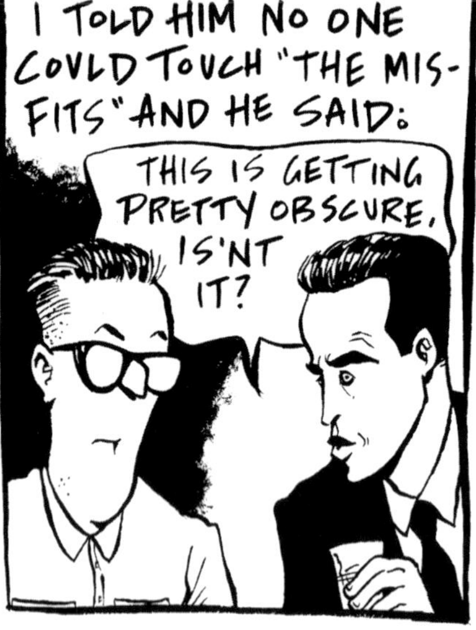
I TOLD HIM NO ONE COULD TOUCH "THE MIS-FITS" AND HE SAID:
THIS IS GETTING PRETTY OBSCURE, IS'NT IT?

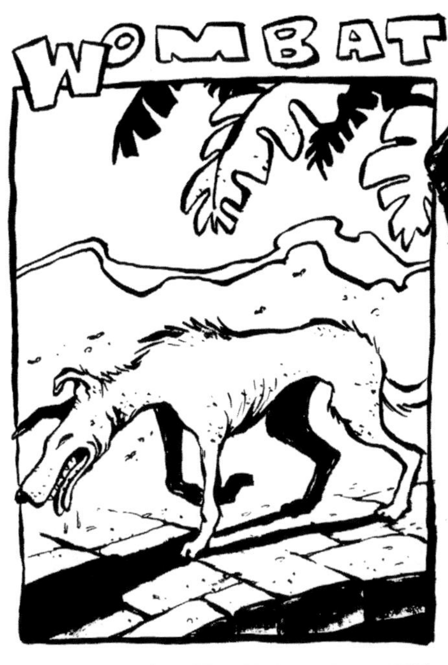
WOMBAT

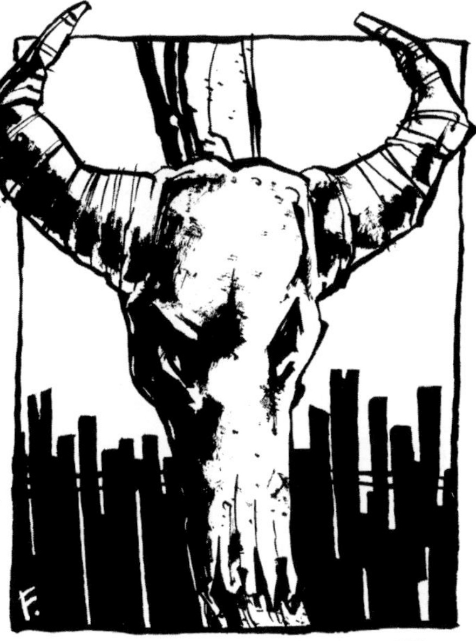

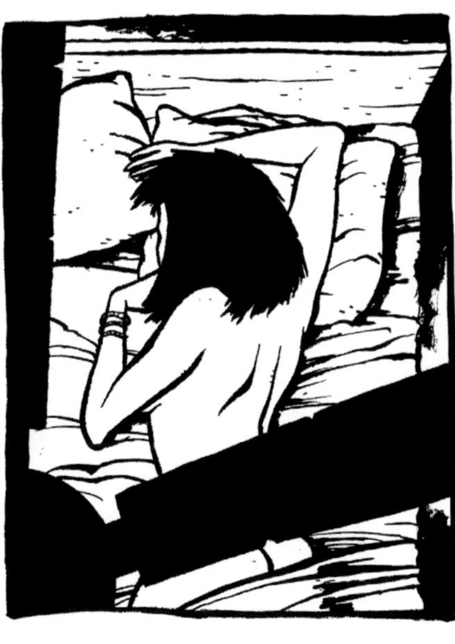

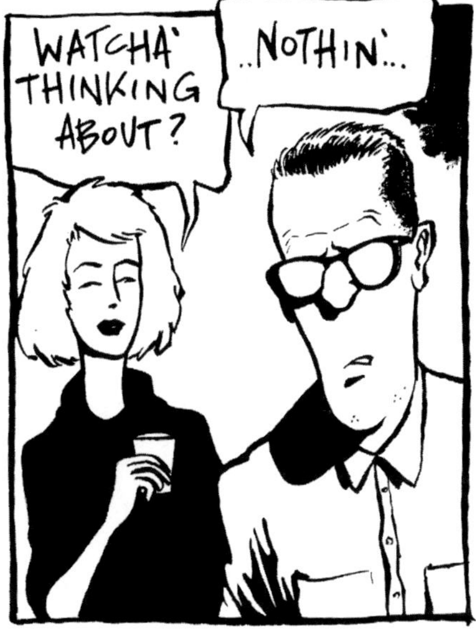
WATCHA' THINKING ABOUT?
..NOTHIN'...

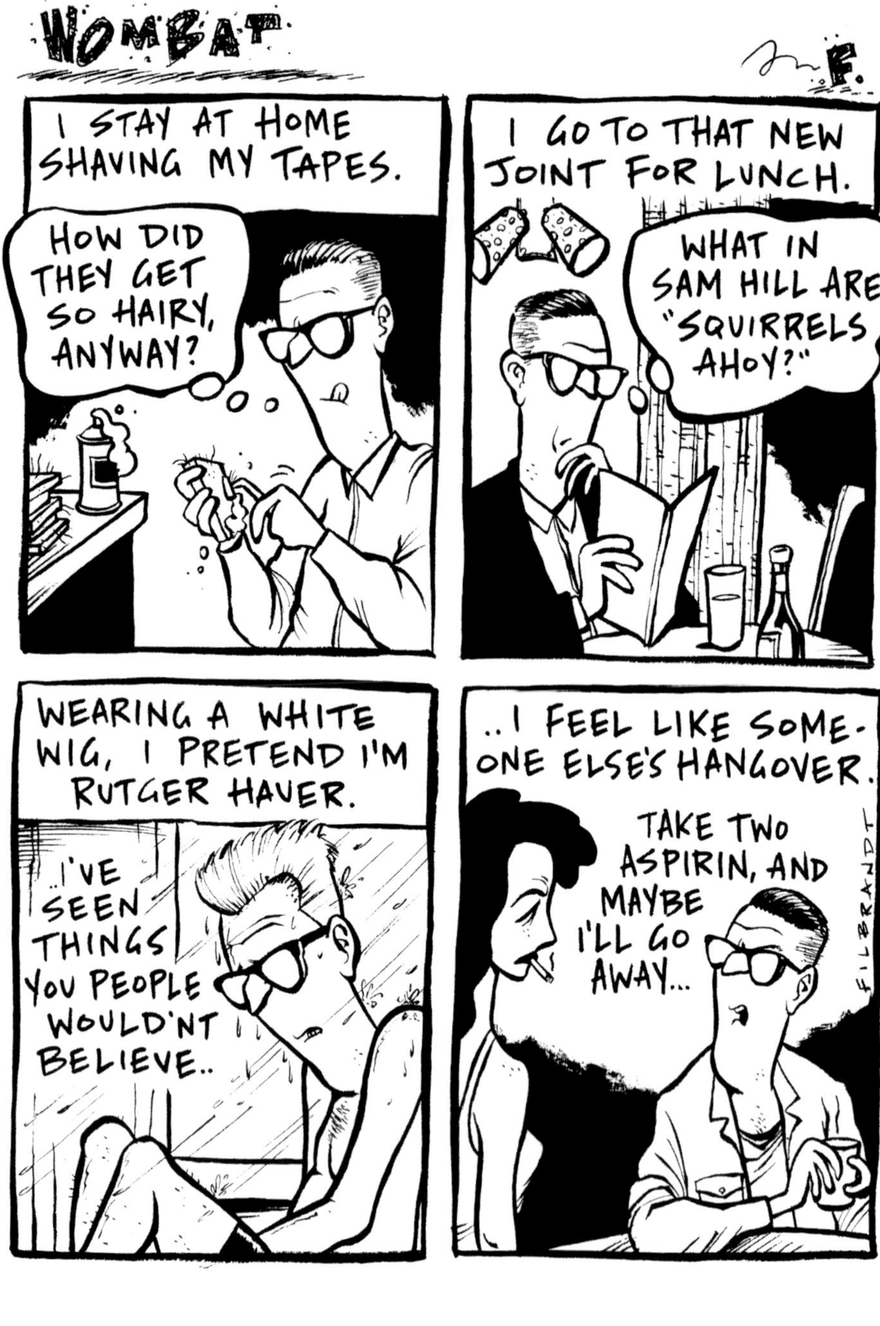

WOMBAT

F.

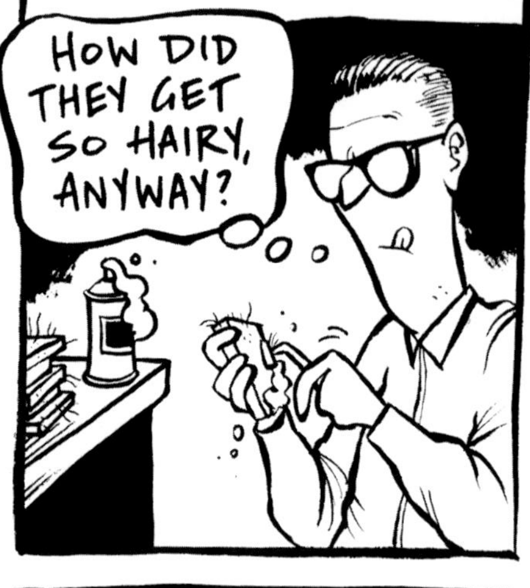

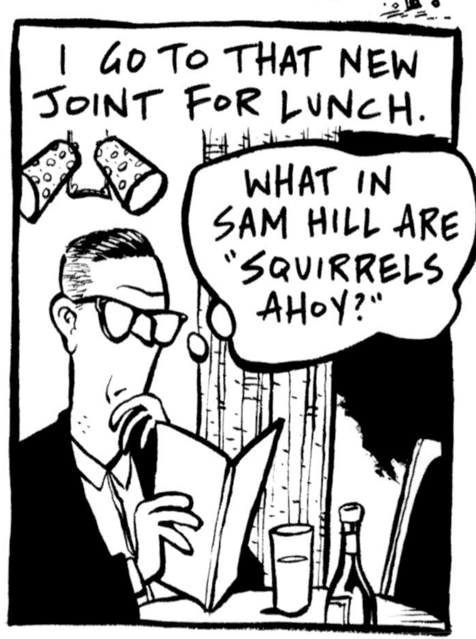

WEARING A WHITE WIG, I PRETEND I'M RUTGER HAUER.

..I'VE SEEN THINGS YOU PEOPLE WOULD'NT BELIEVE..

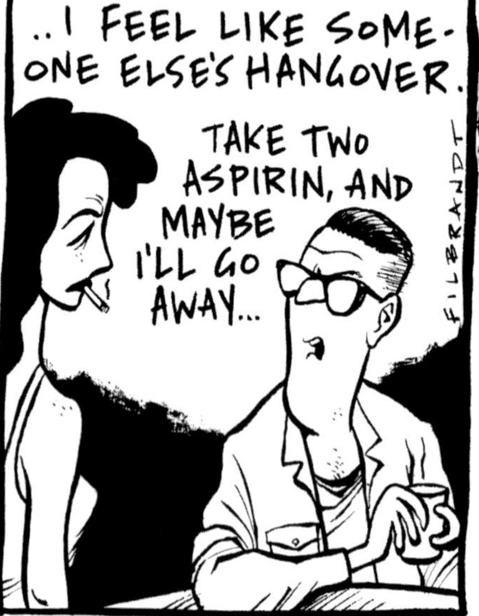

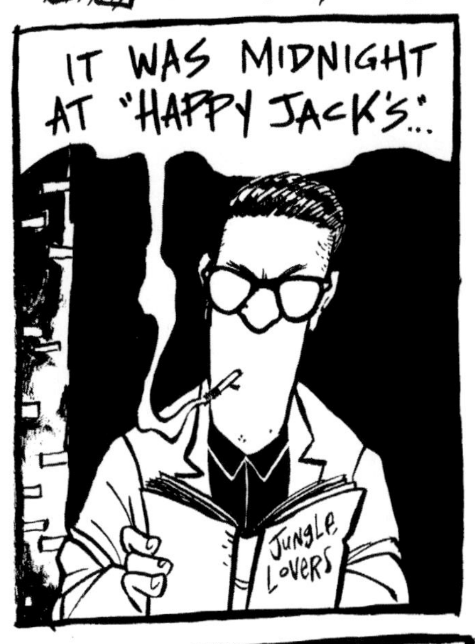
IT WAS MIDNIGHT AT "HAPPY JACK'S"...
JUNGLE LOVERS

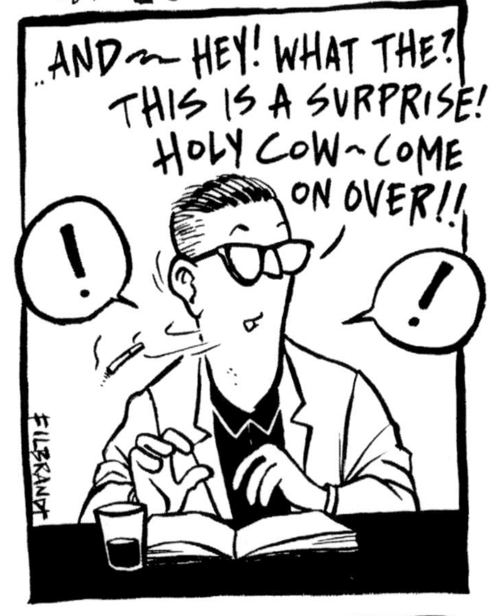
...AND~ HEY! WHAT THE? THIS IS A SURPRISE! HOLY COW~COME ON OVER!!
!
!

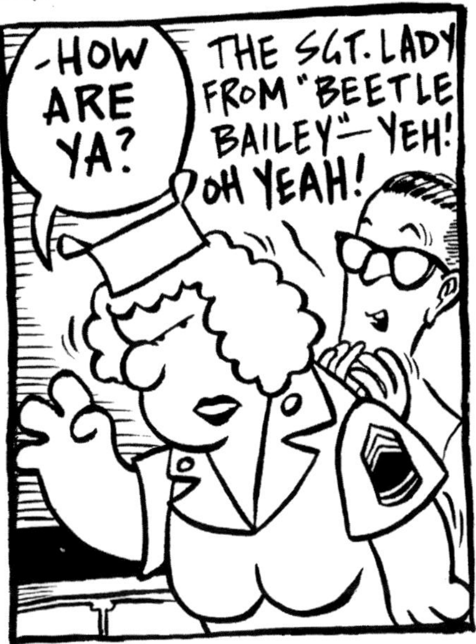
-HOW ARE YA?
THE SGT. LADY FROM "BEETLE BAILEY"— YEH! OH YEAH!

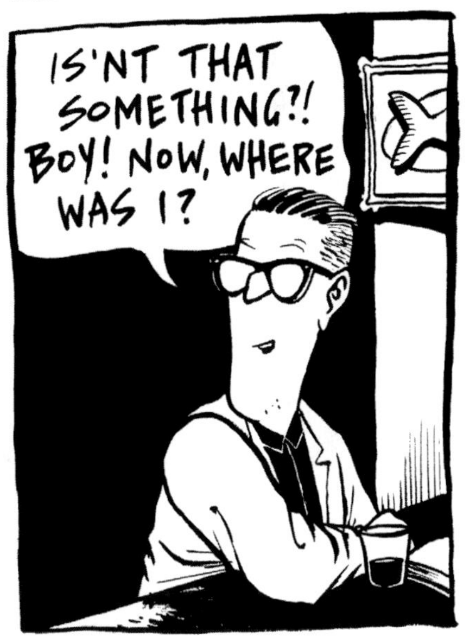
IS'NT THAT SOMETHING?! BOY! NOW, WHERE WAS I?

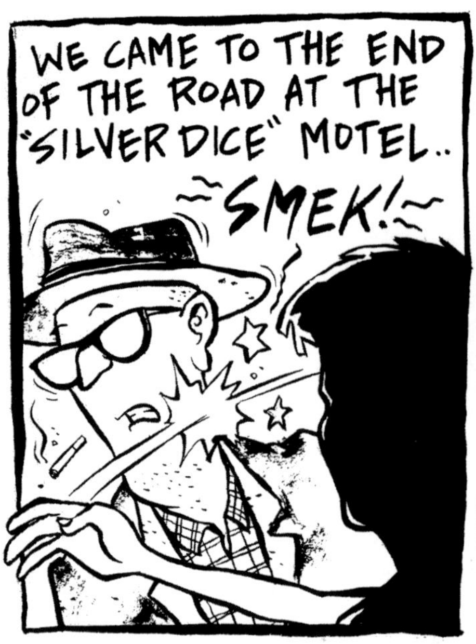
WE CAME TO THE END OF THE ROAD AT THE "SILVER DICE" MOTEL..
SMEK!

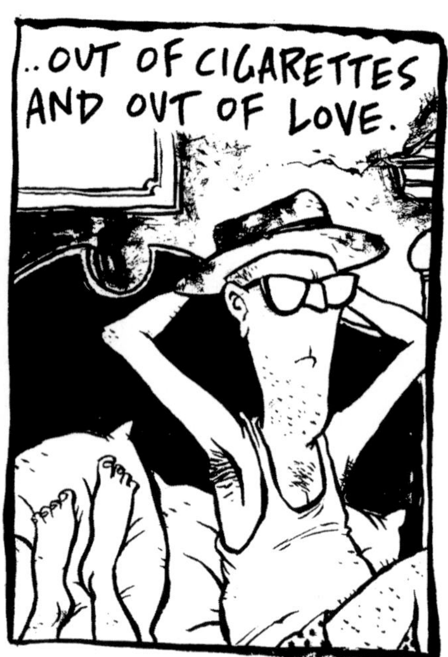
..OUT OF CIGARETTES AND OUT OF LOVE.

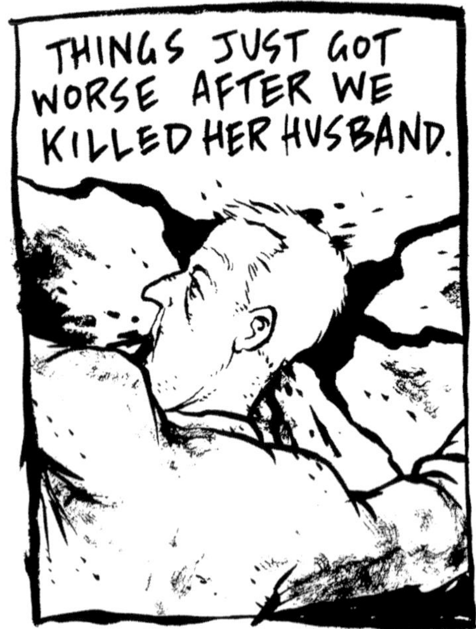
THINGS JUST GOT WORSE AFTER WE KILLED HER HUSBAND.

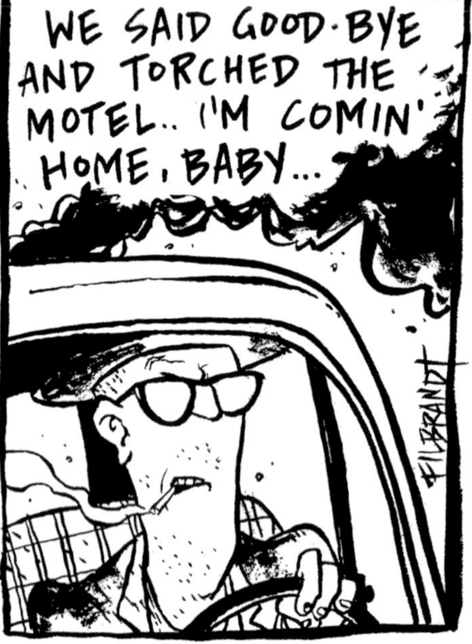
WE SAID GOOD-BYE AND TORCHED THE MOTEL.. I'M COMIN' HOME, BABY...
FILLBRANDT

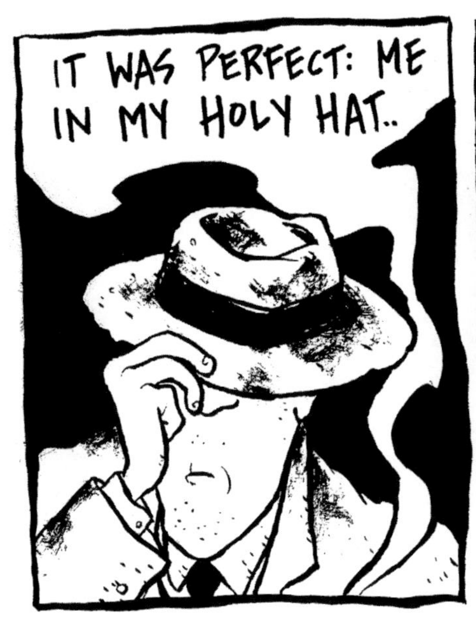
IT WAS PERFECT: ME IN MY HOLY HAT..

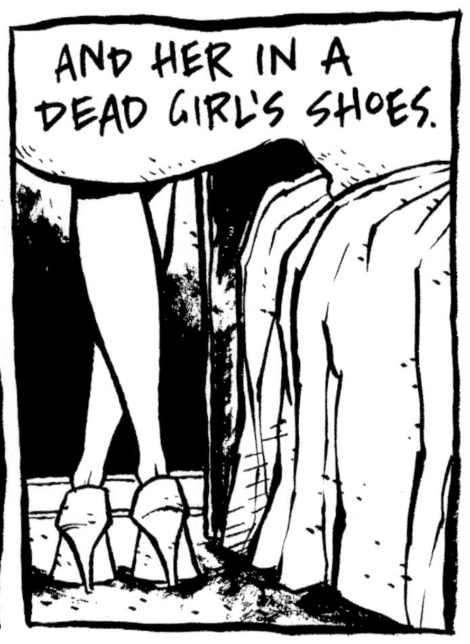
AND HER IN A DEAD GIRL'S SHOES.

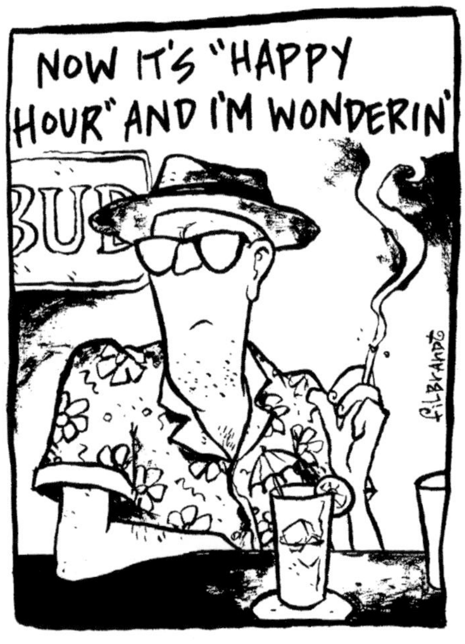
NOW IT'S "HAPPY HOUR" AND I'M WONDERIN'

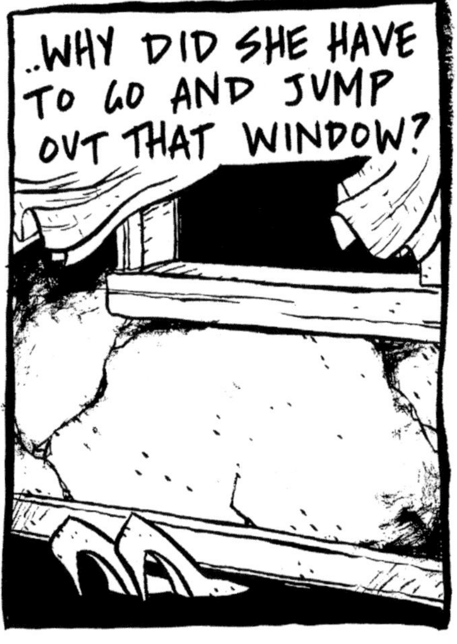
..WHY DID SHE HAVE TO GO AND JUMP OUT THAT WINDOW?

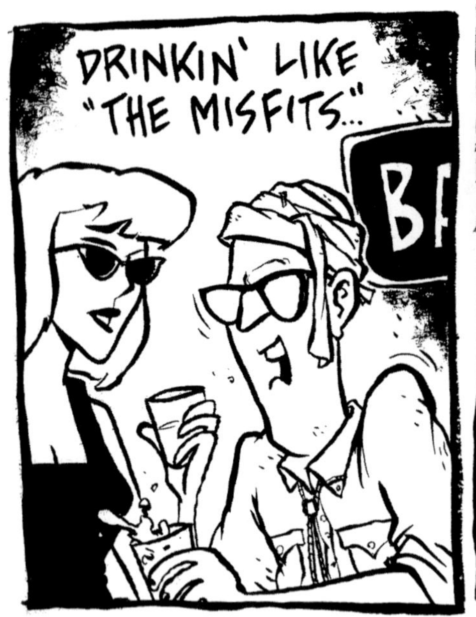
DRINKIN' LIKE "THE MISFITS"...
BA

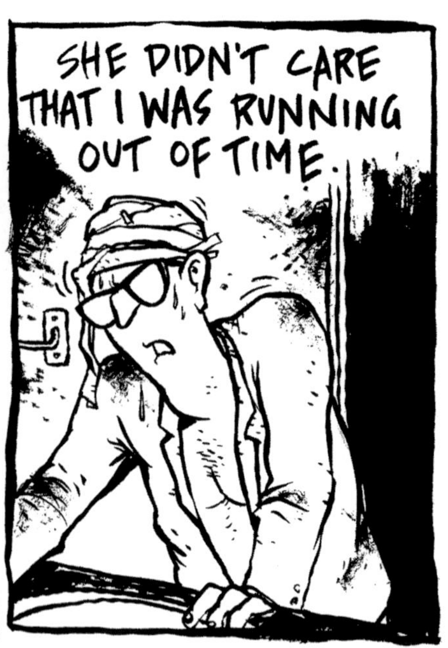
SHE DIDN'T CARE THAT I WAS RUNNING OUT OF TIME.

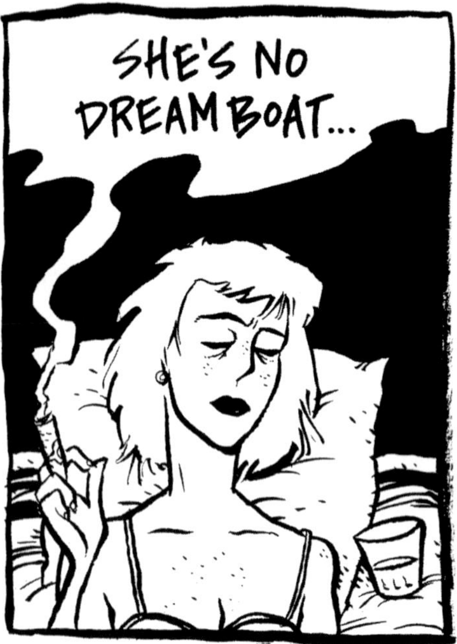
SHE'S NO DREAMBOAT...

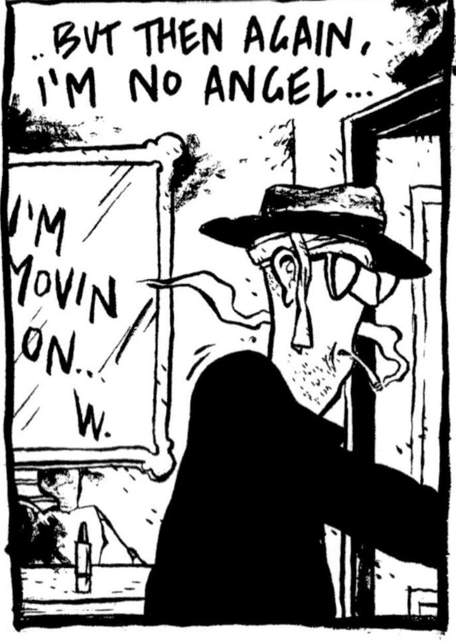
..BUT THEN AGAIN, I'M NO ANGEL...
I'M MOVIN ON..
W.

WOMBAT

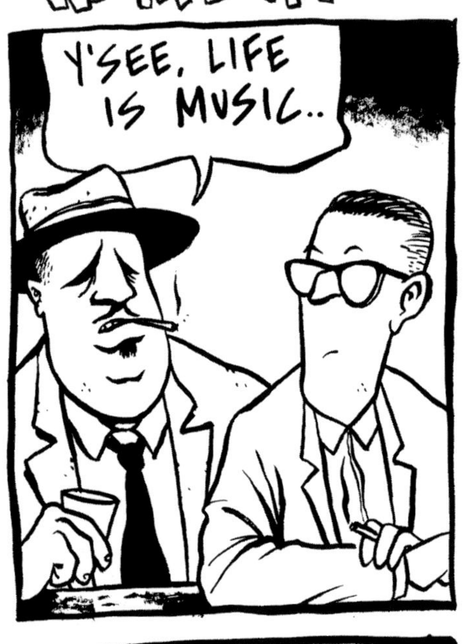
Y'SEE, LIFE IS MUSIC..

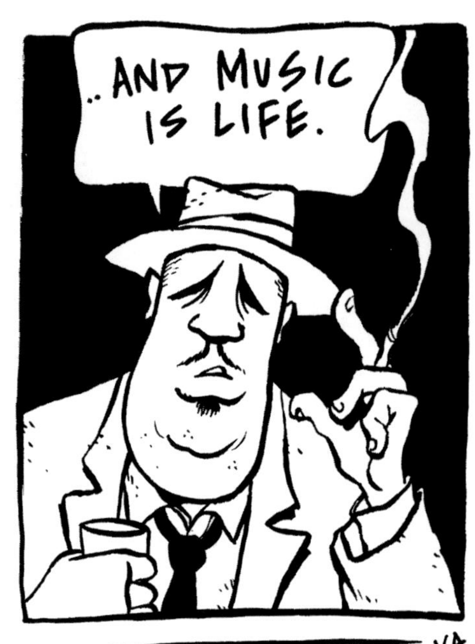
..AND MUSIC IS LIFE.

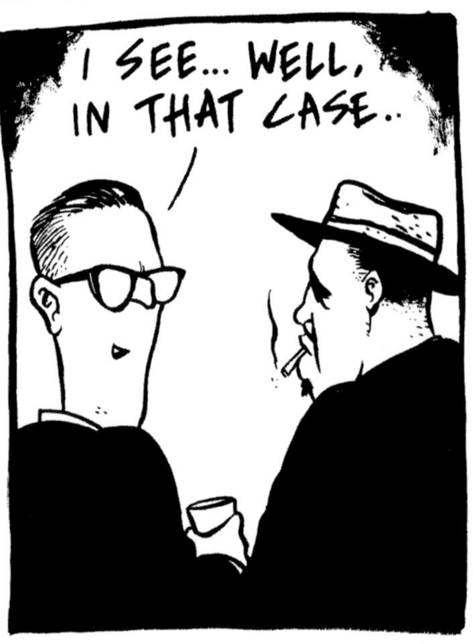
I SEE... WELL, IN THAT CASE..

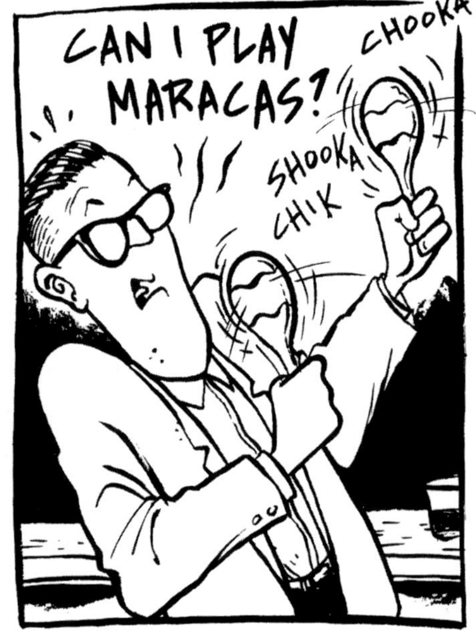
CAN I PLAY MARACAS?
CHOOKA
SHOOKA CHIK

WOMBAT by FILBRANDT·92

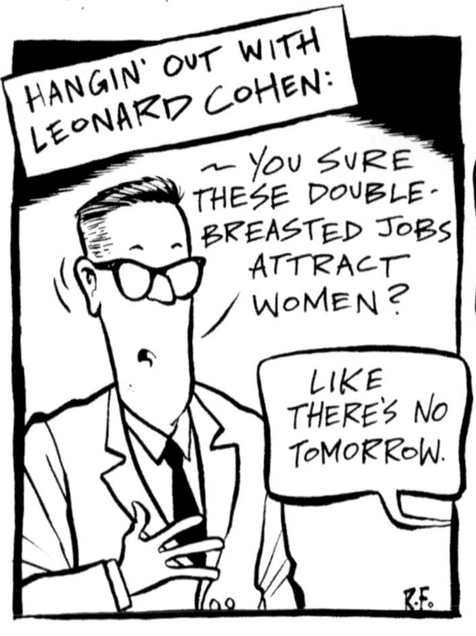

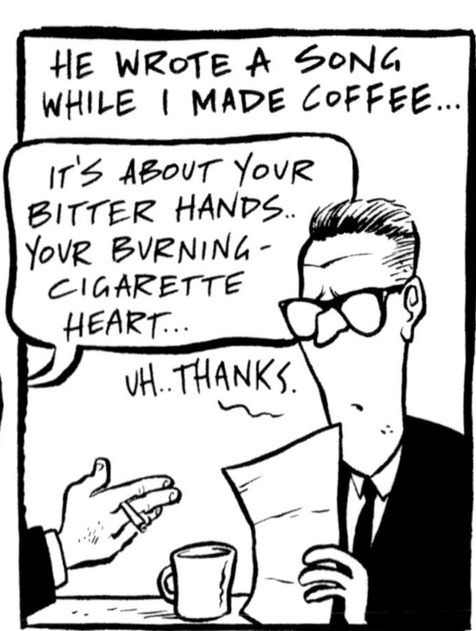

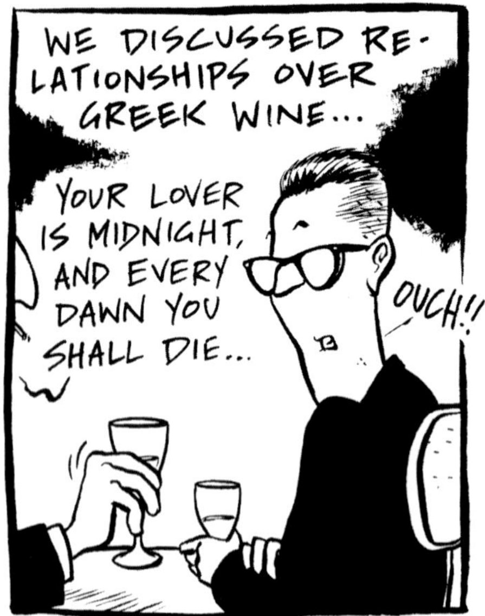

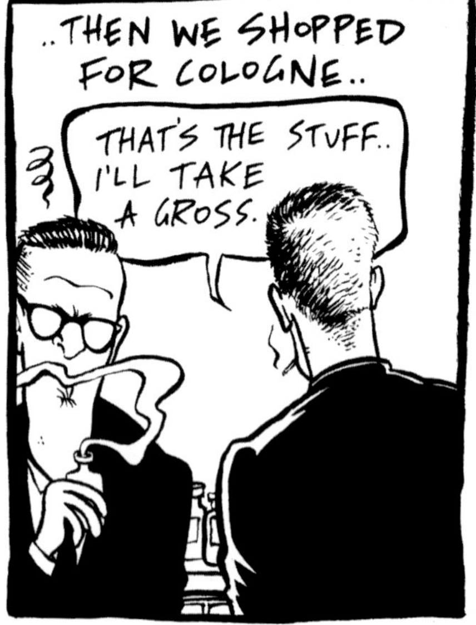

WOMBAT

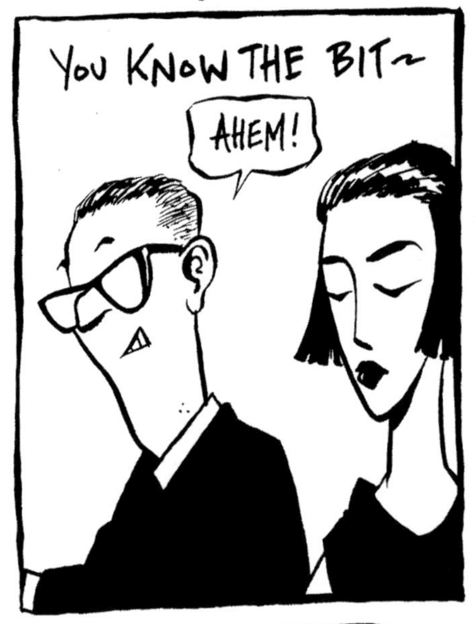
YOU KNOW THE BIT~
AHEM!

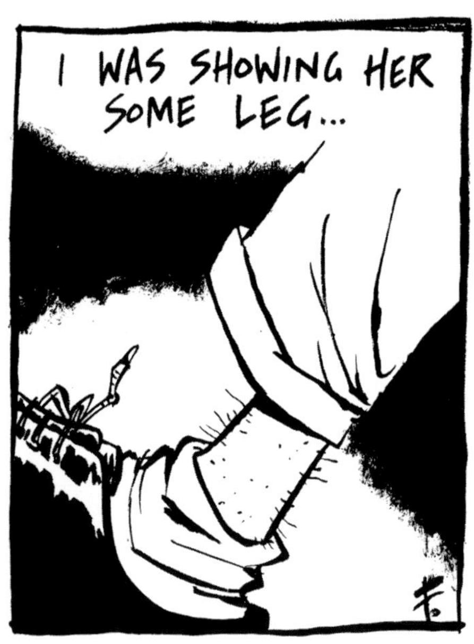
I WAS SHOWING HER SOME LEG...

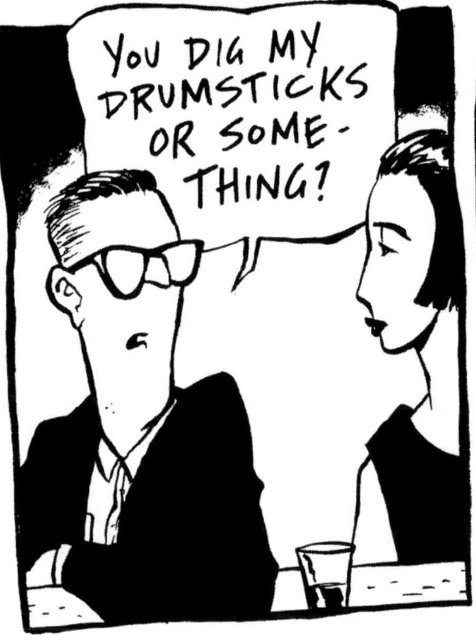
YOU DIG MY DRUMSTICKS OR SOME-THING?

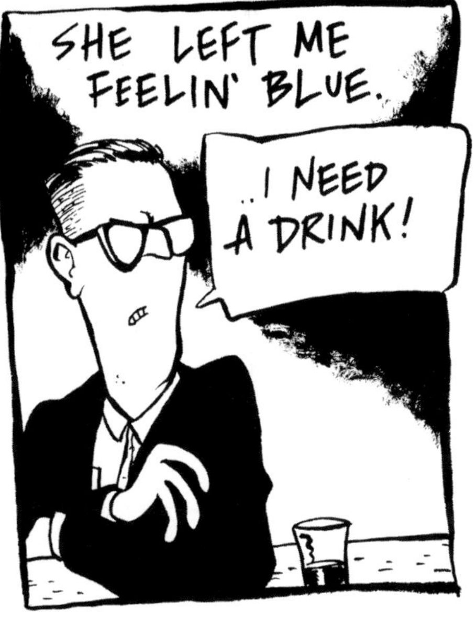
SHE LEFT ME FEELIN' BLUE.
..I NEED A DRINK!

WOMBAT — F.

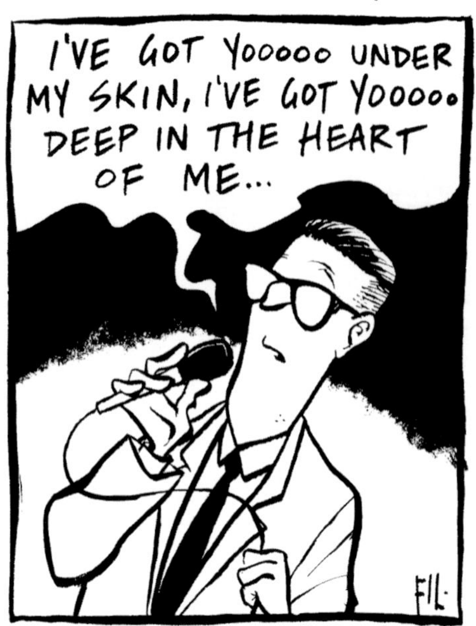
I'VE GOT YOOOOO UNDER MY SKIN, I'VE GOT YOOOOO DEEP IN THE HEART OF ME...
FIL

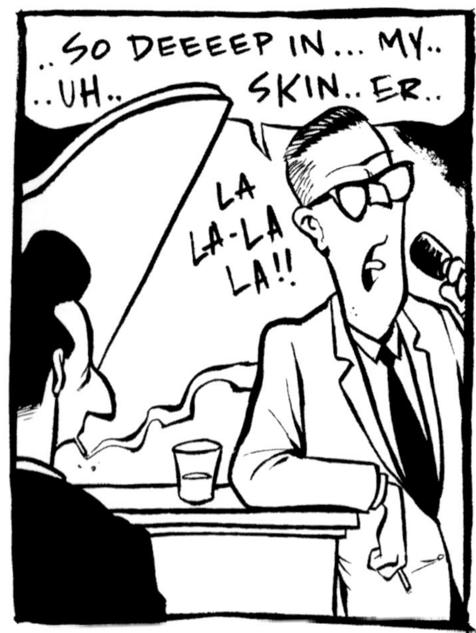
..SO DEEEEP IN... MY.. ..UH.. SKIN.. ER..
LA LA-LA LA!!

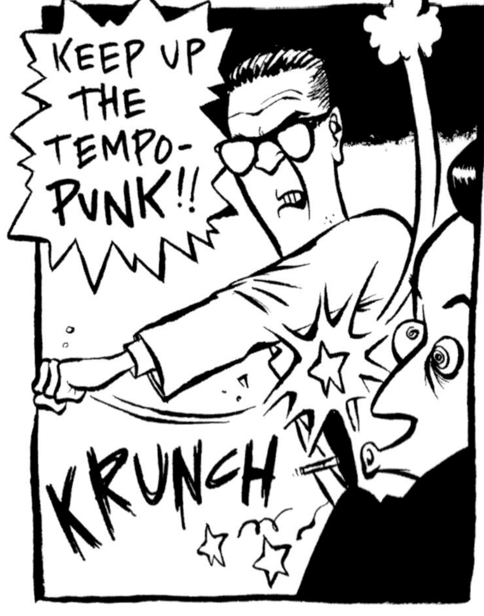
KEEP UP THE TEMPO-PUNK!!
KRUNCH

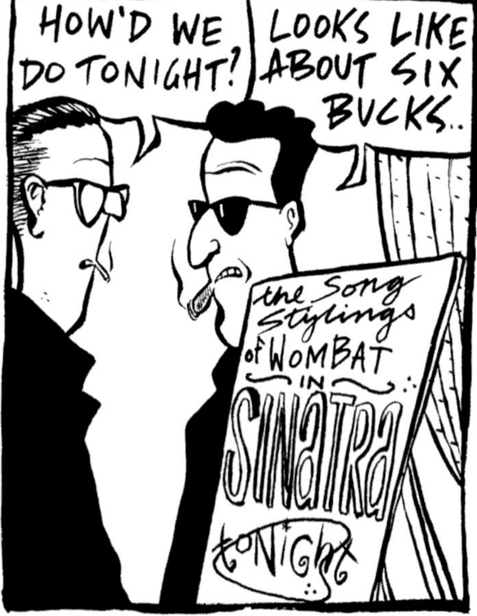
HOW'D WE DO TONIGHT?
LOOKS LIKE ABOUT SIX BUCKS..
the Song Stylings of WOMBAT IN SINATRA tonight

WOMBAT

FILBRANDT

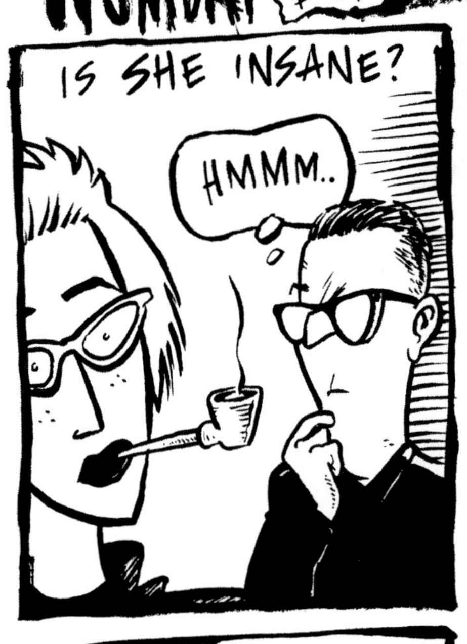

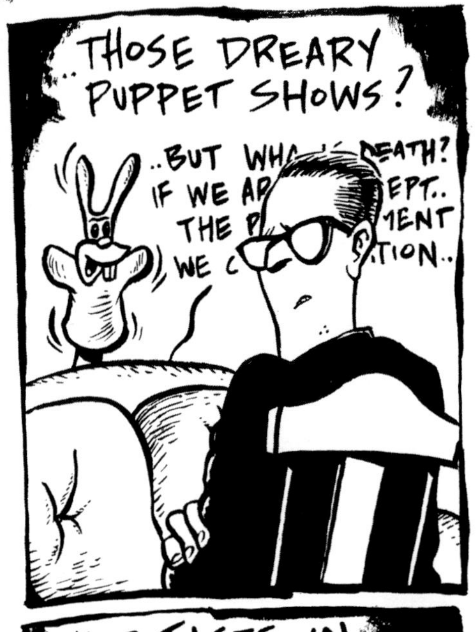

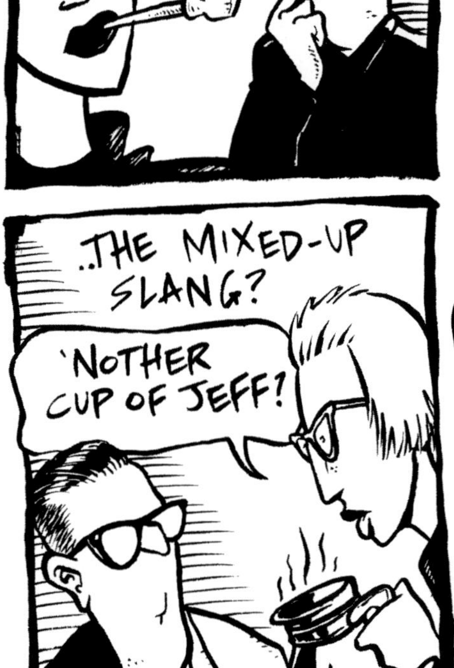

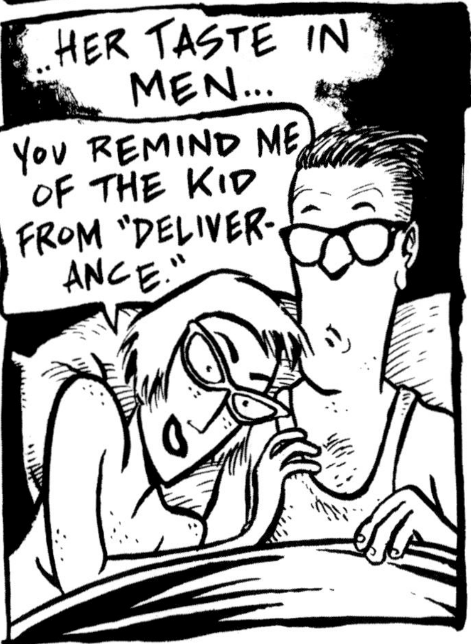

WOMBAT by Rod Filbrandt

FROM THE SERIES "ROT-WEISS"

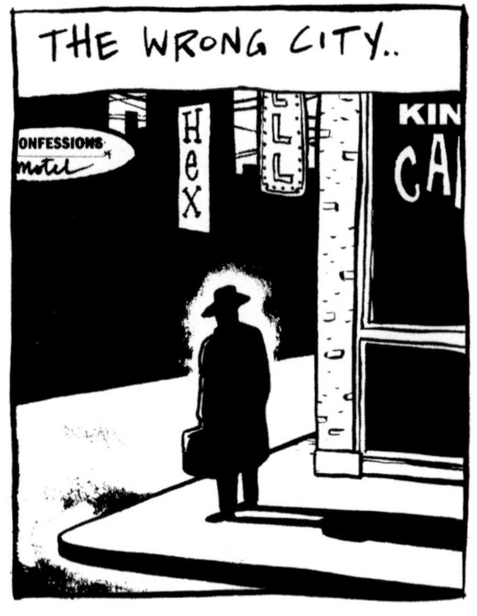

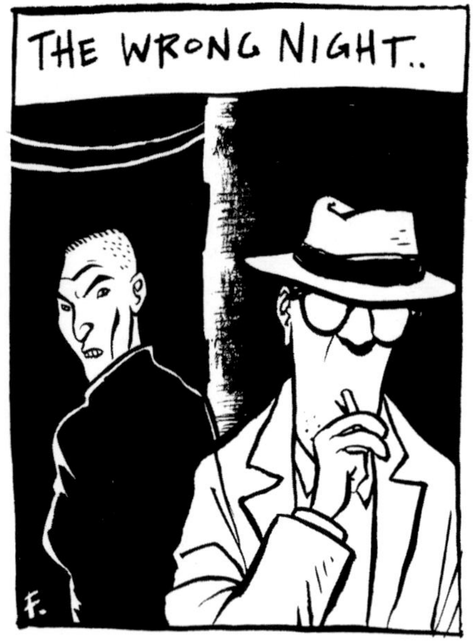

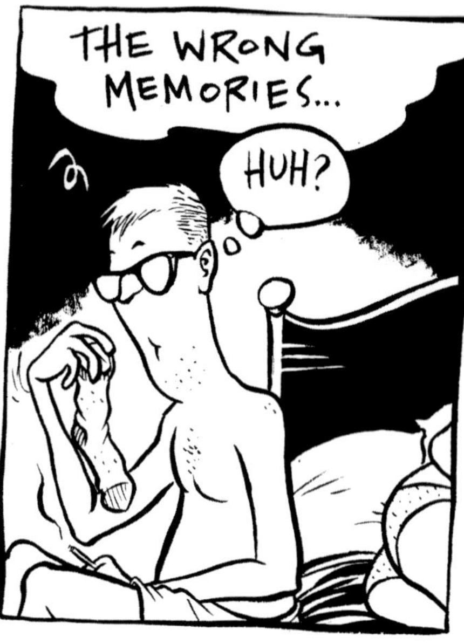

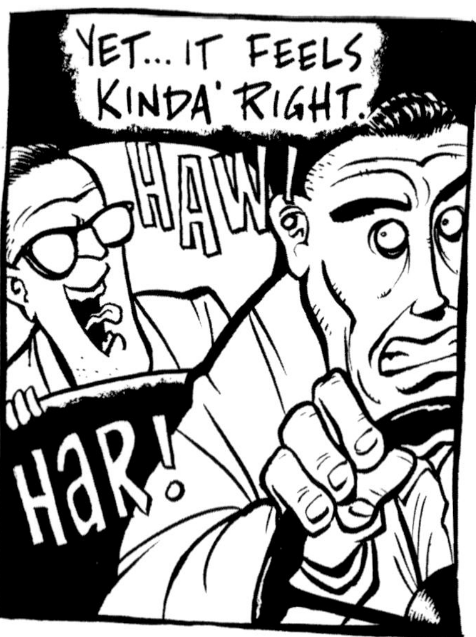

WOMBAT

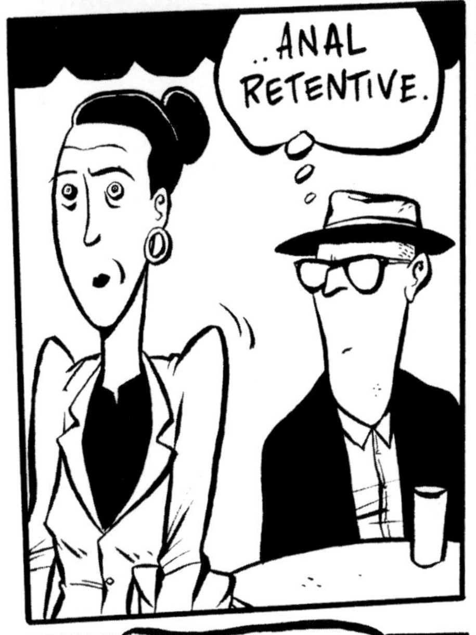
..ANAL RETENTIVE.

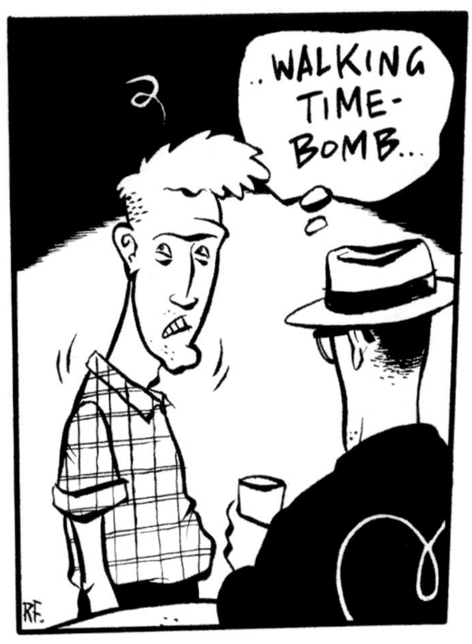
..WALKING TIME-BOMB...
RF.

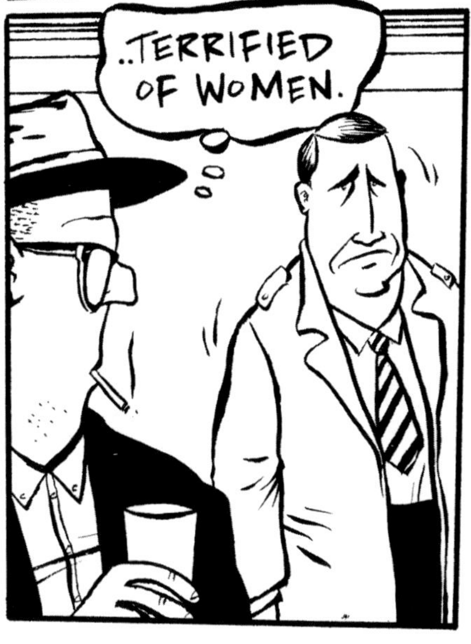
..TERRIFIED OF WOMEN.

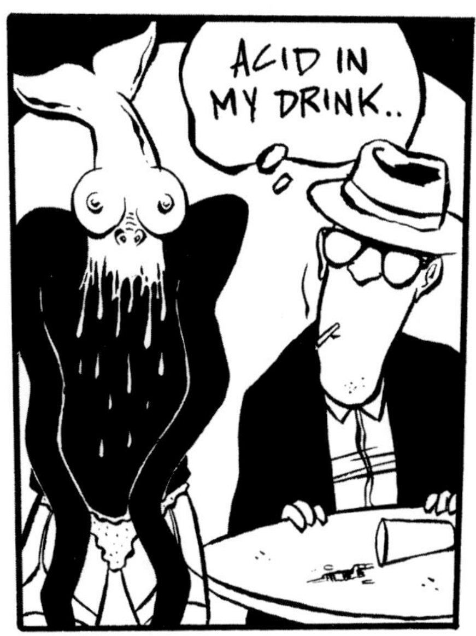
ACID IN MY DRINK..

Wombat

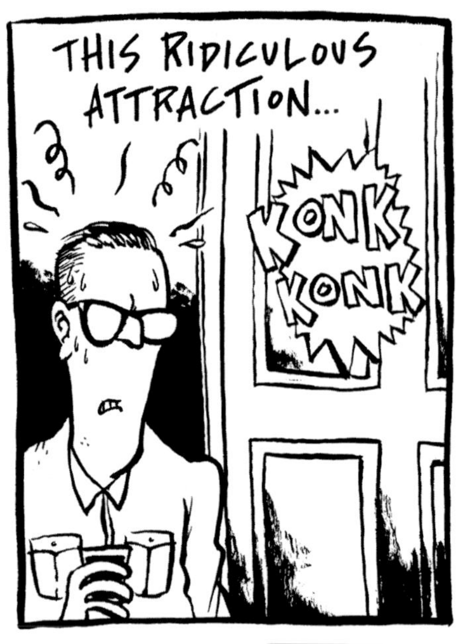
THIS RIDICULOUS ATTRACTION...
KONK KONK

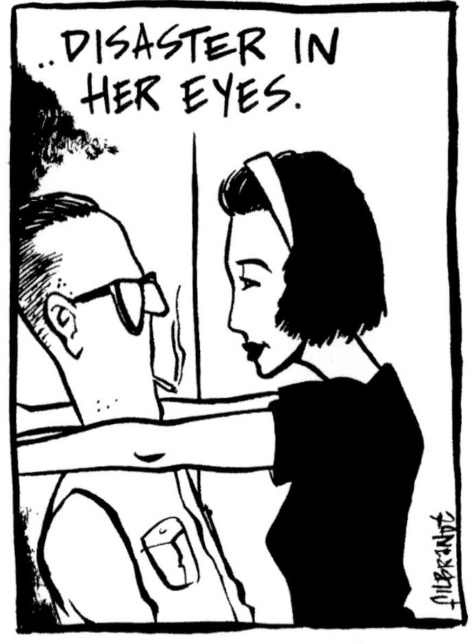
..DISASTER IN HER EYES.

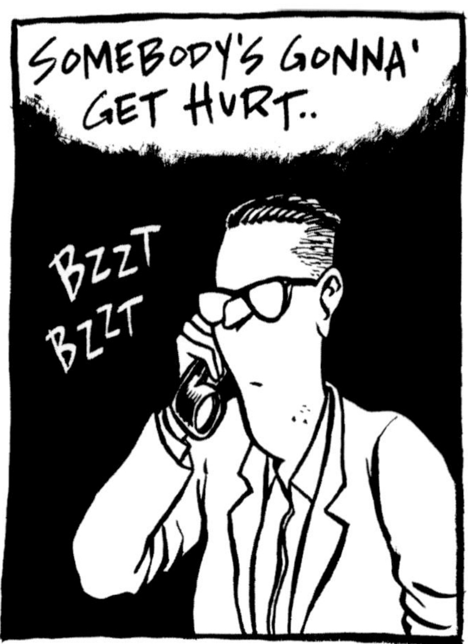
SOMEBODY'S GONNA' GET HURT..
BZZT BZZT

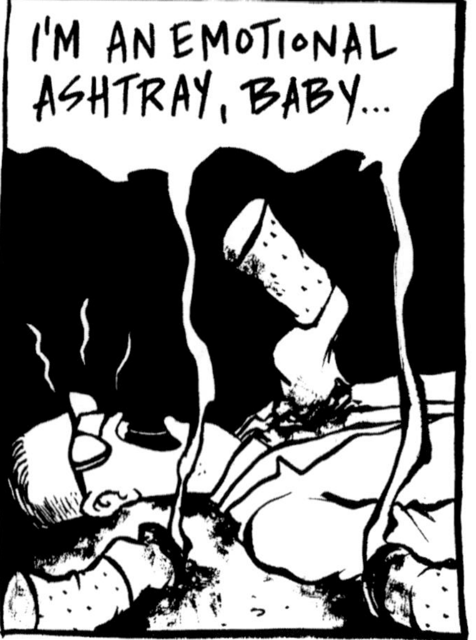
I'M AN EMOTIONAL ASHTRAY, BABY...

"WOMBAT" BY FILBRANDT

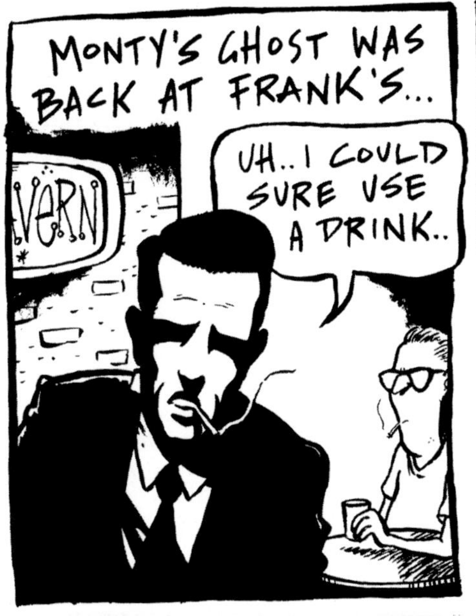

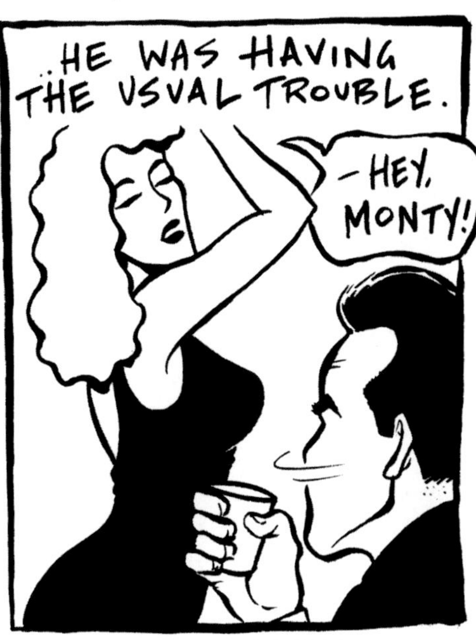

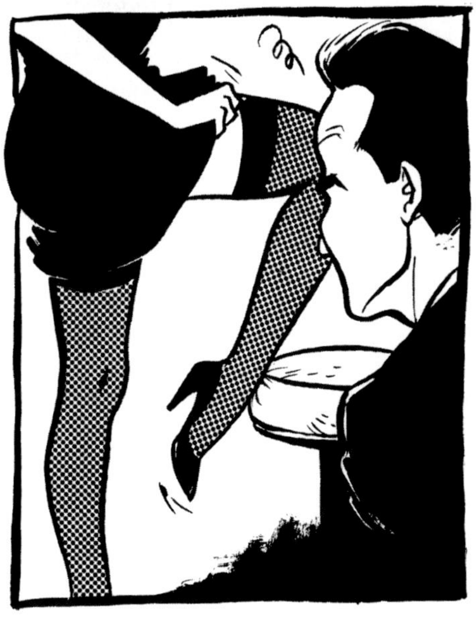

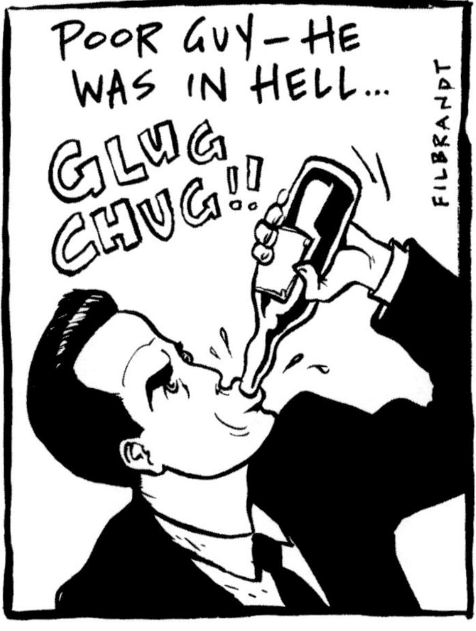

WOMBAT ~ BY FILBRANDT

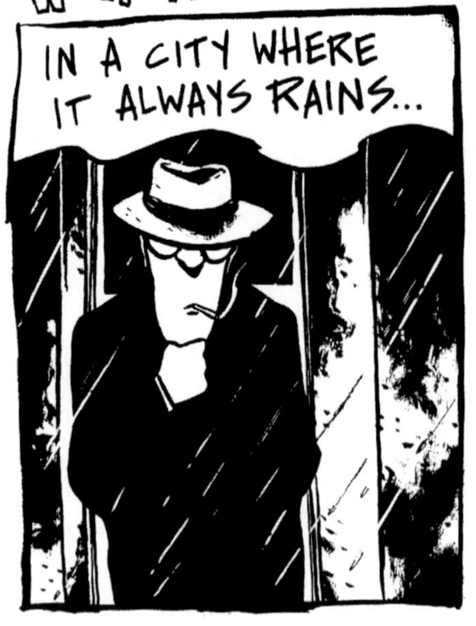

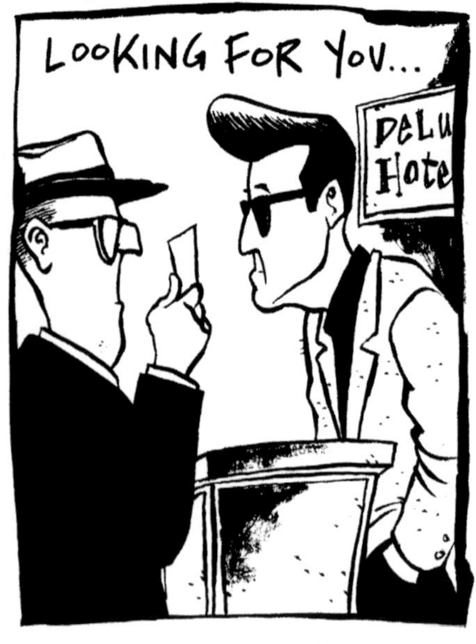

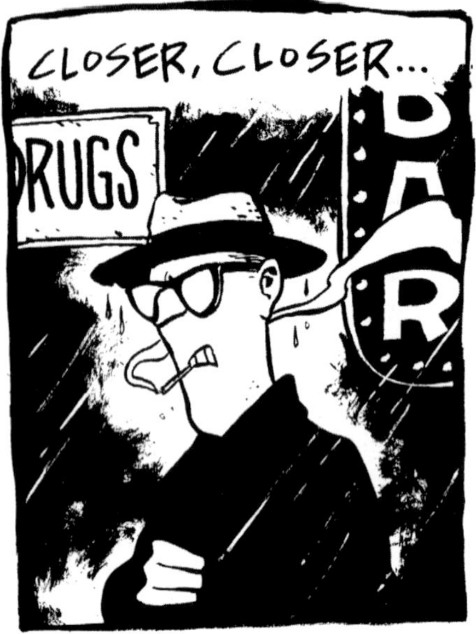

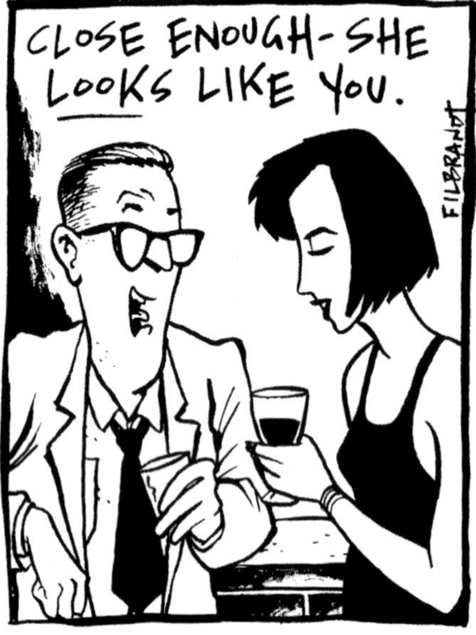

WOMBAT ROGUES' GALLERY OF CONFIRMED BACHELORS!

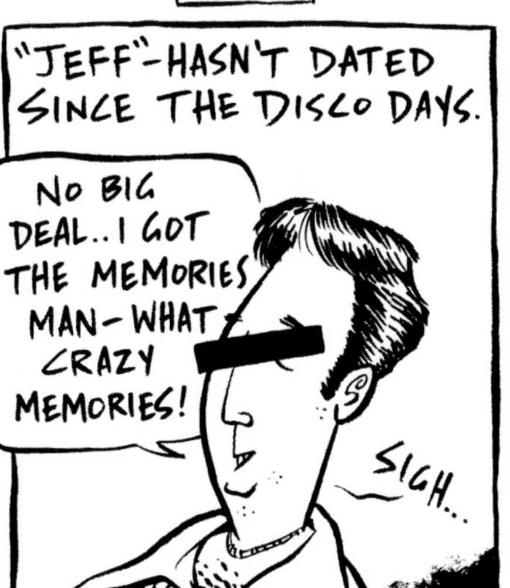

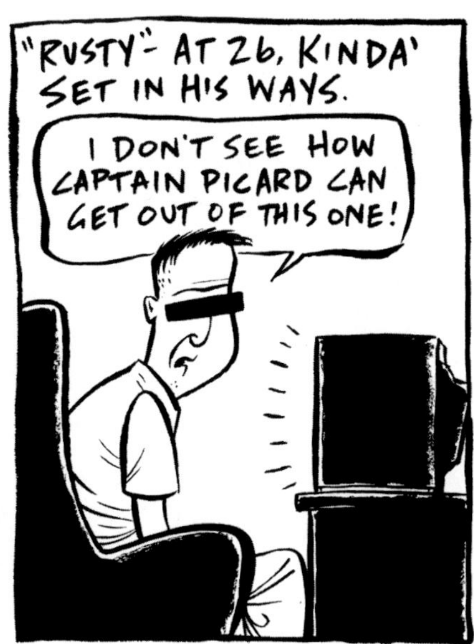

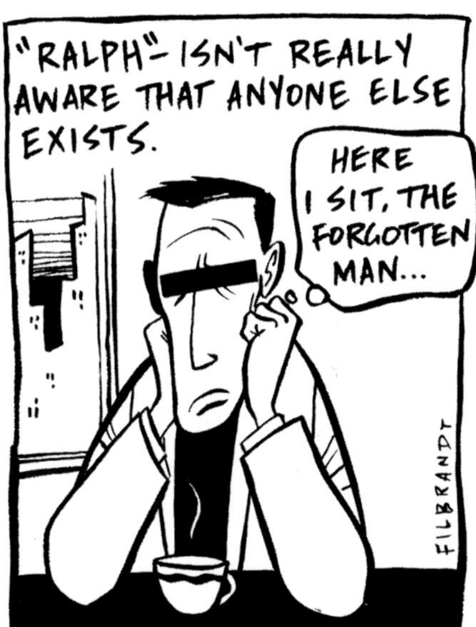

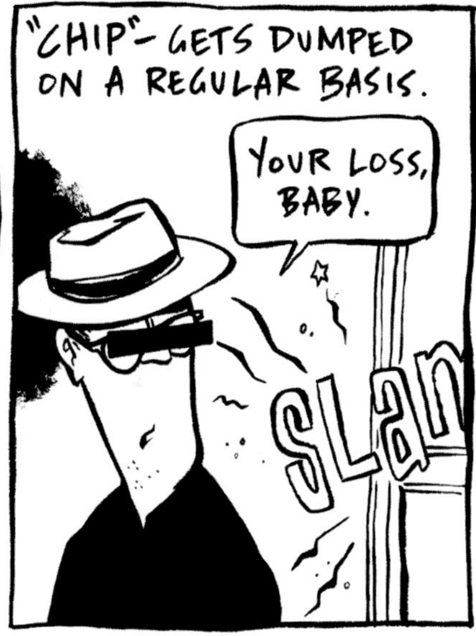

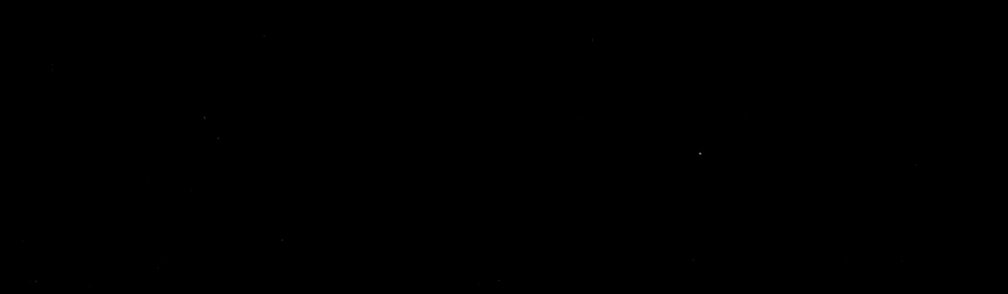

WOMBAT AND THE BURNING CIGARETTE HEART

FILBRaNDT

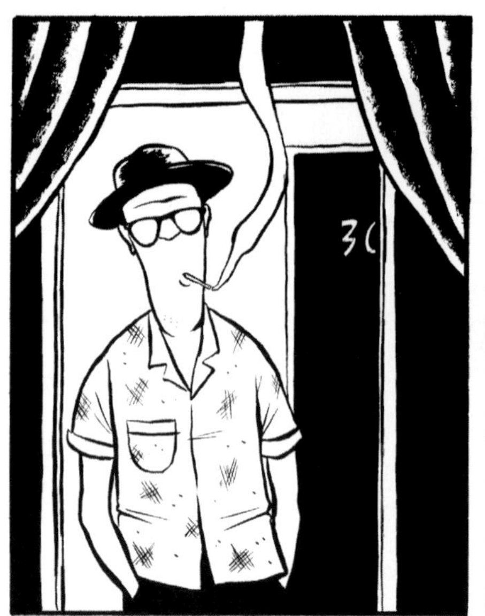
3(

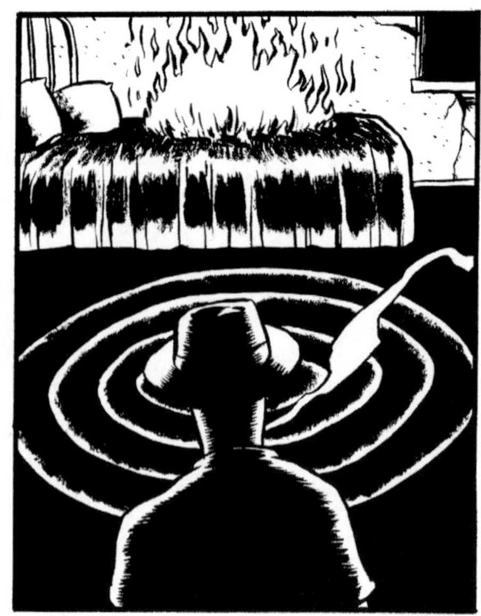

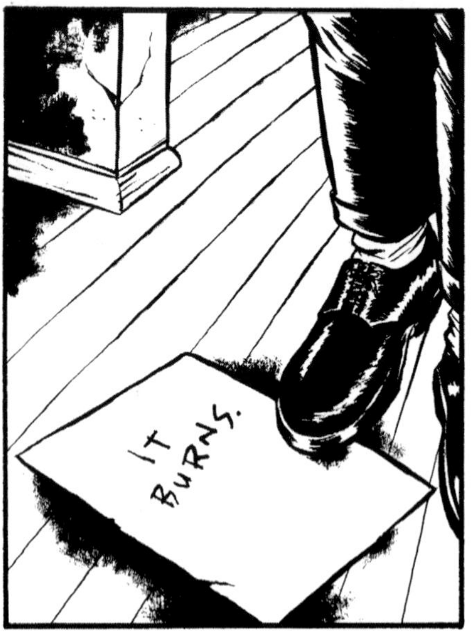
IT BURNS.

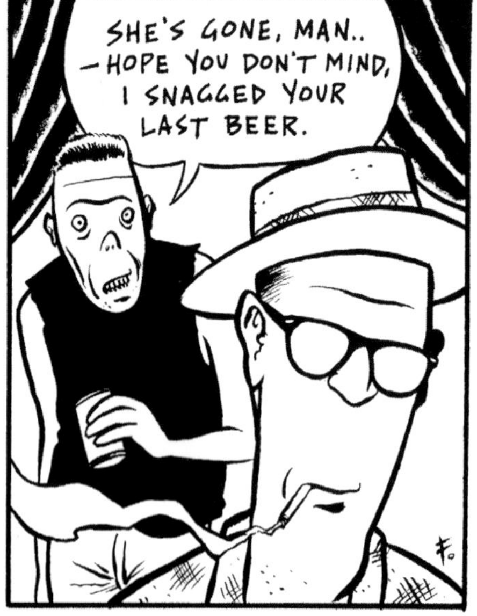
SHE'S GONE, MAN.. —HOPE YOU DON'T MIND, I SNAGGED YOUR LAST BEER.

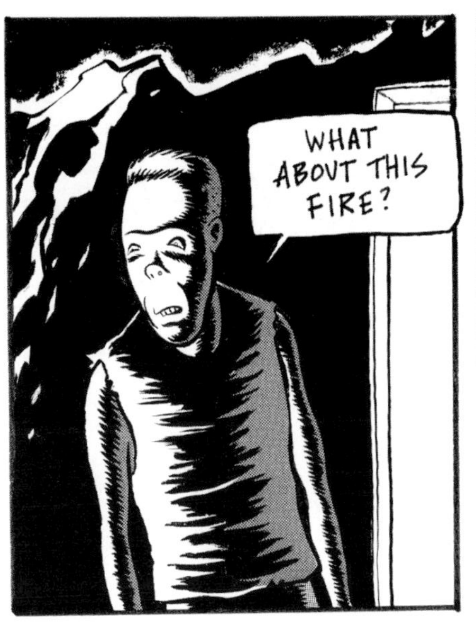
WHAT ABOUT THIS FIRE?

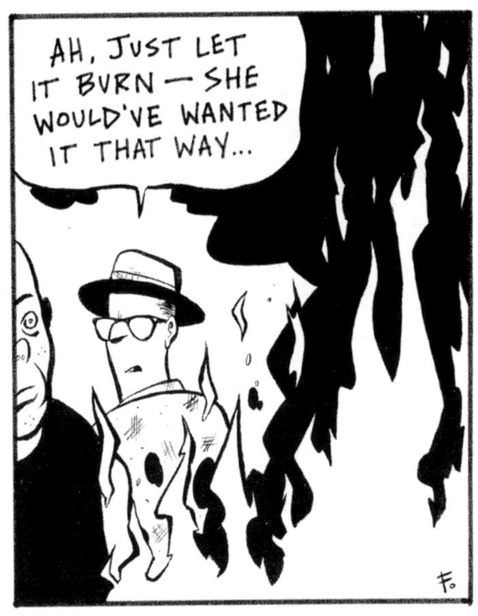
AH, JUST LET IT BURN — SHE WOULD'VE WANTED IT THAT WAY...

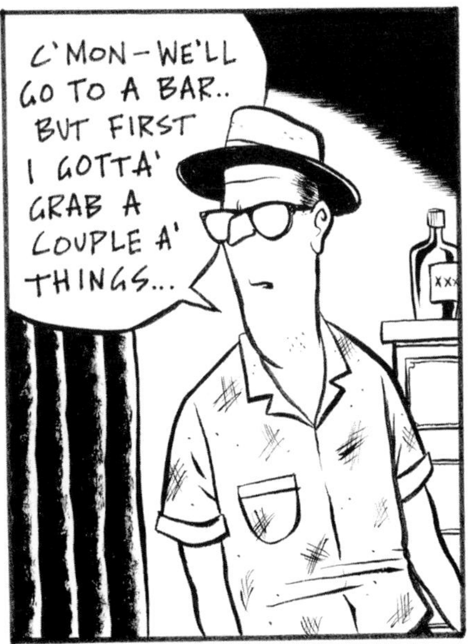
C'MON - WE'LL GO TO A BAR.. BUT FIRST I GOTTA' GRAB A COUPLE A' THINGS...
XXX

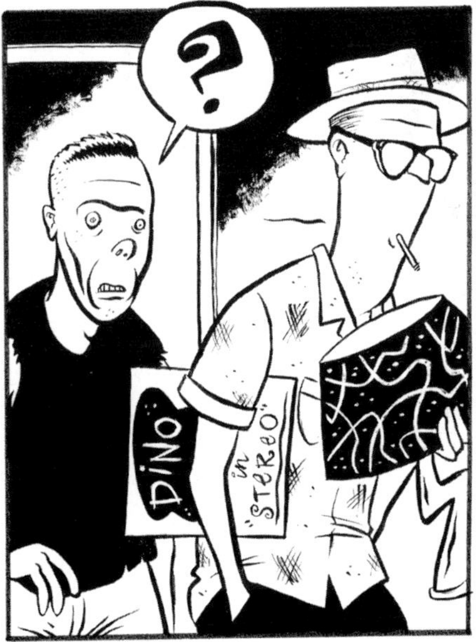
?
DINO
in "STEREO"

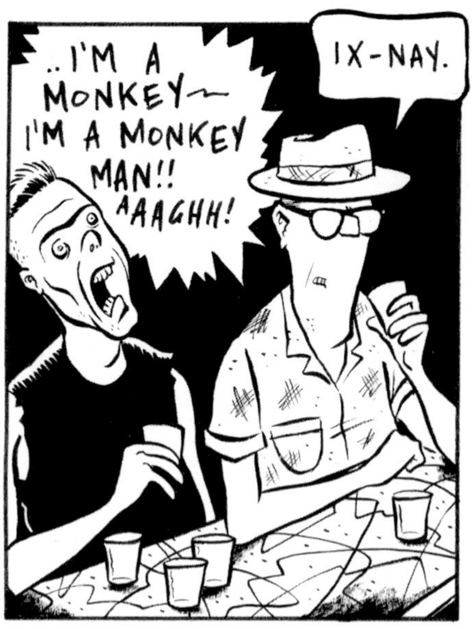
..I'M A MONKEY~ I'M A MONKEY MAN!! AAAGHH!
IX-NAY.

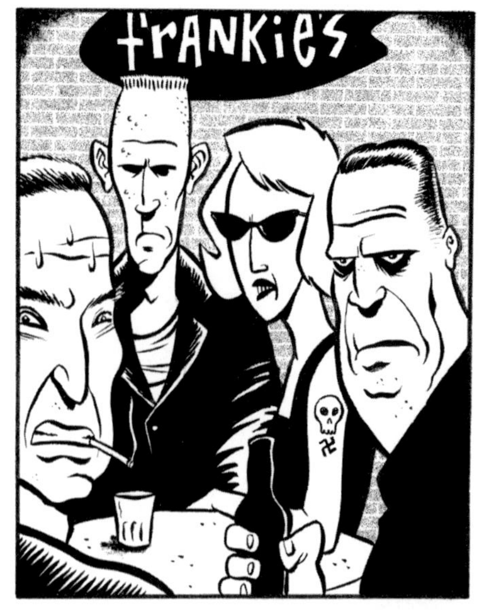
frankie's

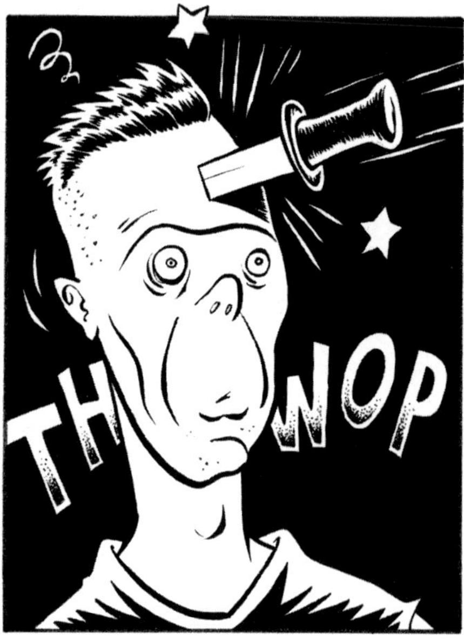
THWOP

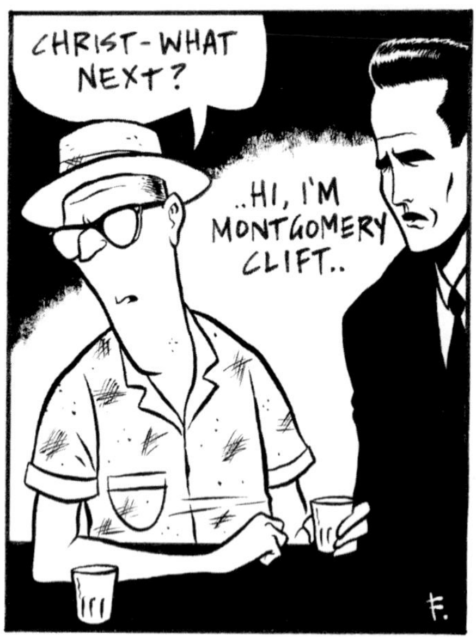
CHRIST-WHAT NEXT?
..HI, I'M MONTGOMERY CLIFT..
F.

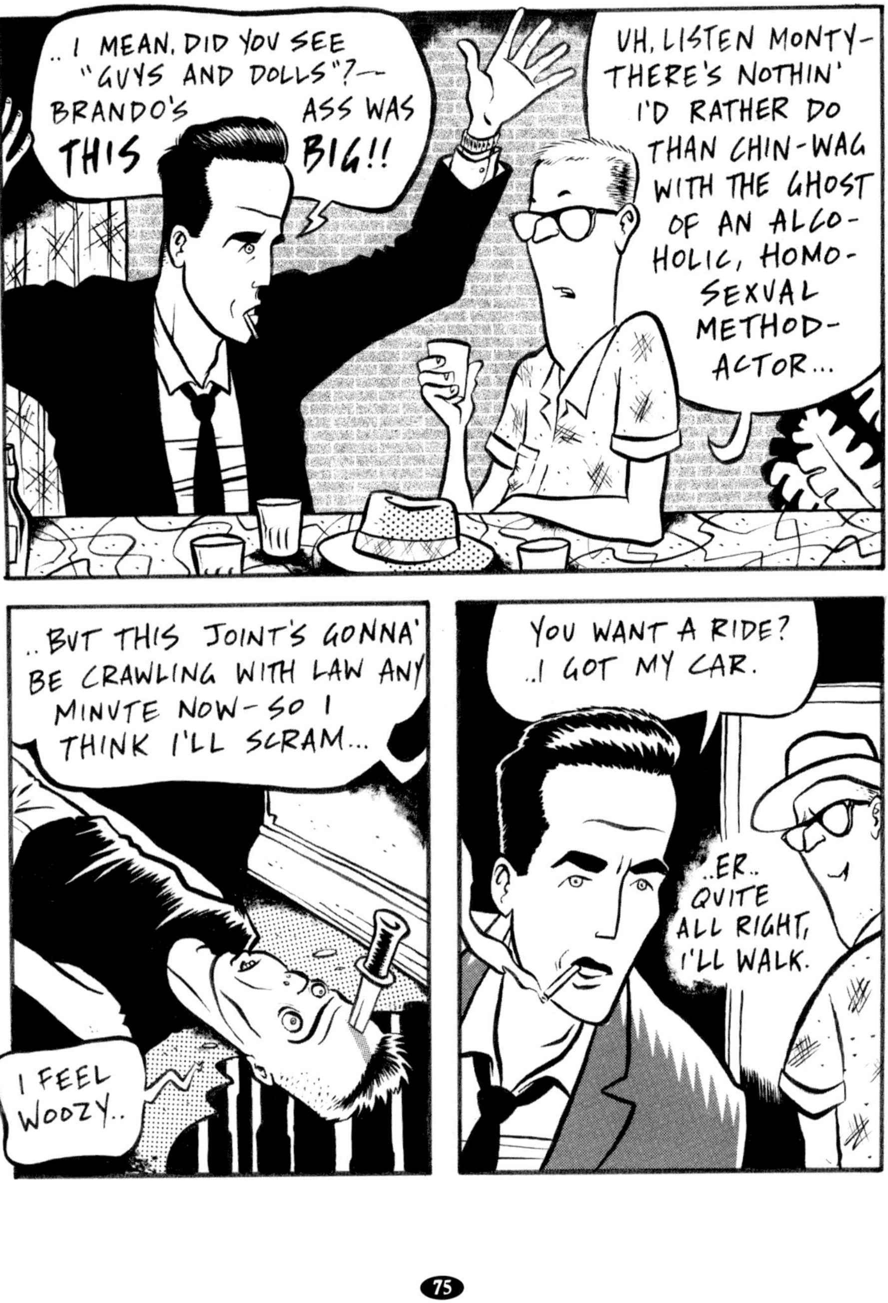

..I MEAN, DID YOU SEE "GUYS AND DOLLS"?— BRANDO'S ASS WAS THIS BIG!!

UH, LISTEN MONTY- THERE'S NOTHIN' I'D RATHER DO THAN CHIN-WAG WITH THE GHOST OF AN ALCO-HOLIC, HOMO-SEXUAL METHOD-ACTOR...

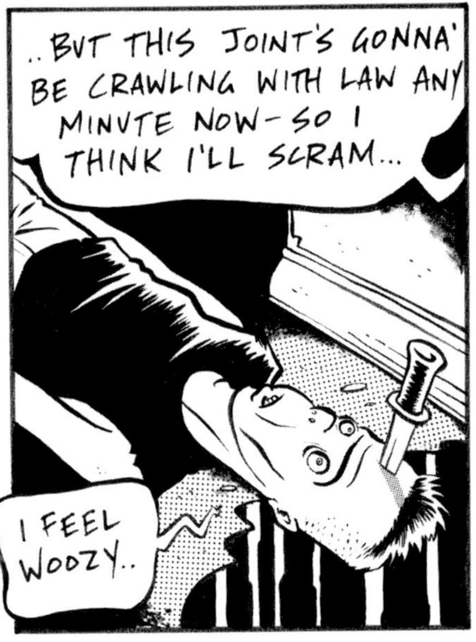

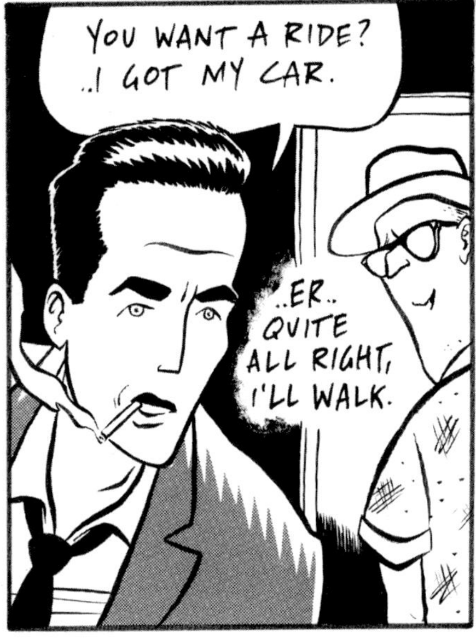

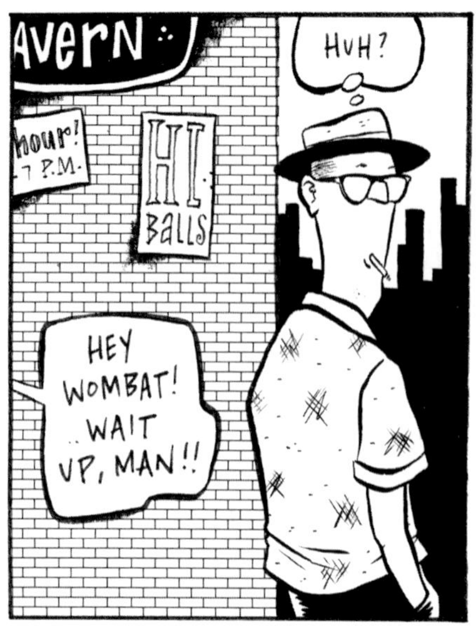
AVERN
HOUR! 7 P.M.
HI BALLS
HUH?
HEY WOMBAT! ..WAIT UP, MAN!!

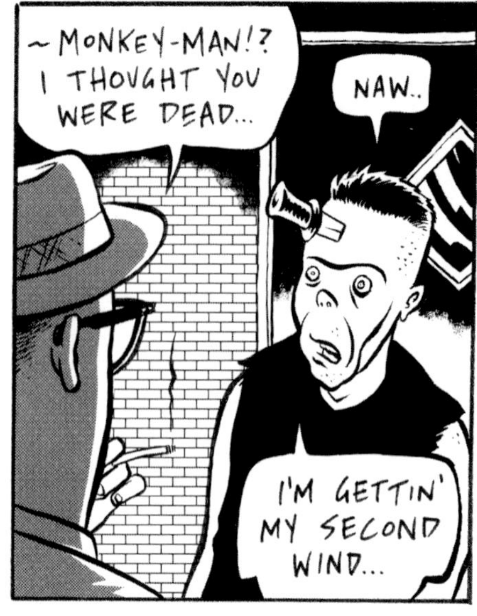
~MONKEY-MAN!? I THOUGHT YOU WERE DEAD...
NAW..
I'M GETTIN' MY SECOND WIND...

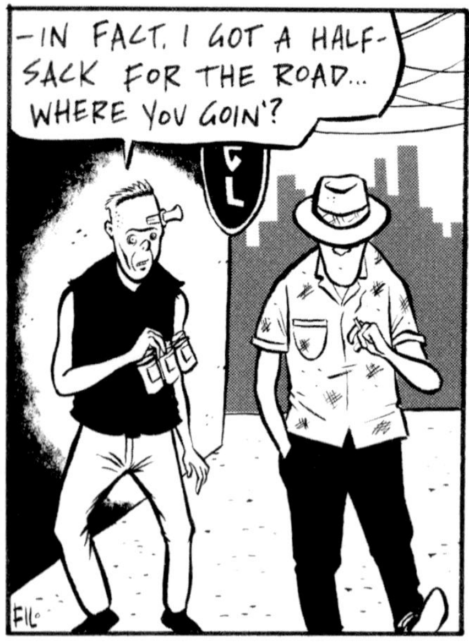
-IN FACT, I GOT A HALF-SACK FOR THE ROAD... WHERE YOU GOIN'?

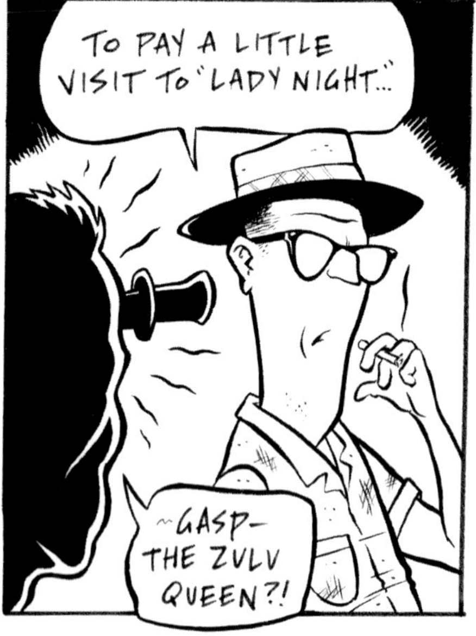
TO PAY A LITTLE VISIT TO "LADY NIGHT."
~GASP- THE ZULU QUEEN?!

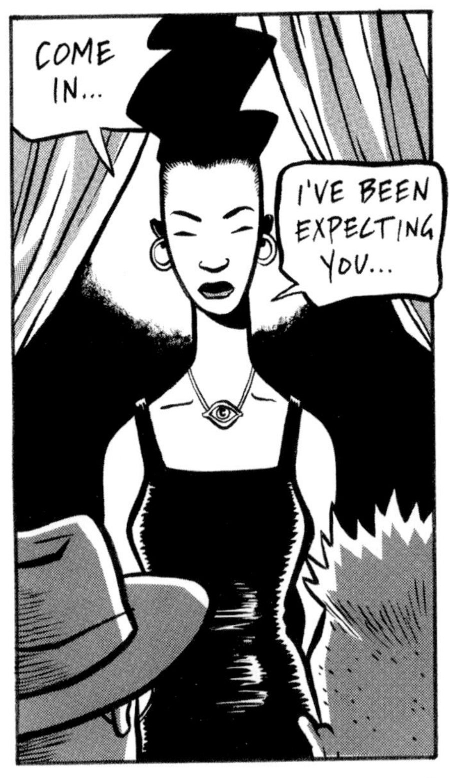
COME IN...
I'VE BEEN EXPECTING YOU...

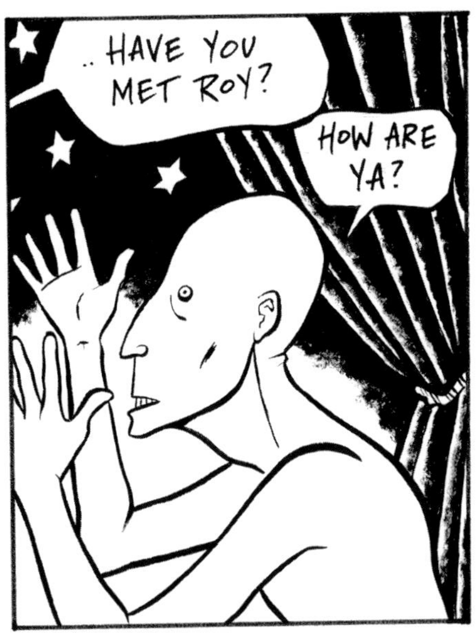
..HAVE YOU MET ROY?
HOW ARE YA?

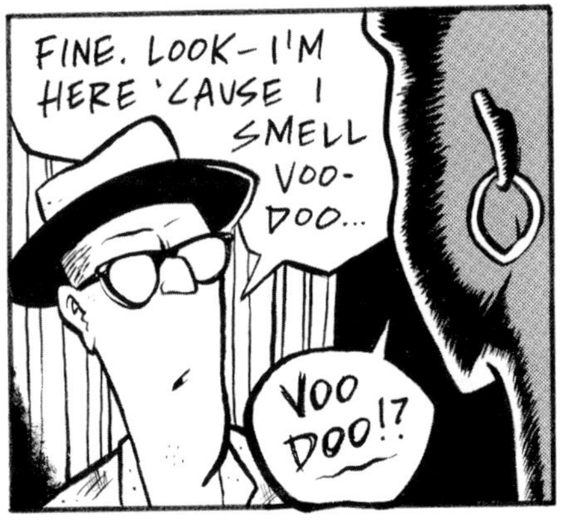
FINE. LOOK- I'M HERE 'CAUSE I SMELL VOO-DOO...
VOO DOO!?

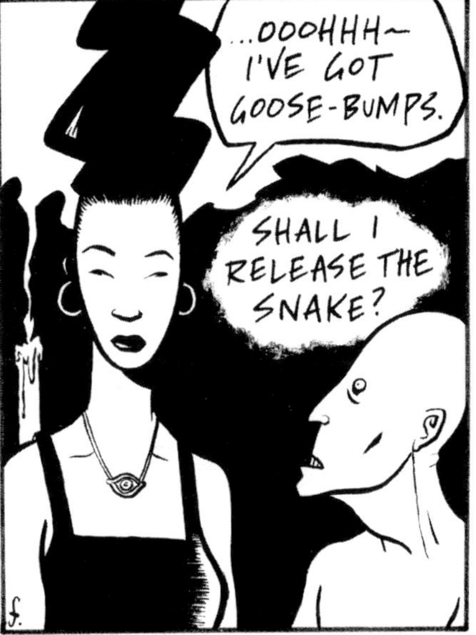
...OOOHHH~ I'VE GOT GOOSE-BUMPS.
SHALL I RELEASE THE SNAKE?

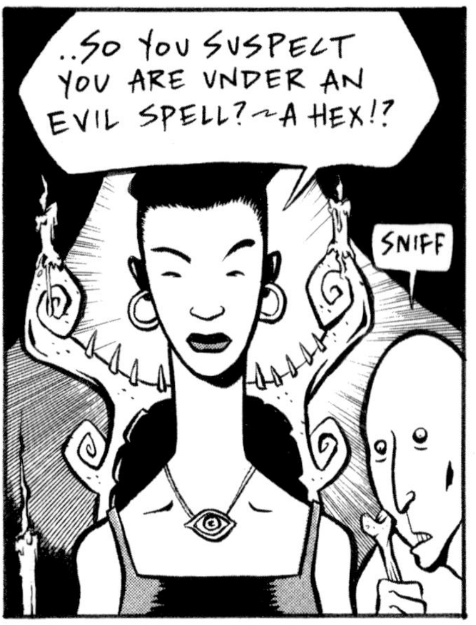
..SO YOU SUSPECT YOU ARE UNDER AN EVIL SPELL?~A HEX!?
SNIFF

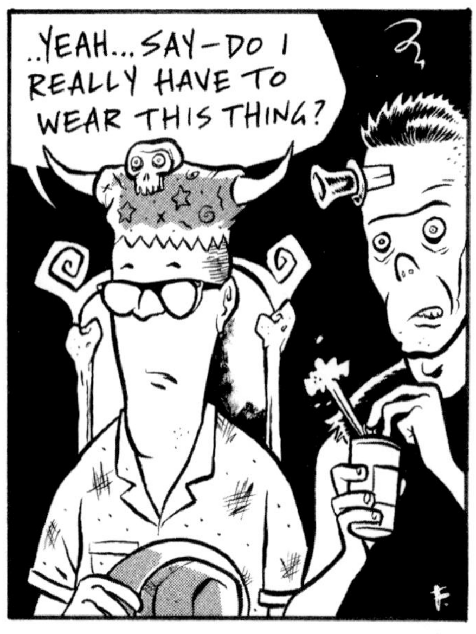
..YEAH... SAY–DO I REALLY HAVE TO WEAR THIS THING?

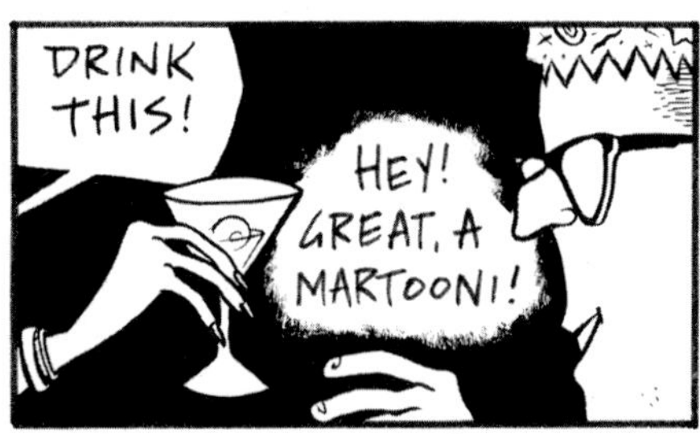
DRINK THIS!
HEY! GREAT, A MARTOONI!

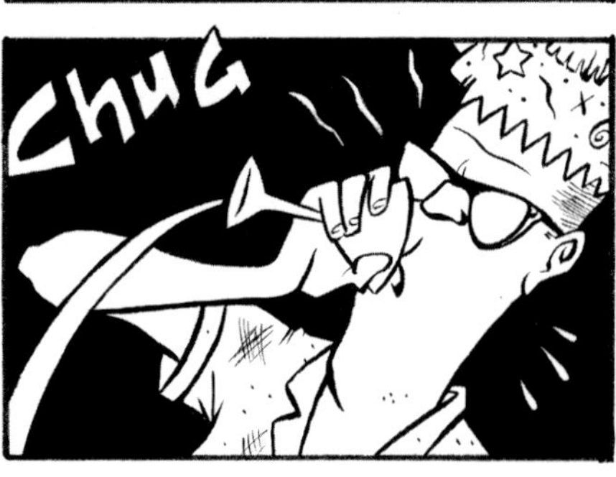
CHUG

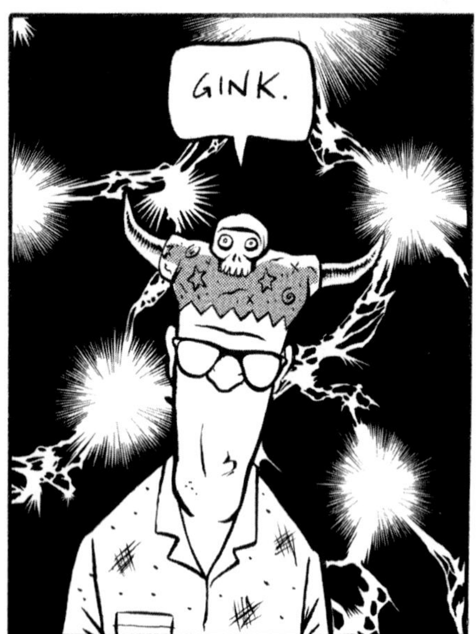
GINK.

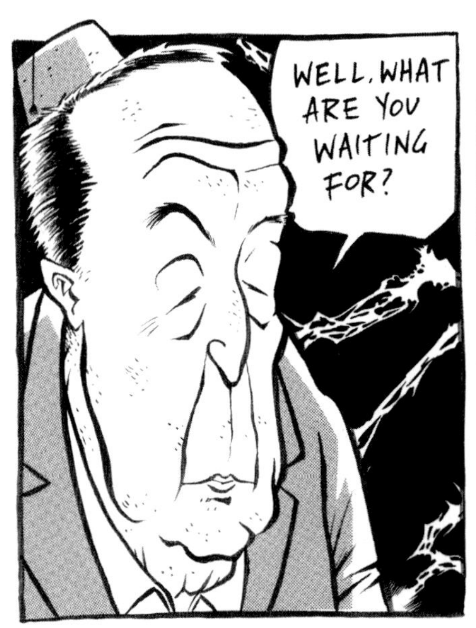
WELL, WHAT ARE YOU WAITING FOR?

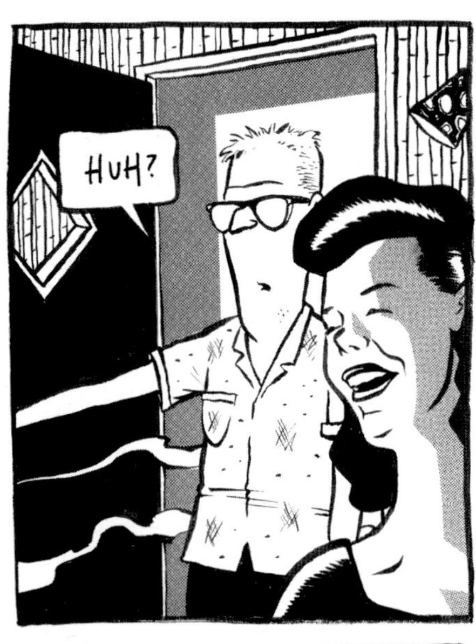
HUH?

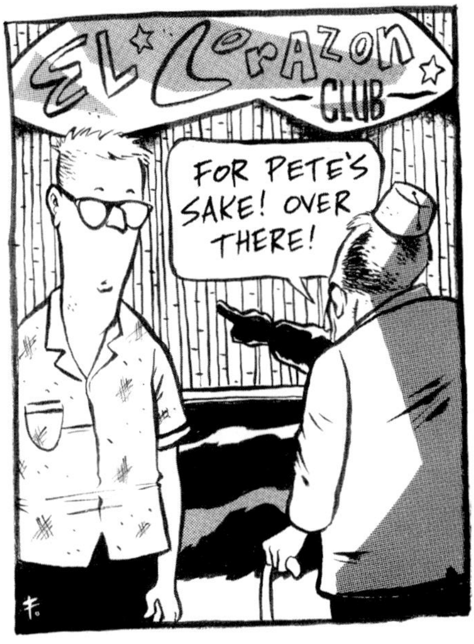
EL CORAZON
CLUB
FOR PETE'S SAKE! OVER THERE!

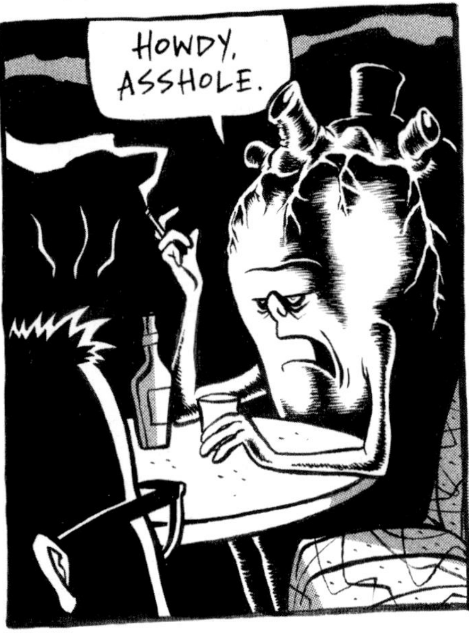
HOWDY, ASSHOLE.

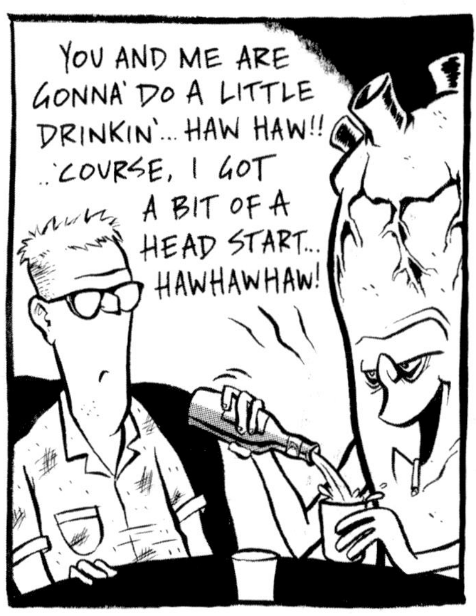
YOU AND ME ARE GONNA' DO A LITTLE DRINKIN'... HAW HAW!! ..'COURSE, I GOT A BIT OF A HEAD START... HAWHAWHAW!

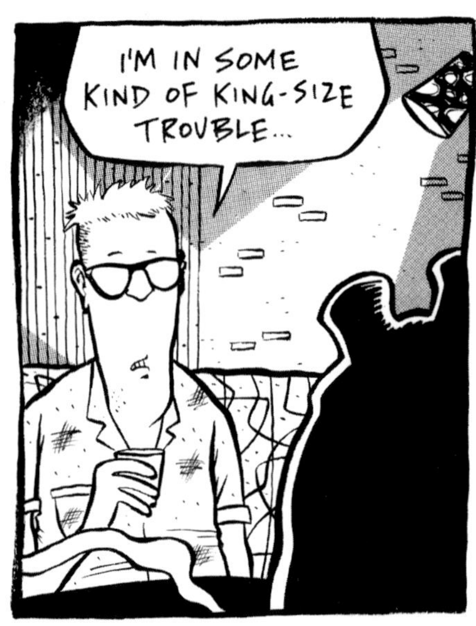
I'M IN SOME KIND OF KING-SIZE TROUBLE...

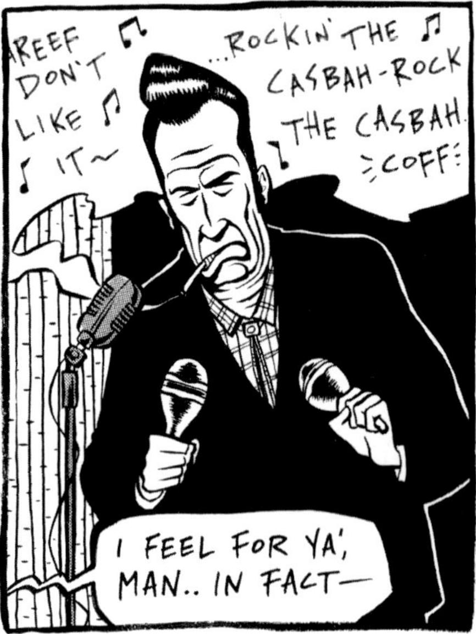
...REEF DON'T LIKE IT~
...ROCKIN' THE CASBAH-ROCK THE CASBAH.
COFF
I FEEL FOR YA', MAN.. IN FACT—

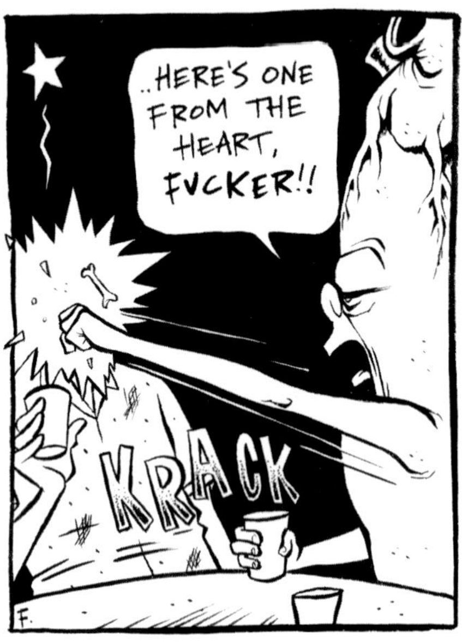
..HERE'S ONE FROM THE HEART, FUCKER!!
KRACK
F.

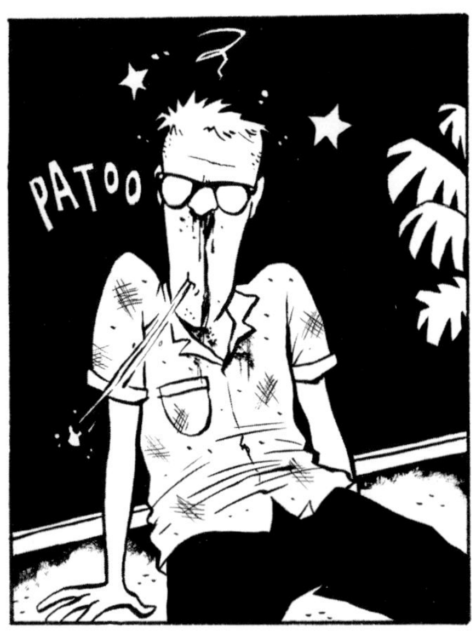
PATOO

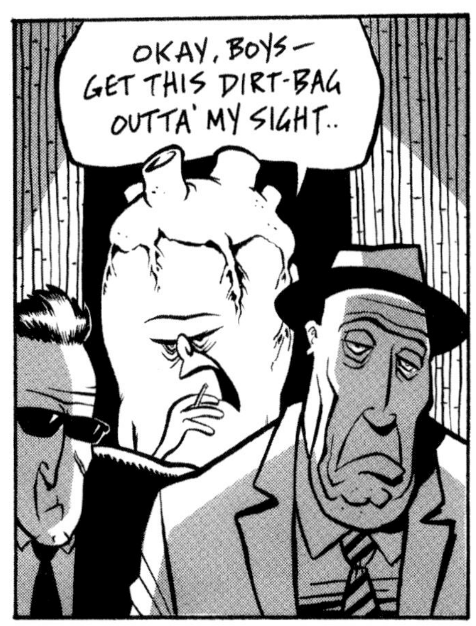
OKAY, BOYS—
GET THIS DIRT-BAG
OUTTA' MY SIGHT..

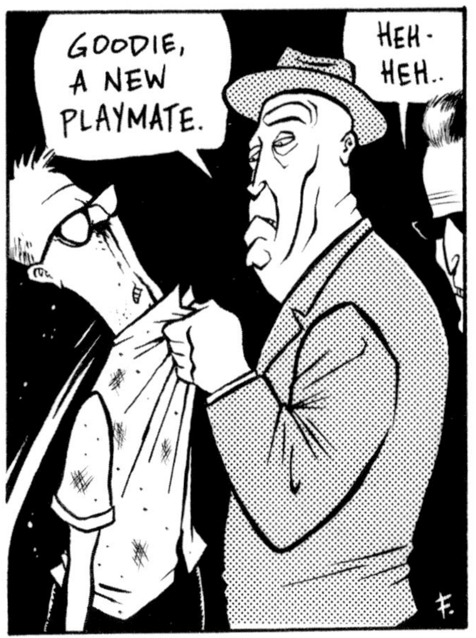
GOODIE,
A NEW
PLAYMATE.
HEH-
HEH..

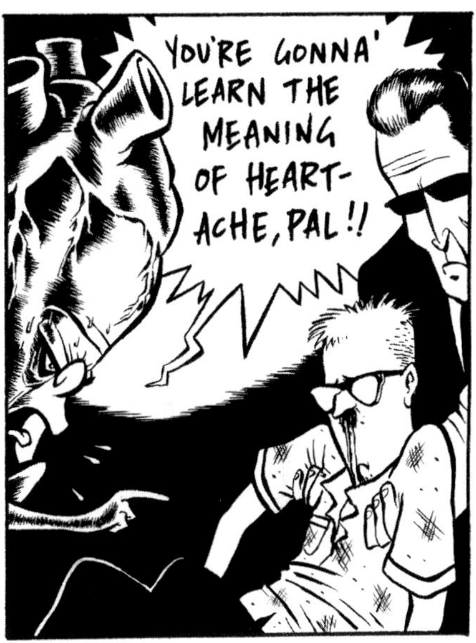
YOU'RE GONNA'
LEARN THE
MEANING
OF HEART-
ACHE, PAL!!

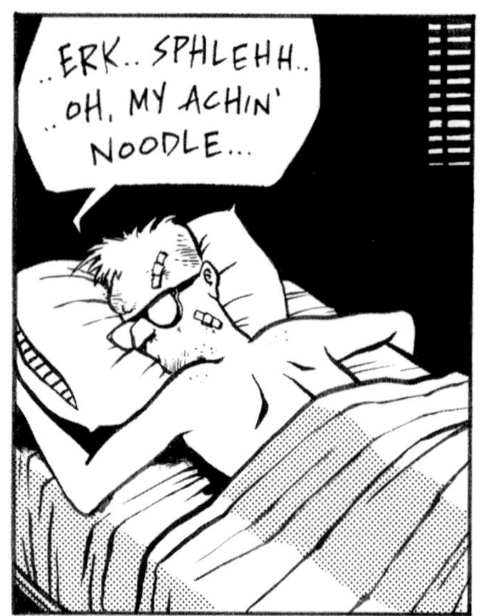
..ERK.. SPHLEHH..
..OH, MY ACHIN'
NOODLE...

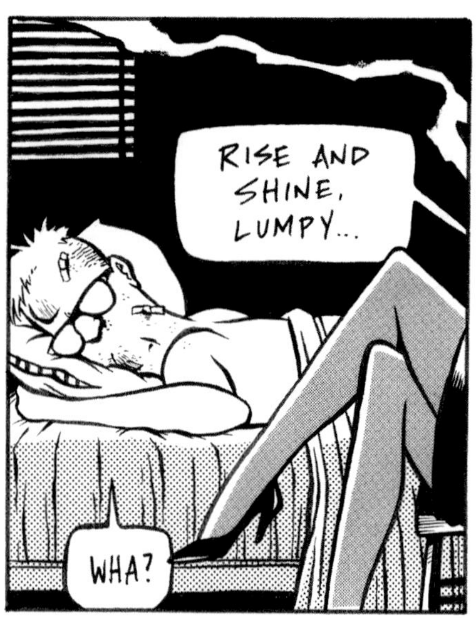
RISE AND
SHINE,
LUMPY...
WHA?

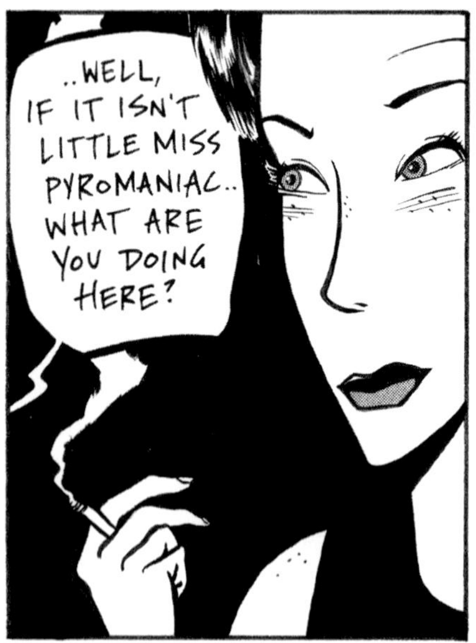
..WELL,
IF IT ISN'T
LITTLE MISS
PYROMANIAC..
WHAT ARE
YOU DOING
HERE?

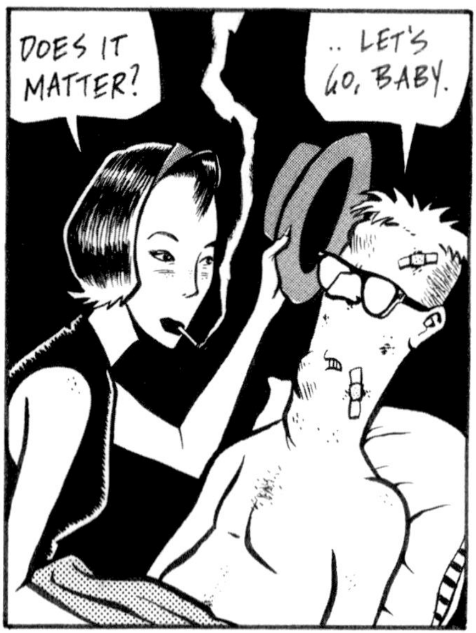
DOES IT
MATTER?
.. LET'S
GO, BABY.

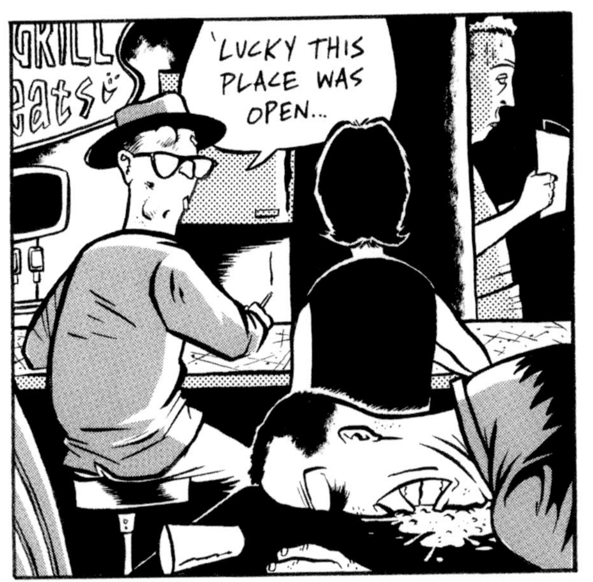
GRILL
eats
"LUCKY THIS PLACE WAS OPEN...

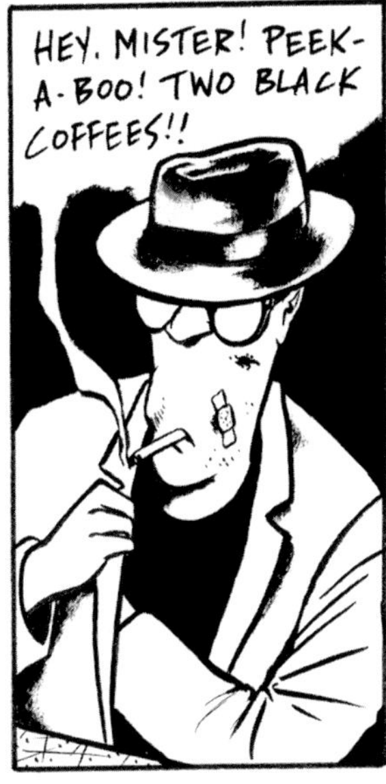
HEY, MISTER! PEEK-A-BOO! TWO BLACK COFFEES!!

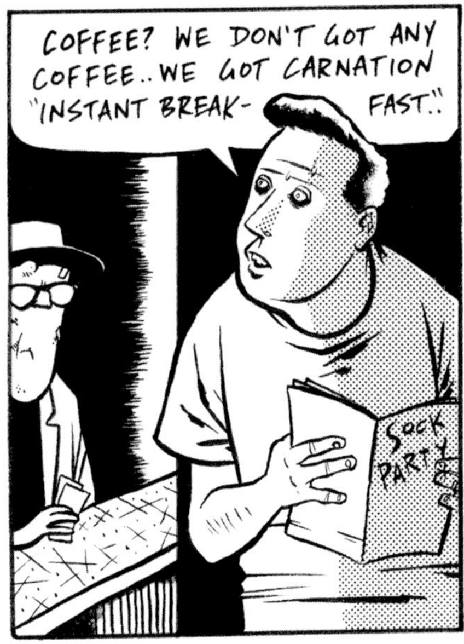
COFFEE? WE DON'T GOT ANY COFFEE.. WE GOT CARNATION "INSTANT BREAK-FAST."
SOCK PARTY

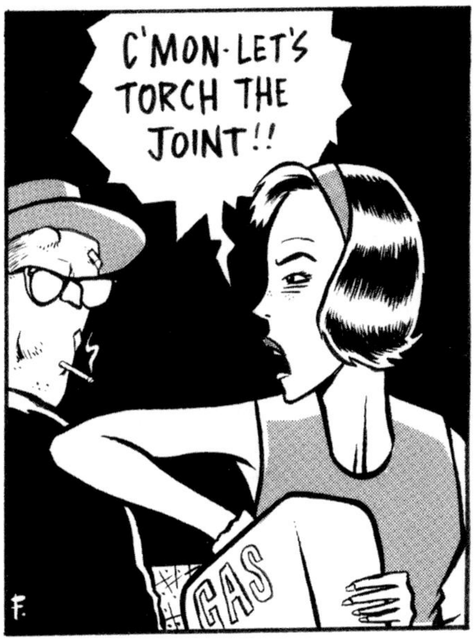
C'MON-LET'S TORCH THE JOINT!!
GAS
F.

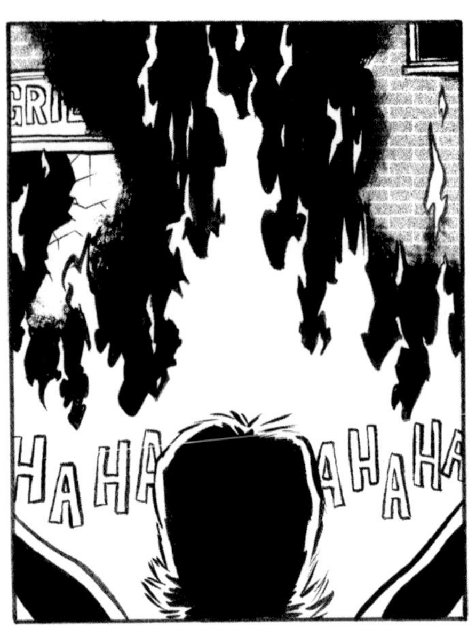
GRIL
HAHAHAHAHAHA

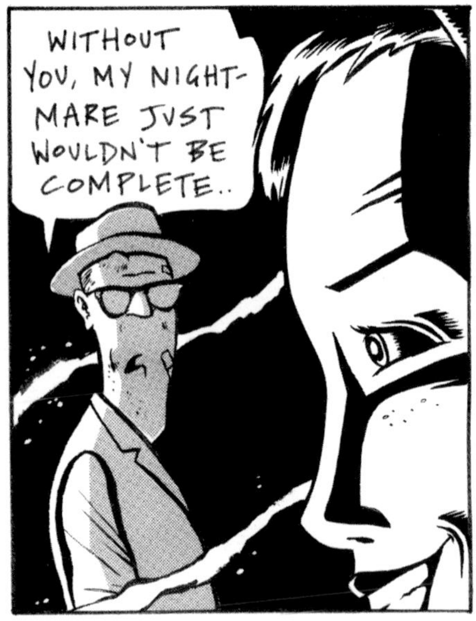
WITHOUT YOU, MY NIGHT-MARE JUST WOULDN'T BE COMPLETE..

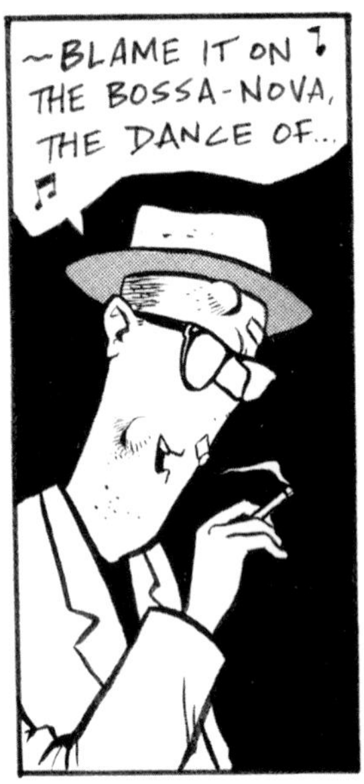
~BLAME IT ON THE BOSSA-NOVA, THE DANCE OF..

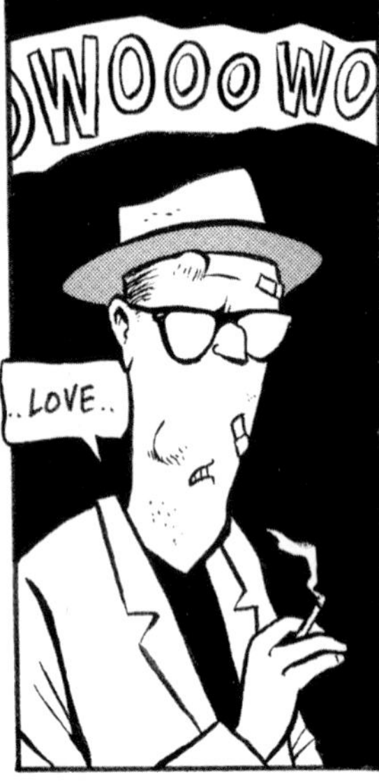
OWOOOWO
..LOVE..

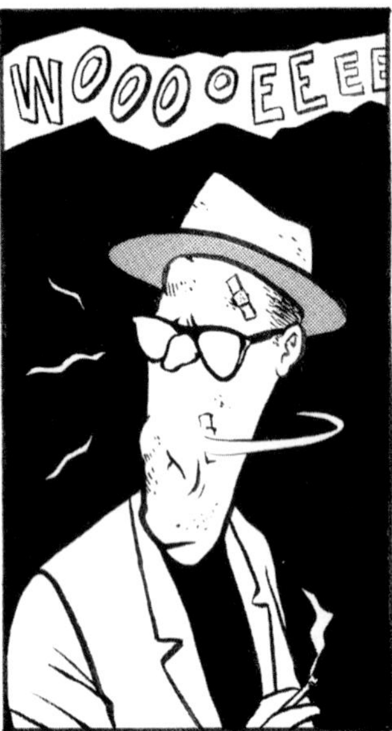
WOOOOEEEE

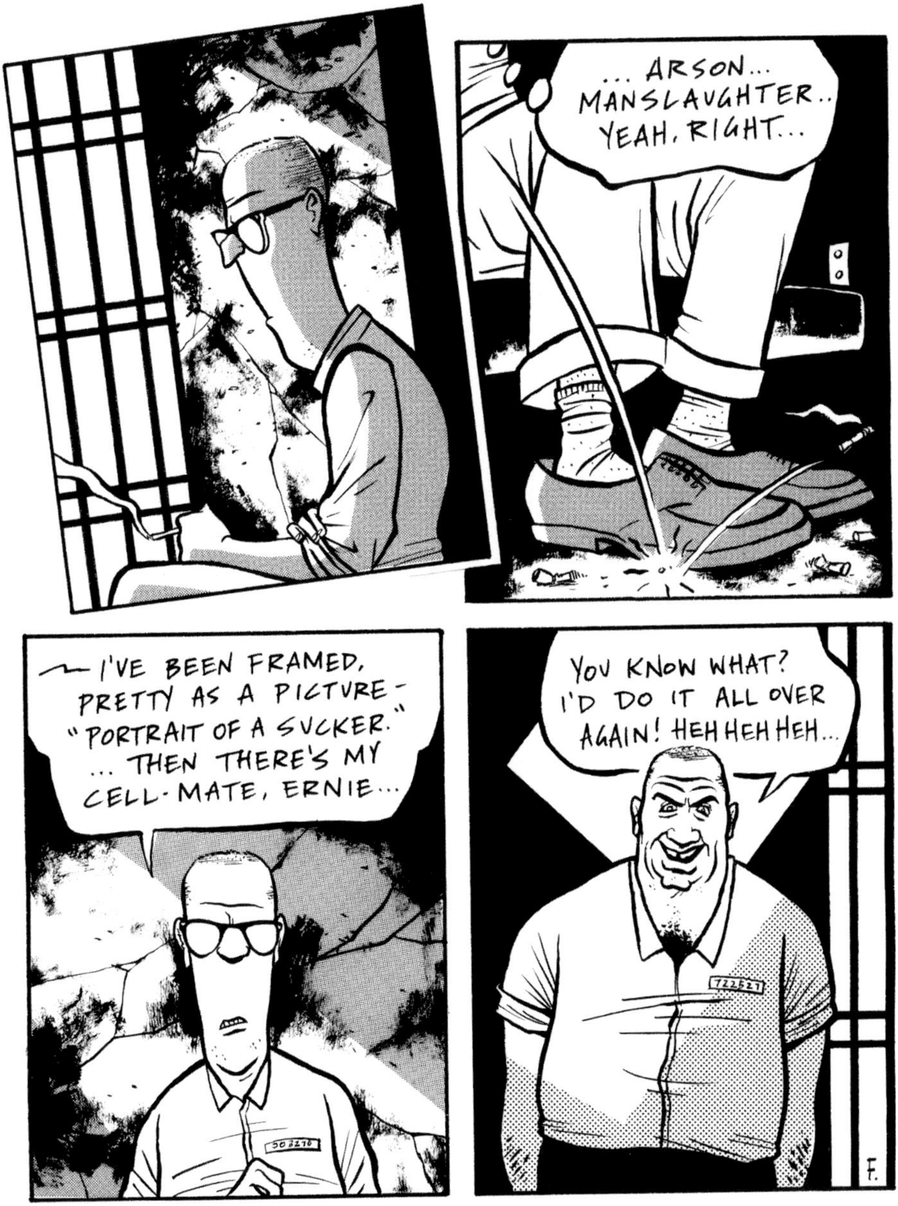

... ARSON... MANSLAUGHTER.. YEAH, RIGHT...

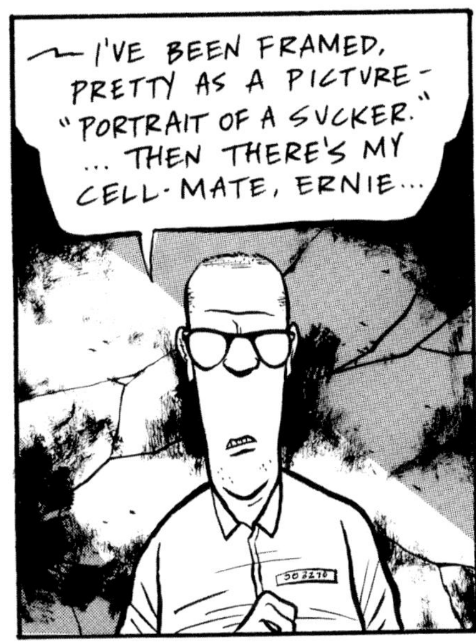

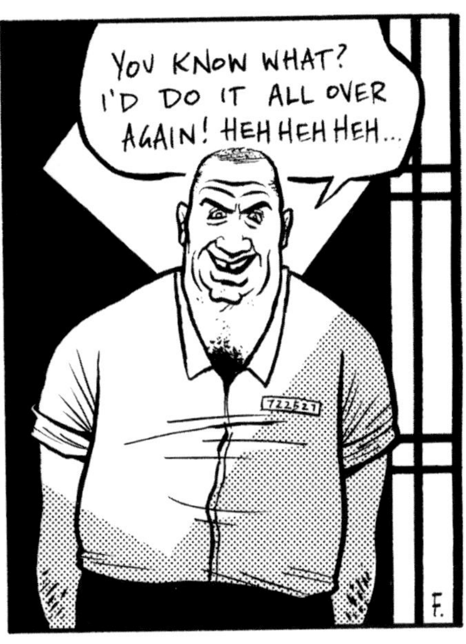

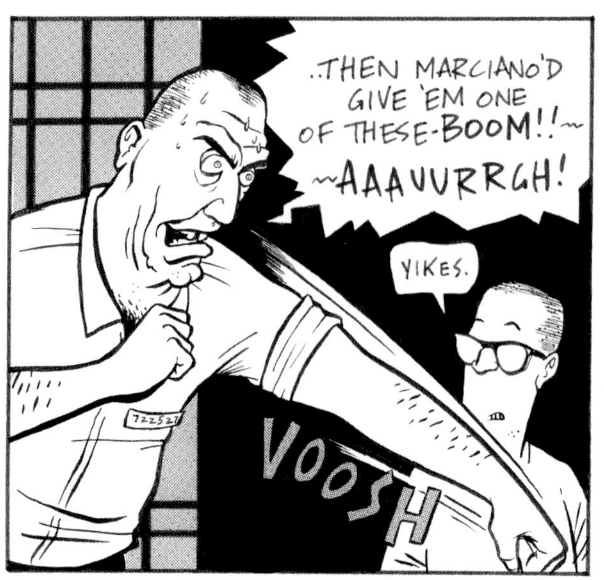
..THEN MARCIANO'D GIVE 'EM ONE OF THESE-BOOM!!~
~AAAUURRGH!
YIKES.
VOOSH

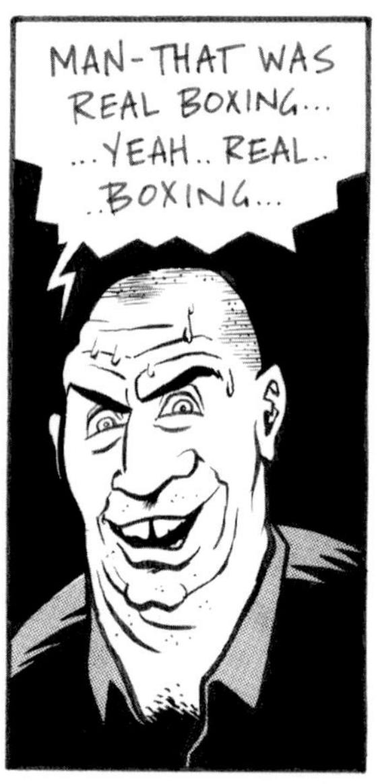
MAN-THAT WAS REAL BOXING... ...YEAH.. REAL.. ..BOXING...

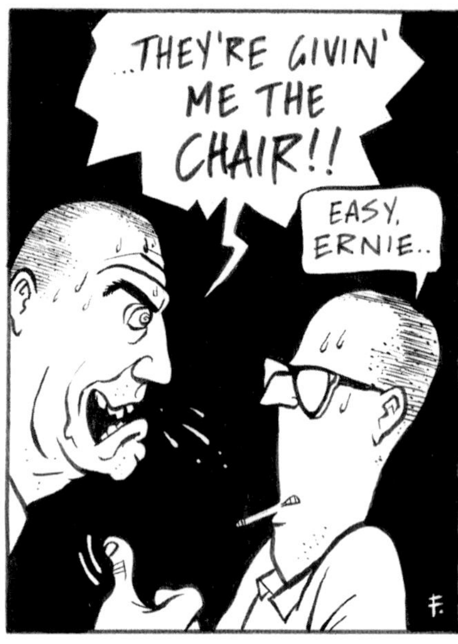
...THEY'RE GIVIN' ME THE CHAIR!!
EASY, ERNIE..

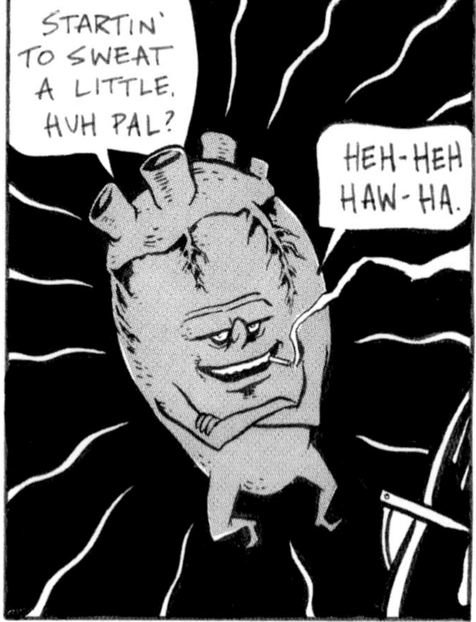
STARTIN' TO SWEAT A LITTLE, HUH PAL?
HEH-HEH HAW-HA.

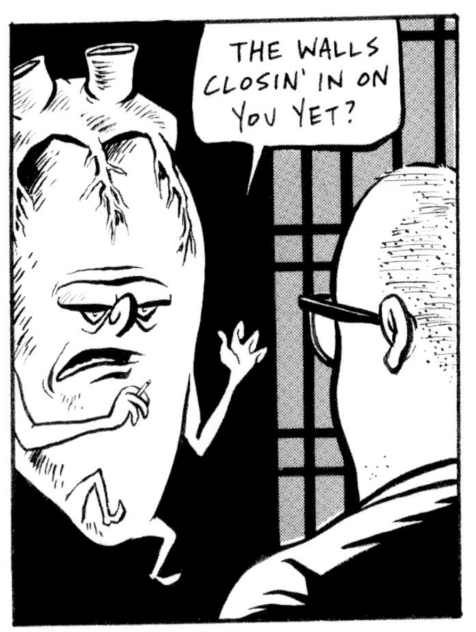
THE WALLS CLOSIN' IN ON YOU YET?

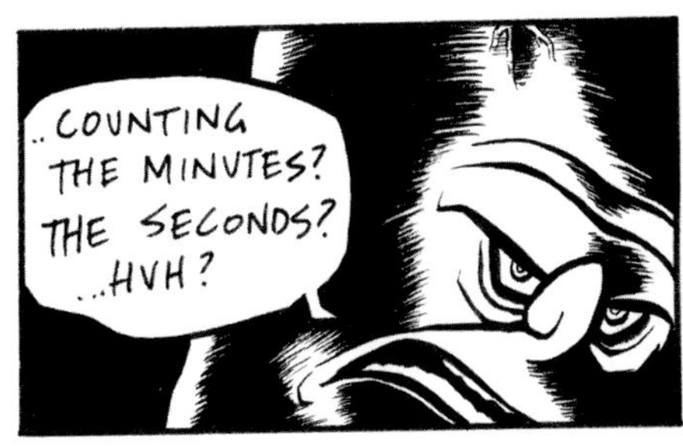
..COUNTING THE MINUTES? THE SECONDS? ...HUH?

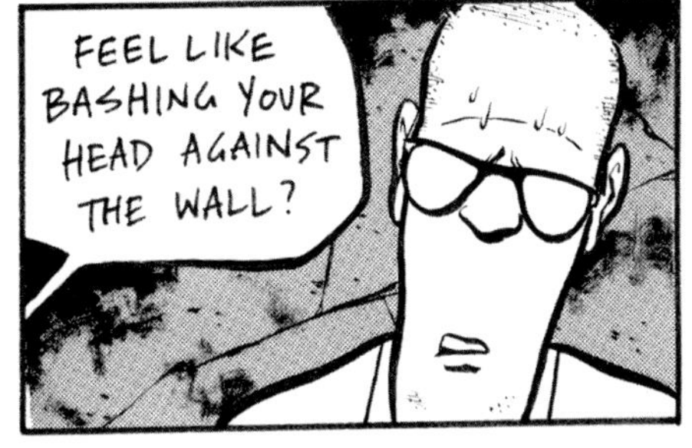
FEEL LIKE BASHING YOUR HEAD AGAINST THE WALL?

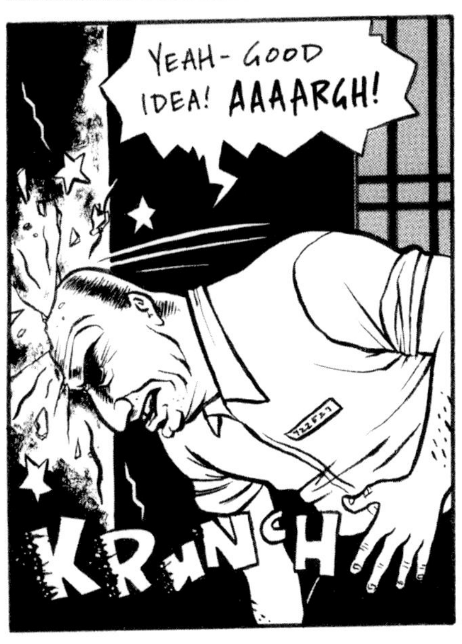
YEAH- GOOD IDEA! AAAARGH!
KRUNCH

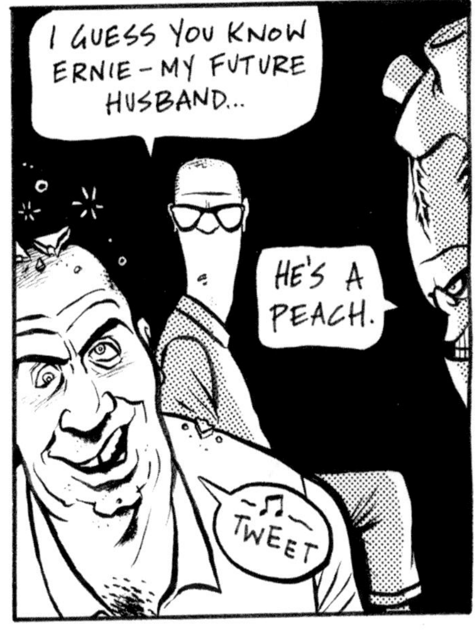
I GUESS YOU KNOW ERNIE - MY FUTURE HUSBAND...
HE'S A PEACH.
TWEET

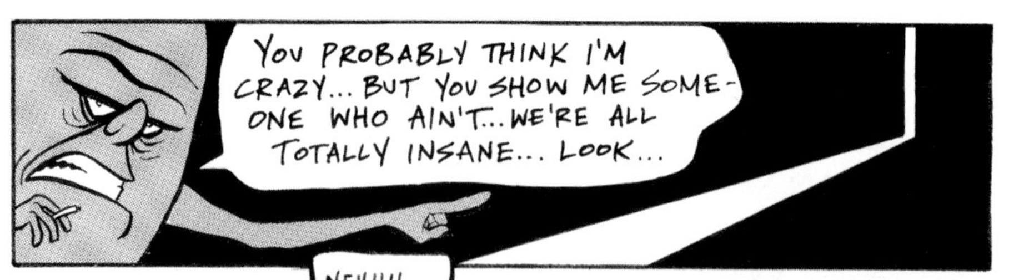
YOU PROBABLY THINK I'M CRAZY... BUT YOU SHOW ME SOME-ONE WHO AIN'T...WE'RE ALL TOTALLY INSANE... LOOK...

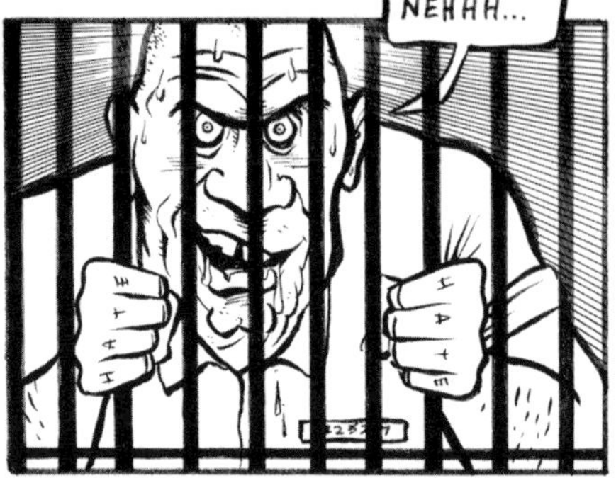
NEHHH...
HATE
HATE

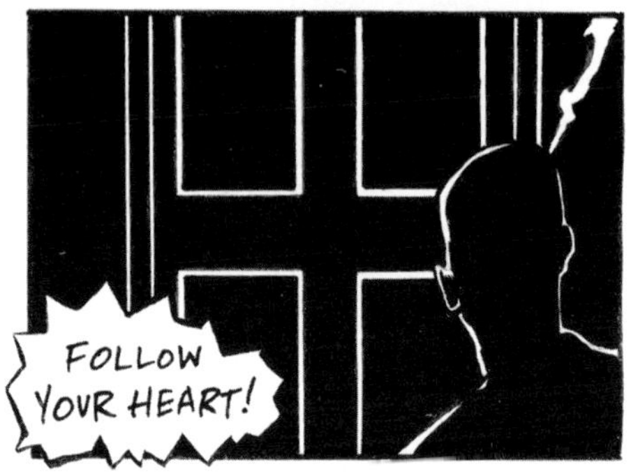
FOLLOW YOUR HEART!

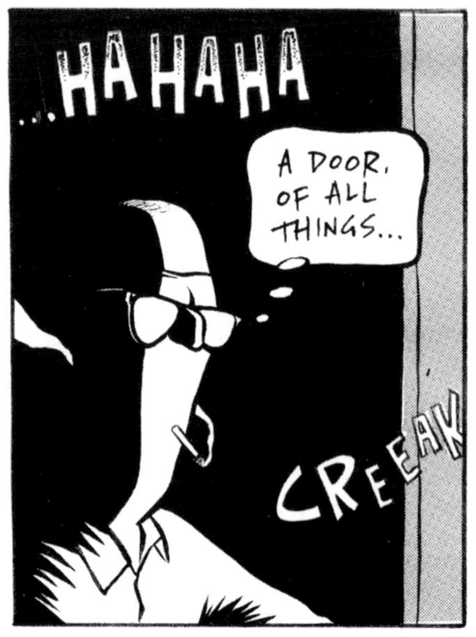
...HAHAHA
A DOOR, OF ALL THINGS...
CREEAK

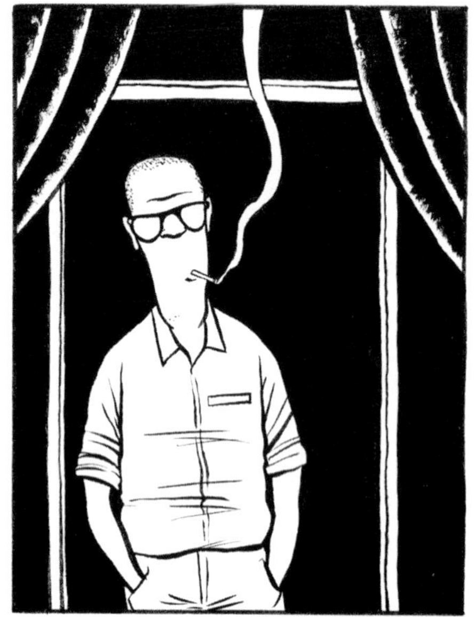

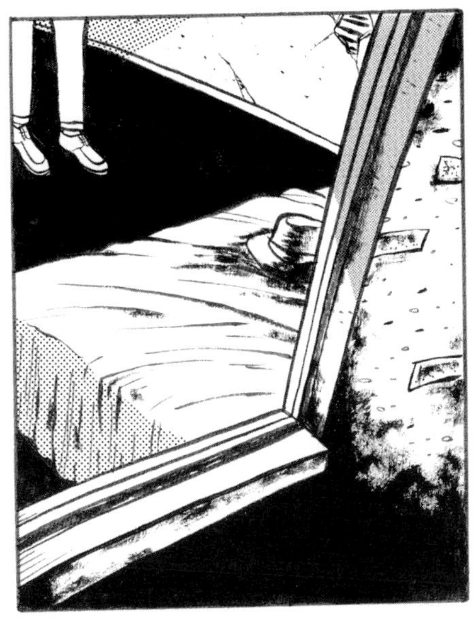

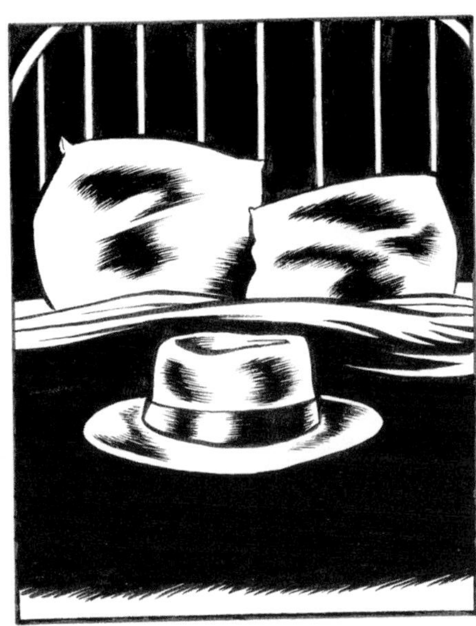

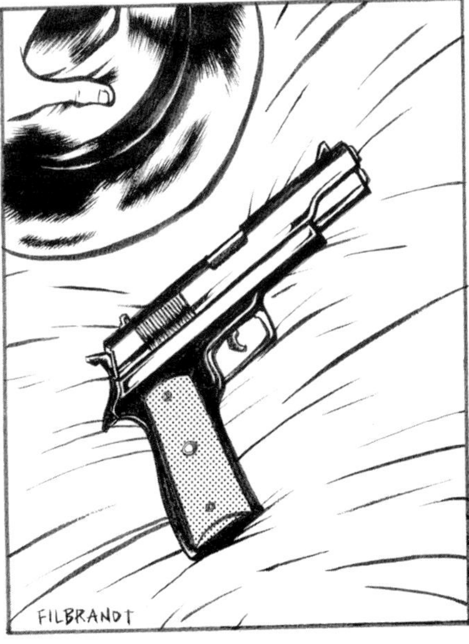

FILBRANDT

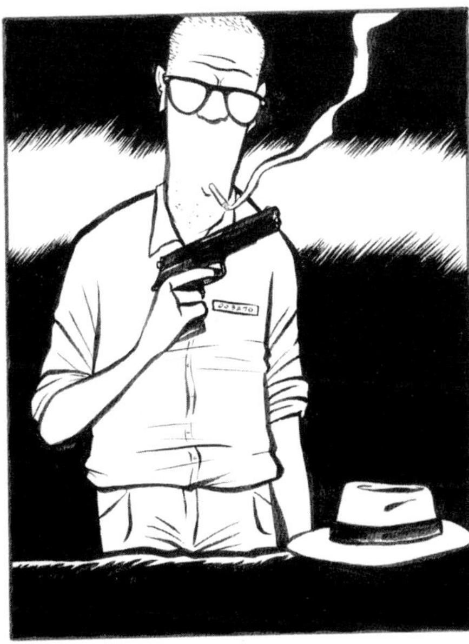

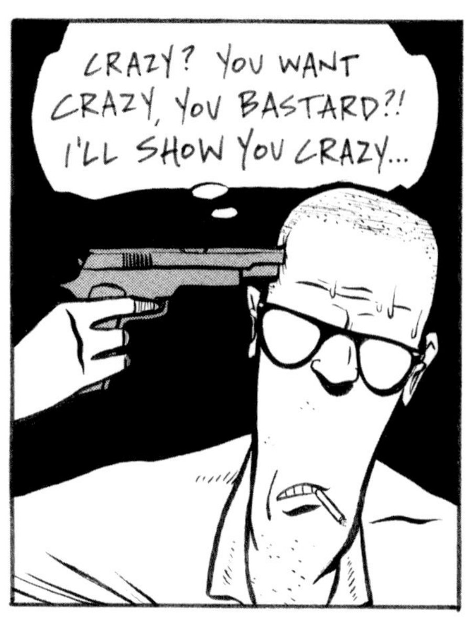

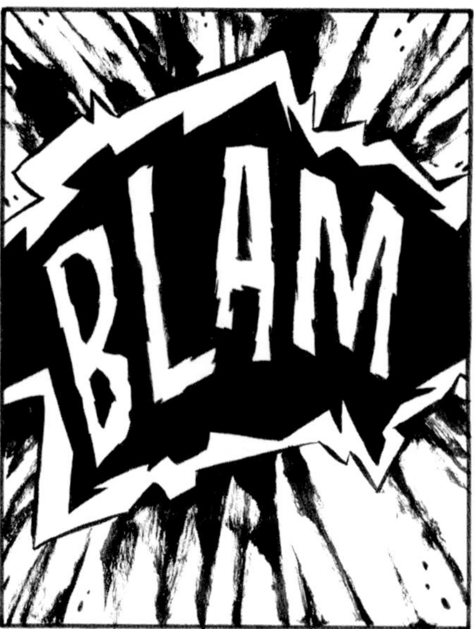

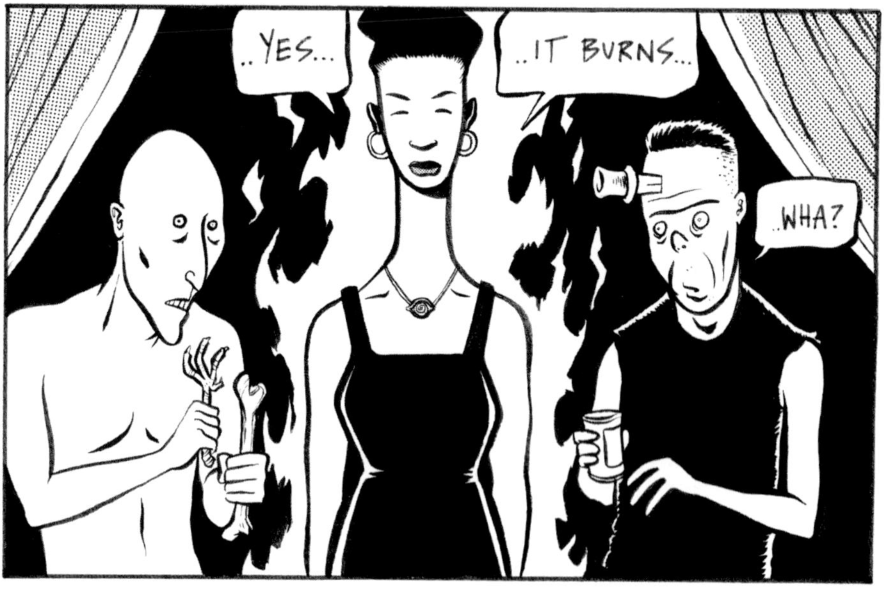

..YES...

..IT BURNS...

..WHA?

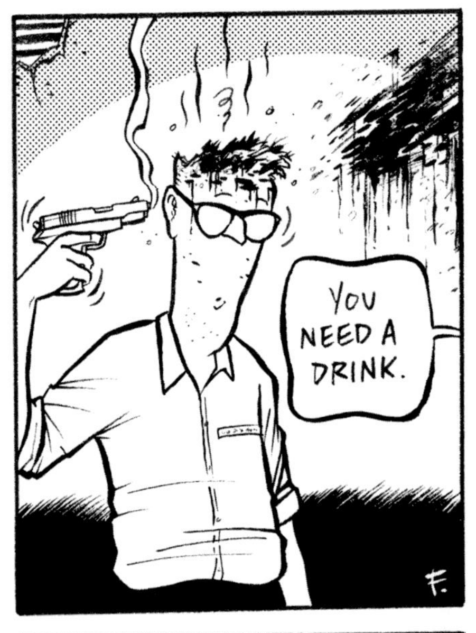
YOU NEED A DRINK.
F.

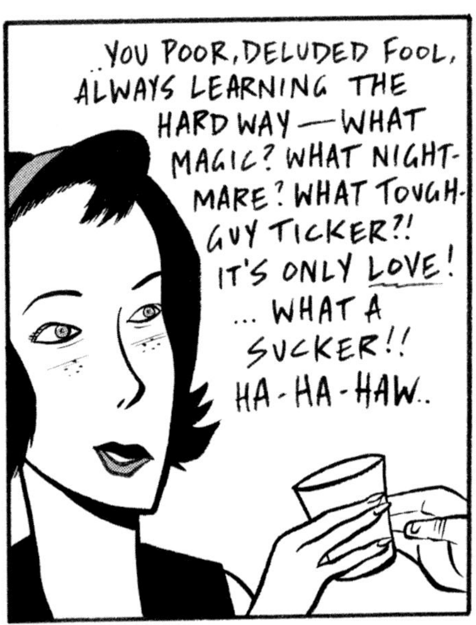
..YOU POOR, DELUDED FOOL, ALWAYS LEARNING THE HARD WAY — WHAT MAGIC? WHAT NIGHT-MARE? WHAT TOUGH-GUY TICKER?! IT'S ONLY LOVE! ... WHAT A SUCKER!! HA-HA-HAW..

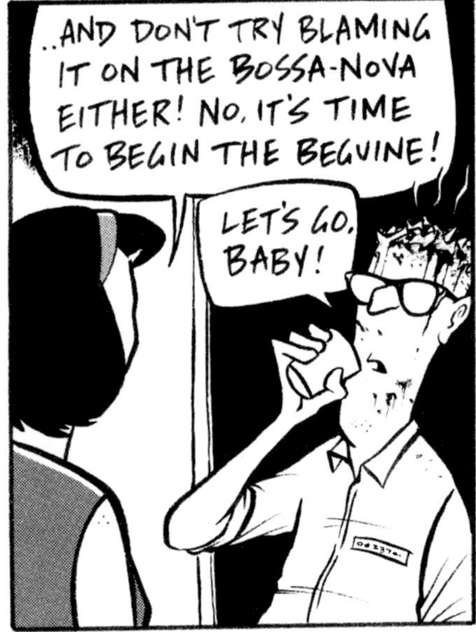
..AND DON'T TRY BLAMING IT ON THE BOSSA-NOVA EITHER! NO, IT'S TIME TO BEGIN THE BEGUINE!
LET'S GO, BABY!

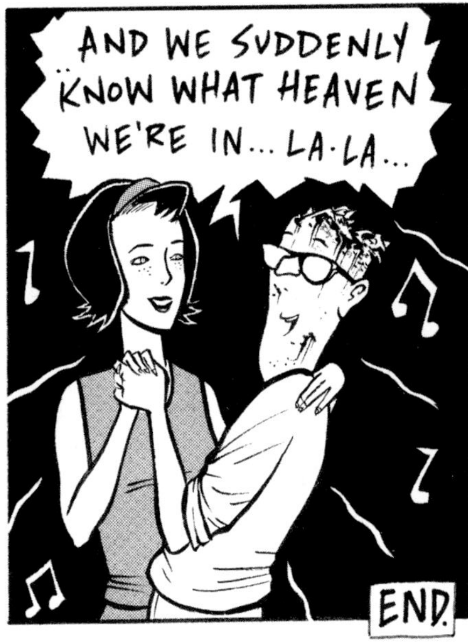
..AND WE SUDDENLY KNOW WHAT HEAVEN WE'RE IN... LA-LA...
END.

WOMBAT 5000 KÖLN / filbrändtz*

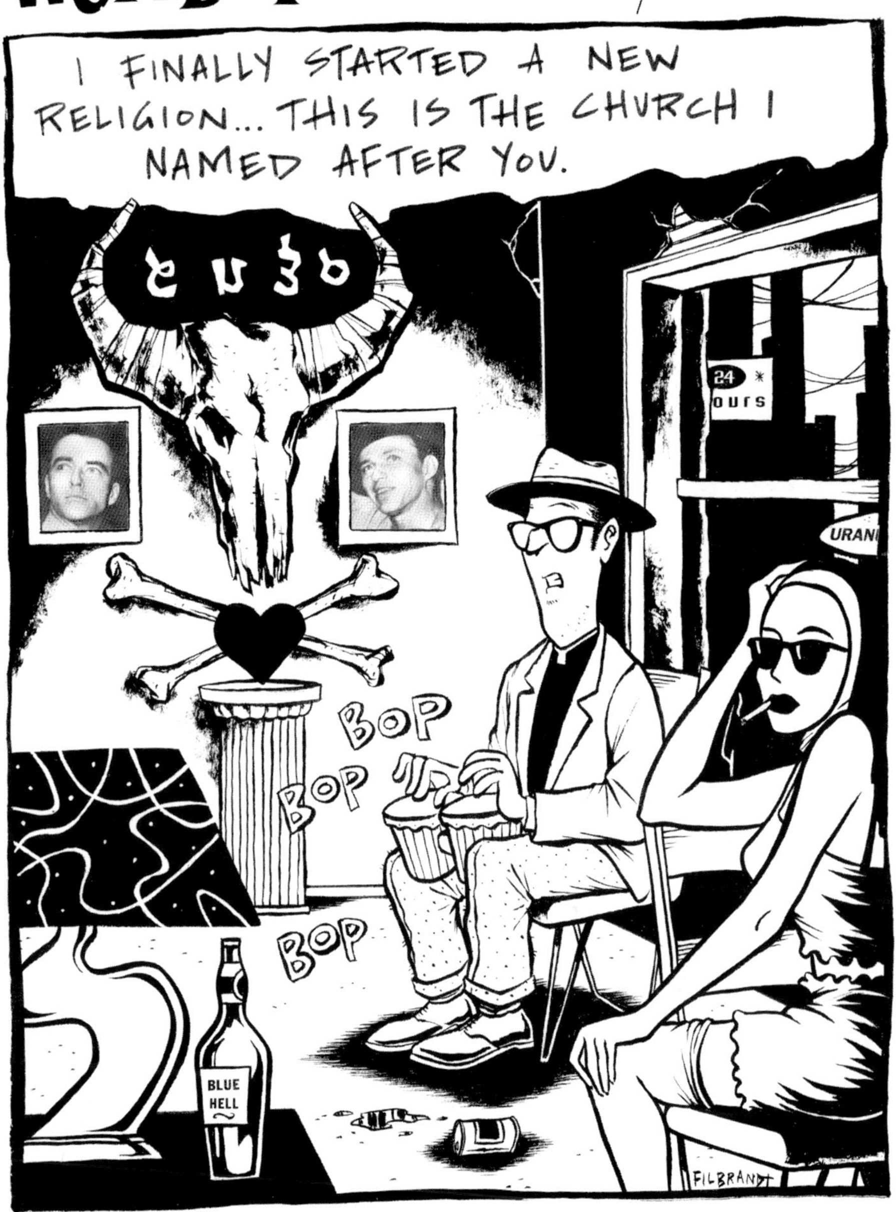

WOMBAT

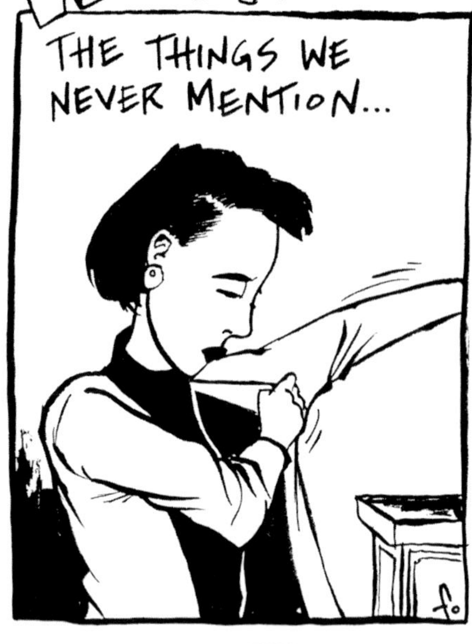
THE THINGS WE NEVER MENTION...

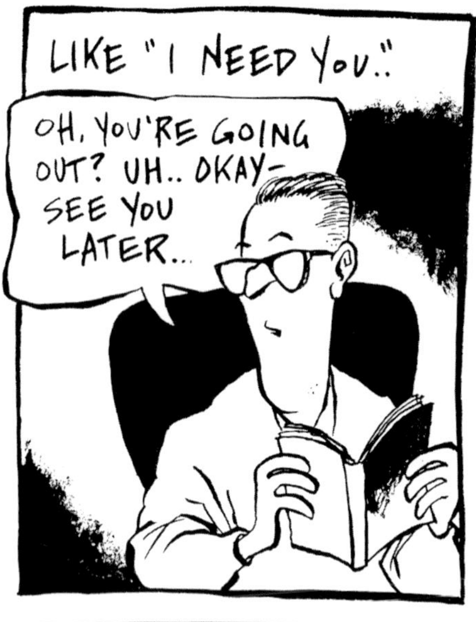
LIKE "I NEED YOU."
OH, YOU'RE GOING OUT? UH.. OKAY- SEE YOU LATER...

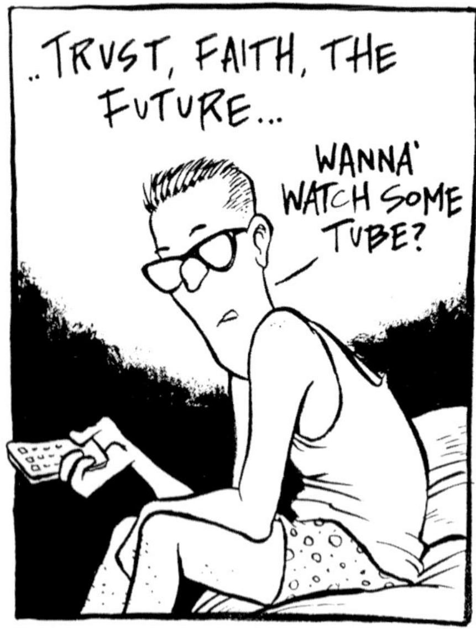
..TRUST, FAITH, THE FUTURE...
WANNA' WATCH SOME TUBE?

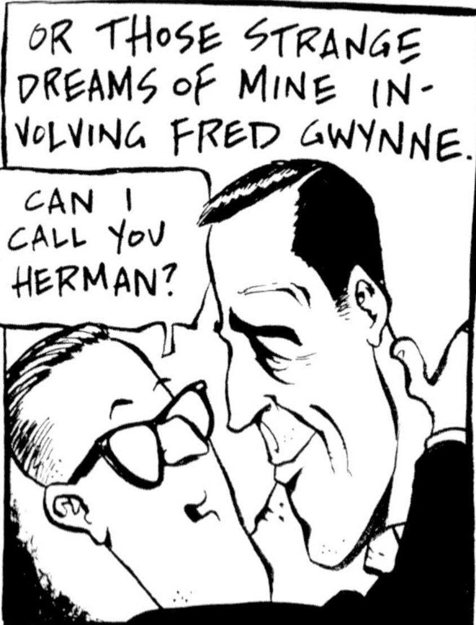
OR THOSE STRANGE DREAMS OF MINE IN-VOLVING FRED GWYNNE.
CAN I CALL YOU HERMAN?

WOMBAT

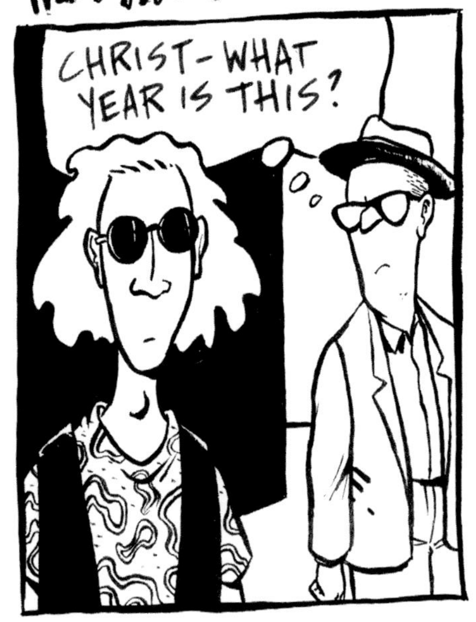
CHRIST- WHAT YEAR IS THIS?

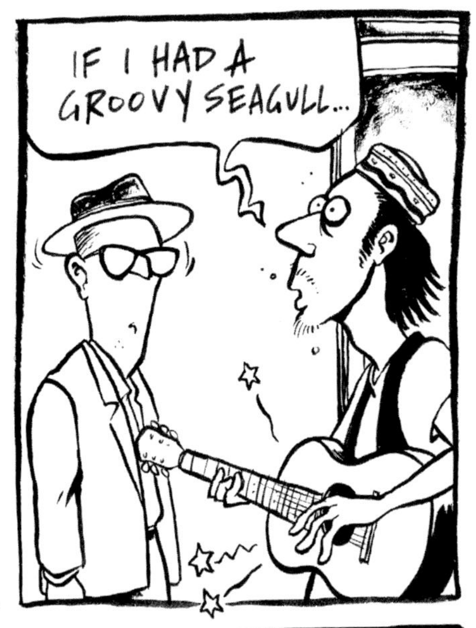
IF I HAD A GROOVY SEAGULL...

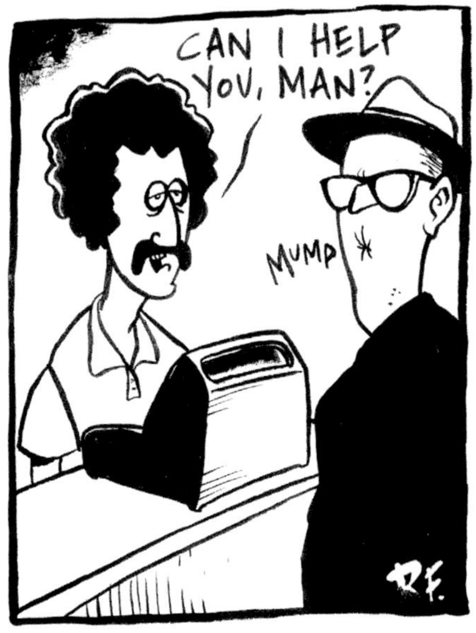
CAN I HELP YOU, MAN?
MUMP
P.F.

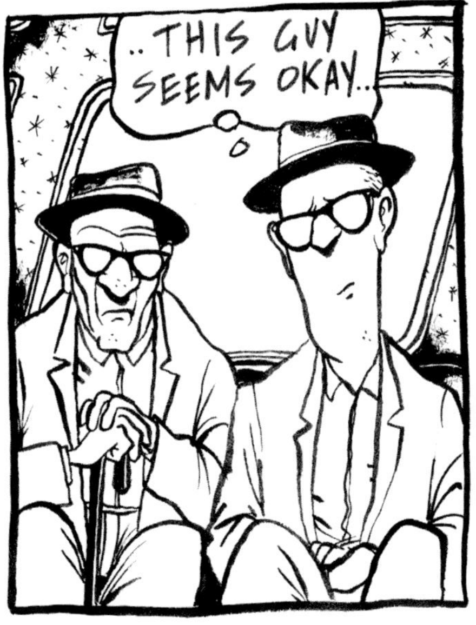
..THIS GUY SEEMS OKAY..

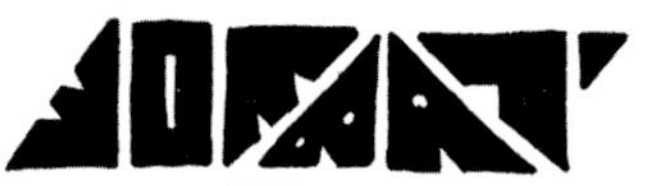

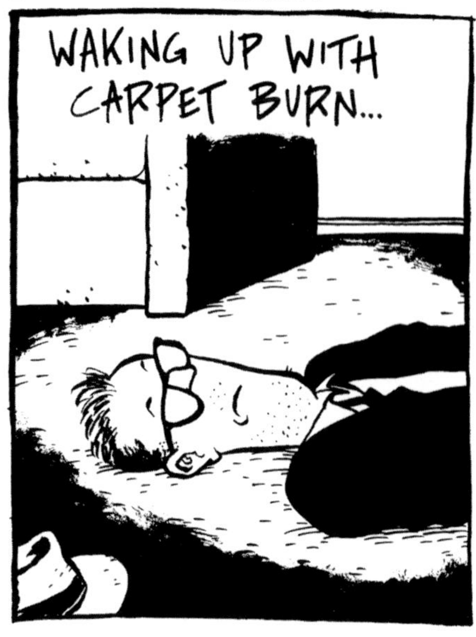
WAKING UP WITH CARPET BURN...

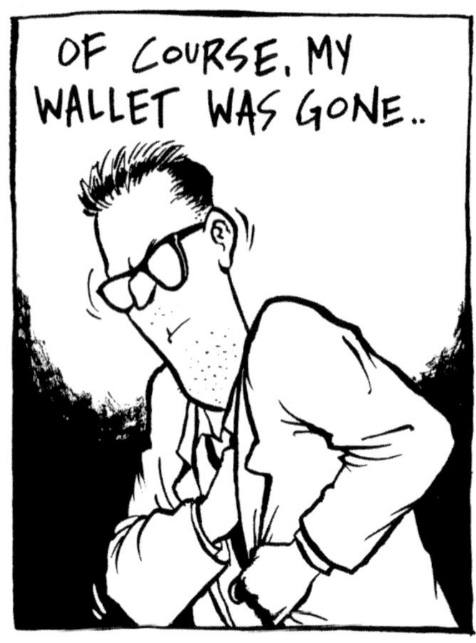
OF COURSE, MY WALLET WAS GONE..

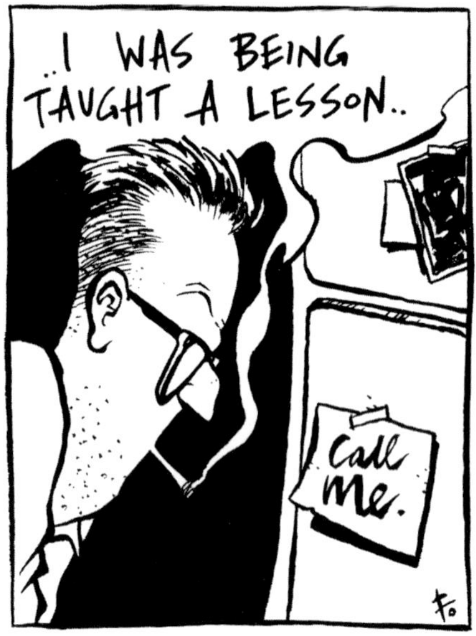
..I WAS BEING TAUGHT A LESSON..
Call Me.

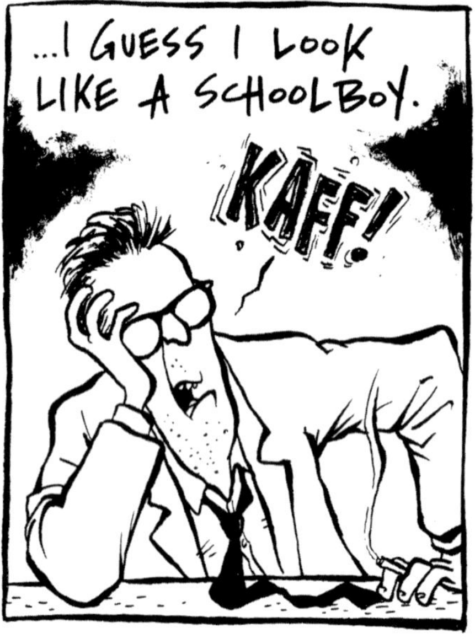
...I GUESS I LOOK LIKE A SCHOOLBOY.
KAFF!

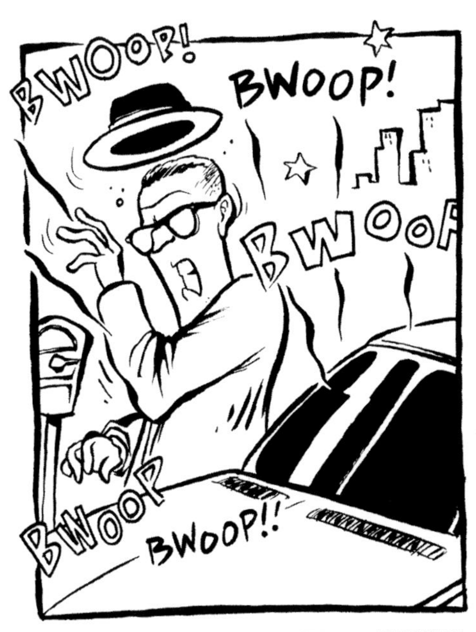
BWOOP!
BWOOP!
BWOOP
BWOOP
BWOOP!!

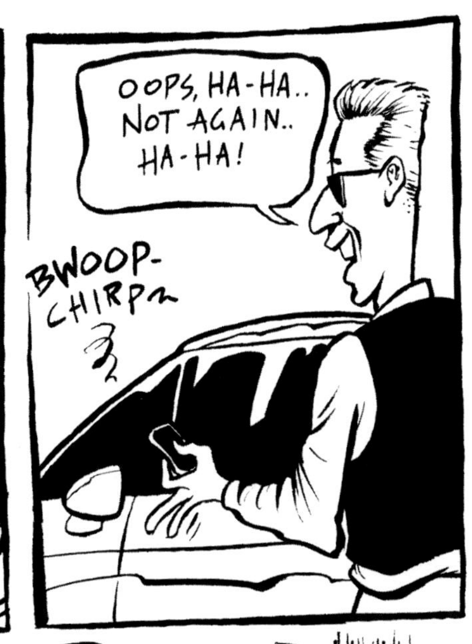
OOPS, HA-HA..
NOT AGAIN..
HA-HA!
BWOOP-
CHIRP

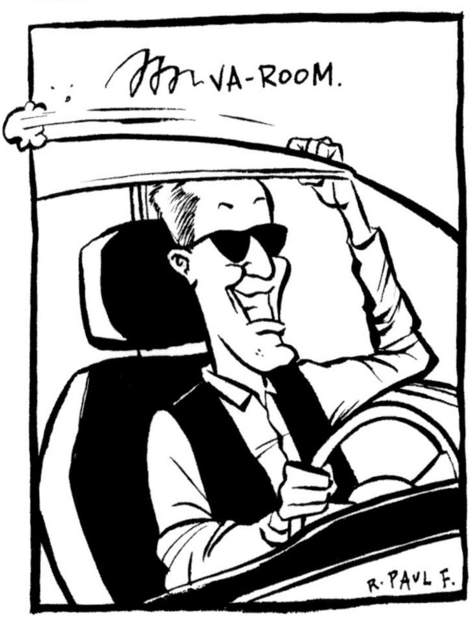
VA-ROOM.
R. PAUL F.

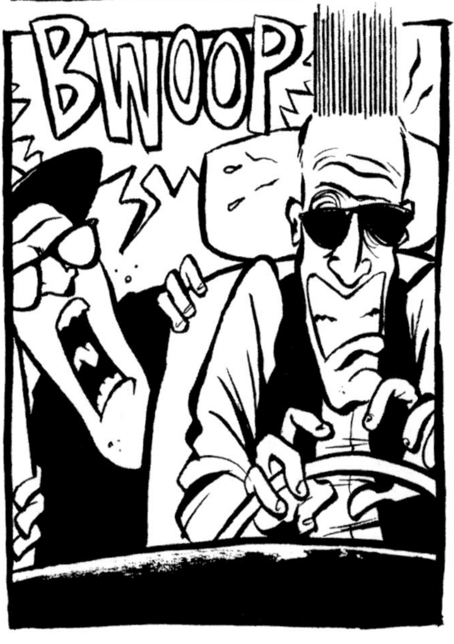
BWOOP

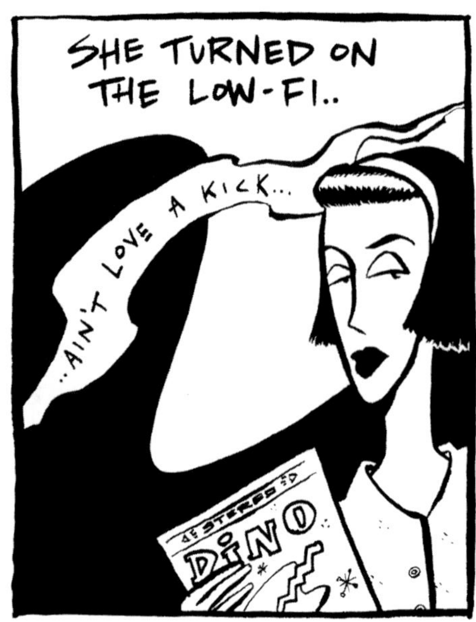
SHE TURNED ON THE LOW-FI..
..AIN'T LOVE A KICK...
STEREO
DINO

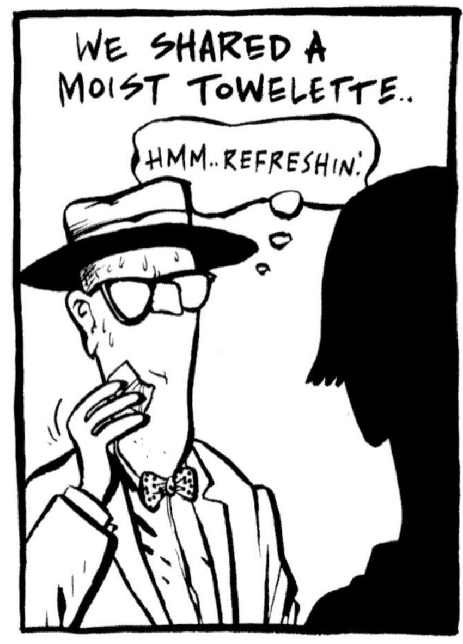
WE SHARED A MOIST TOWELETTE..
HMM.. REFRESHIN'.

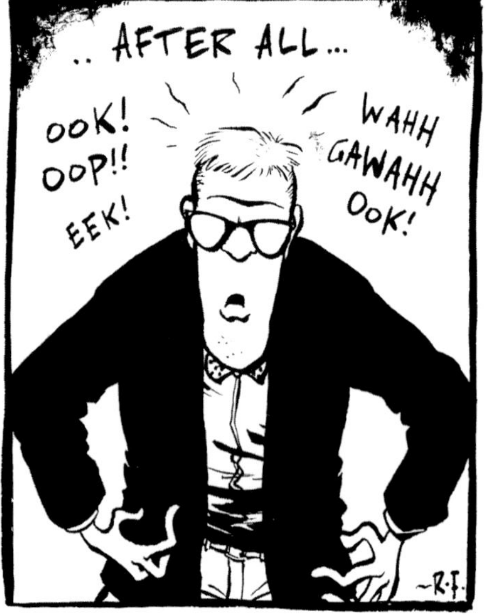
.. AFTER ALL...
OOK! OOP!! EEK!
WAHH GAWAHH OOK!
~R.F.

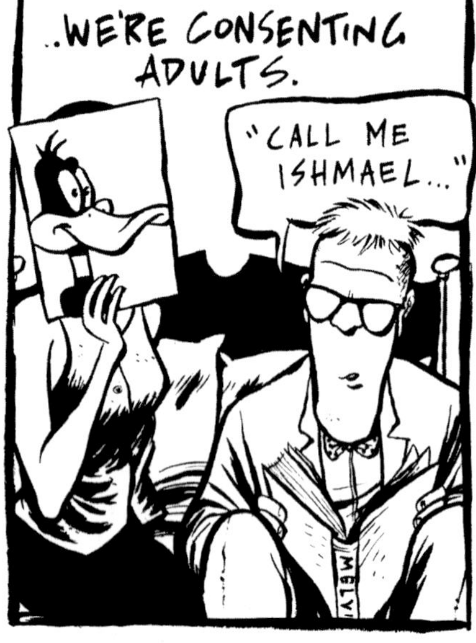
..WE'RE CONSENTING ADULTS.
"CALL ME ISHMAEL..."

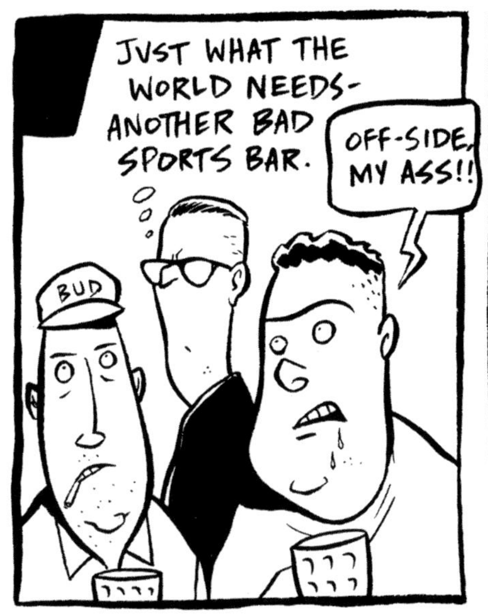
JUST WHAT THE WORLD NEEDS- ANOTHER BAD SPORTS BAR.
OFF-SIDE, MY ASS!!
BUD

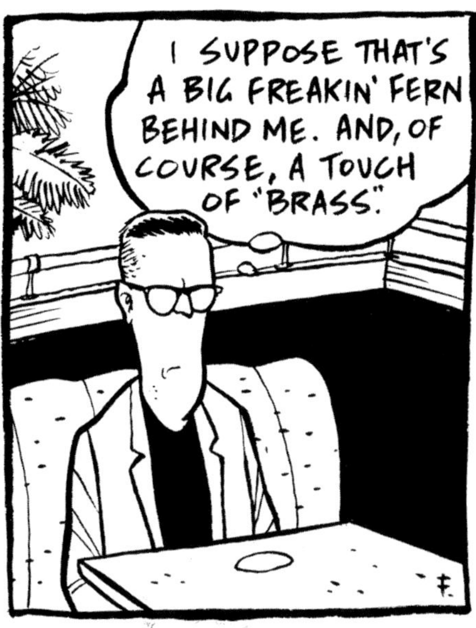
I SUPPOSE THAT'S A BIG FREAKIN' FERN BEHIND ME. AND, OF COURSE, A TOUCH OF "BRASS."

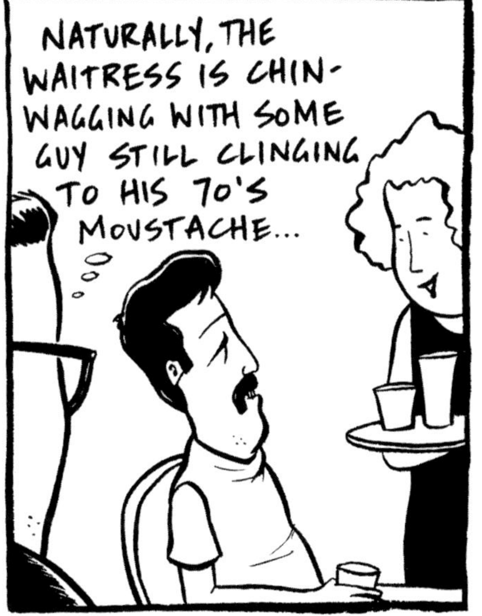
NATURALLY, THE WAITRESS IS CHIN-WAGGING WITH SOME GUY STILL CLINGING TO HIS 70'S MOUSTACHE...

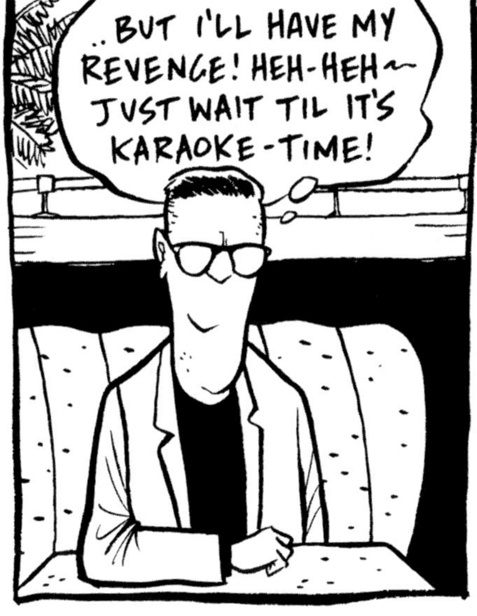
..BUT I'LL HAVE MY REVENGE! HEH-HEH~ JUST WAIT TIL IT'S KARAOKE-TIME!

WOMBAT BY R. FILBRANDT

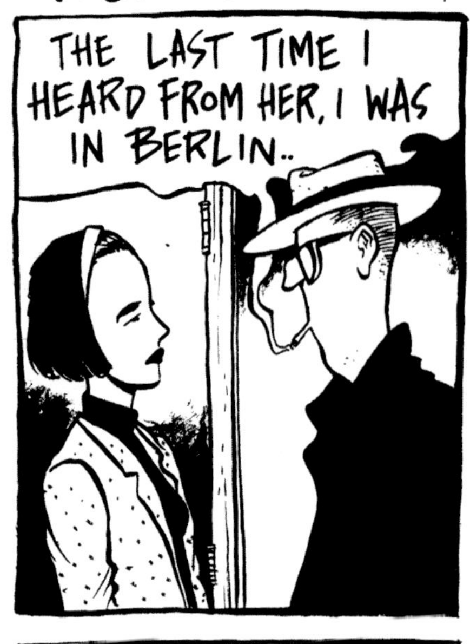

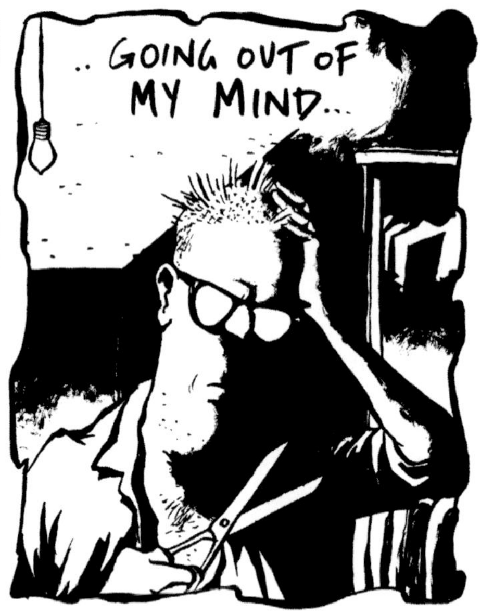

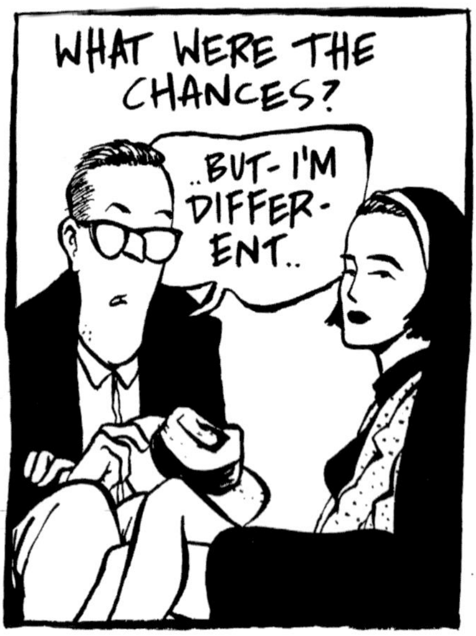

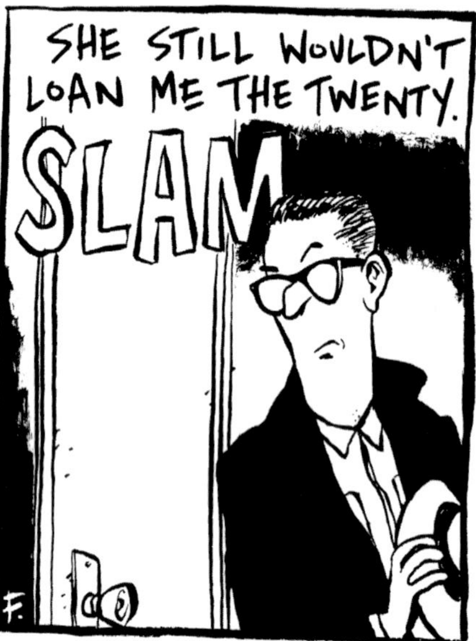

WOMBAT

by "RAGIN' DOILY"
(PHONEY TUFF-ARTIST ALIAS. YOU GOT A PROBLEM WITH THAT?)

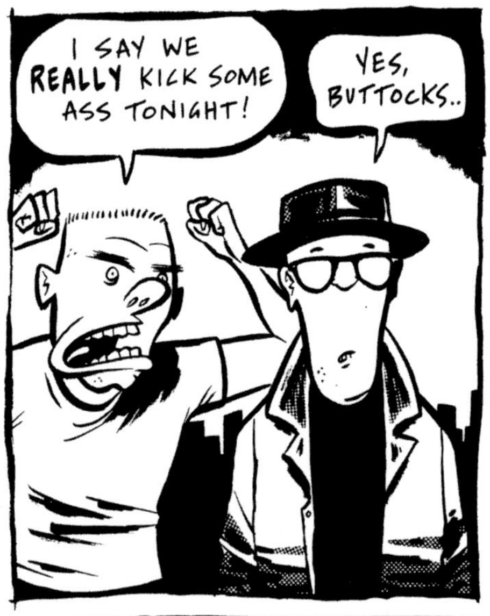

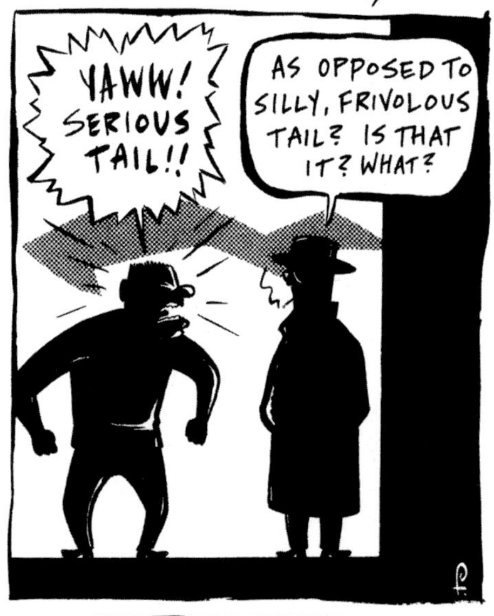

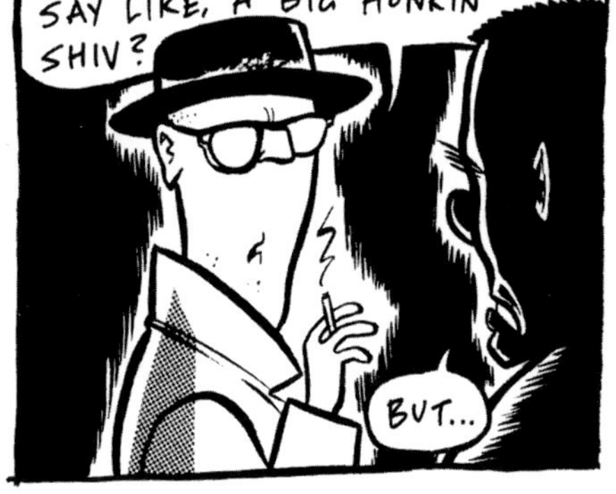

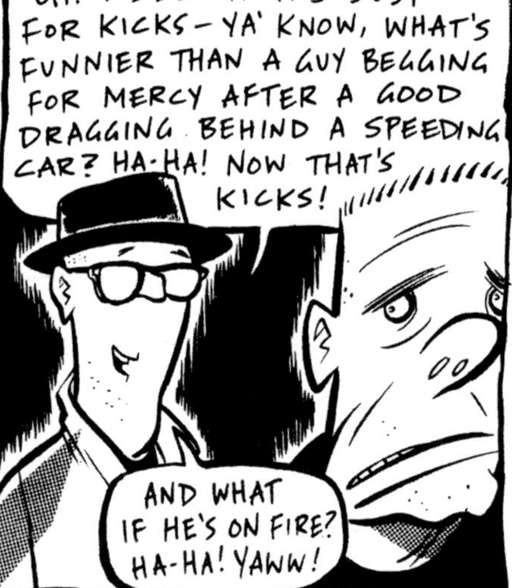

the WOMBAT JUNGLE

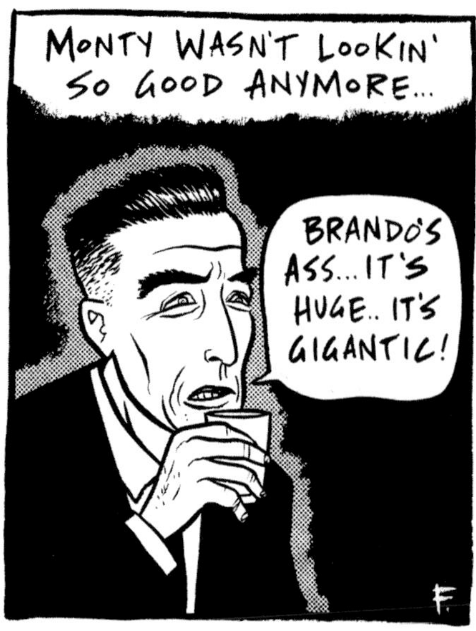

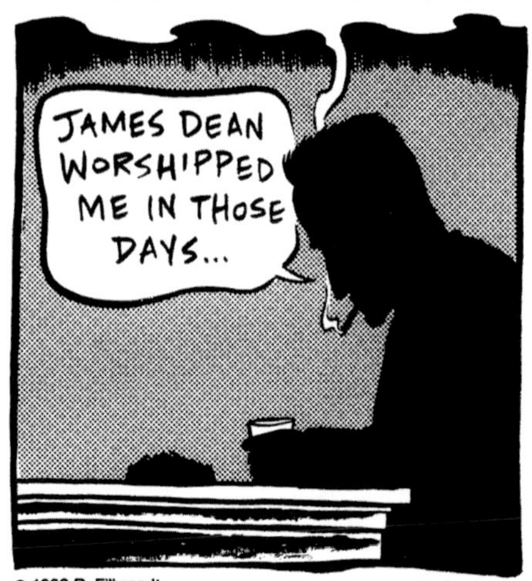

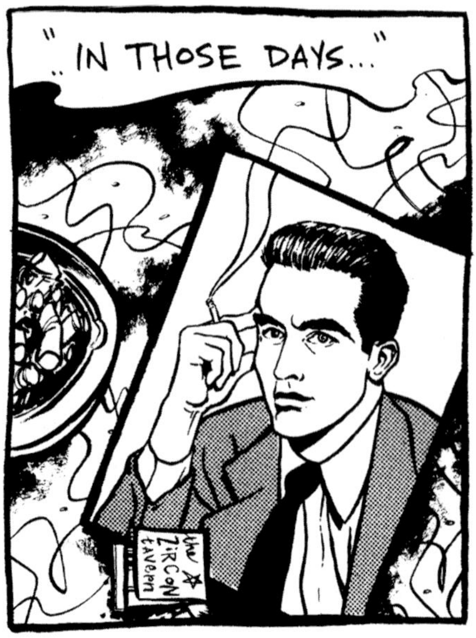

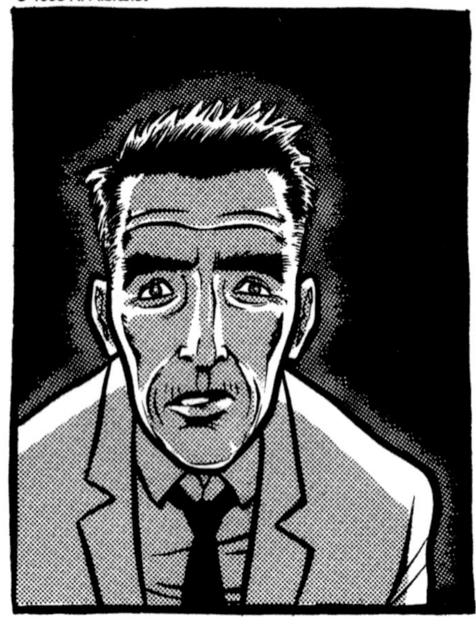

WOMBAT ~ SPECIAL GUEST-STAR: ROY!

R. FILBRANDT

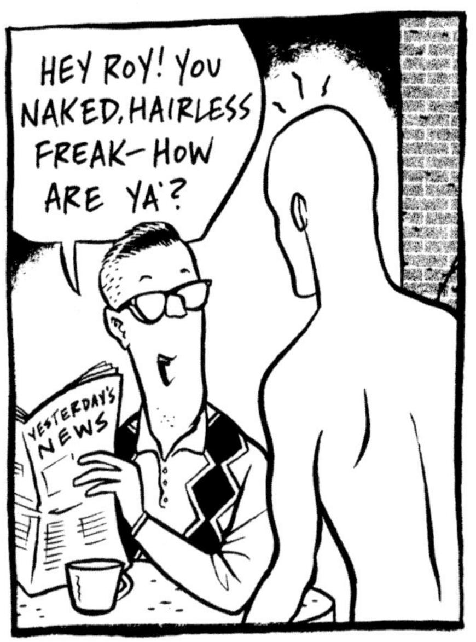

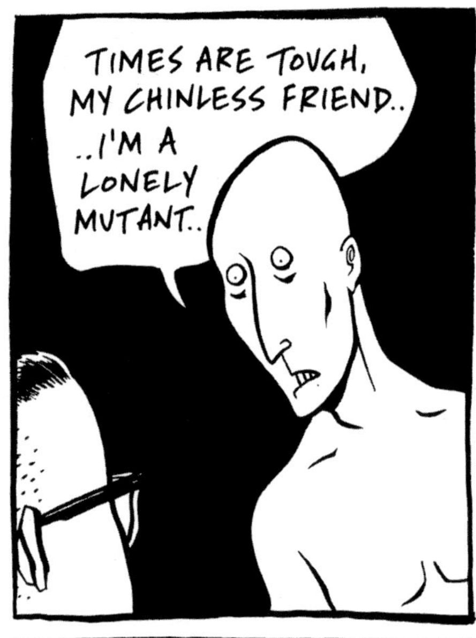

..I THOUGHT I HAD A "HI AND LOIS" GIG, BUT IT FELL THROUGH.. "NANCY" AIN'T EVEN HIRING—BUT YA' KNOW, I THINK I GOT A SHOT AT SOME "GARFIELD" ACTION!

F.

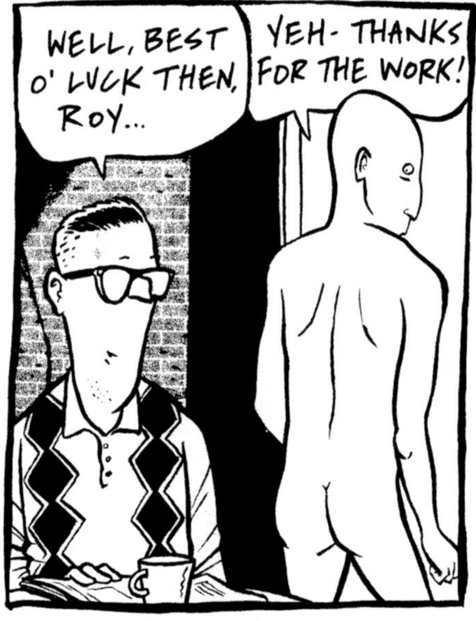

WOMBAT

BY ROD

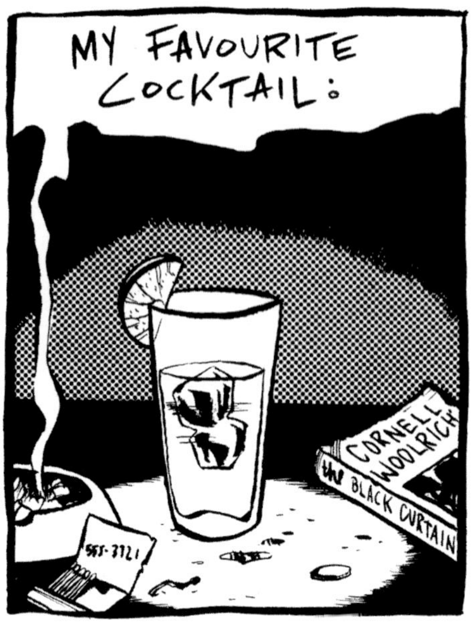

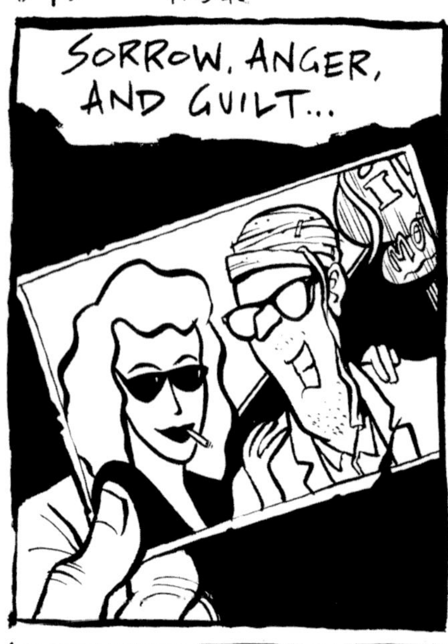

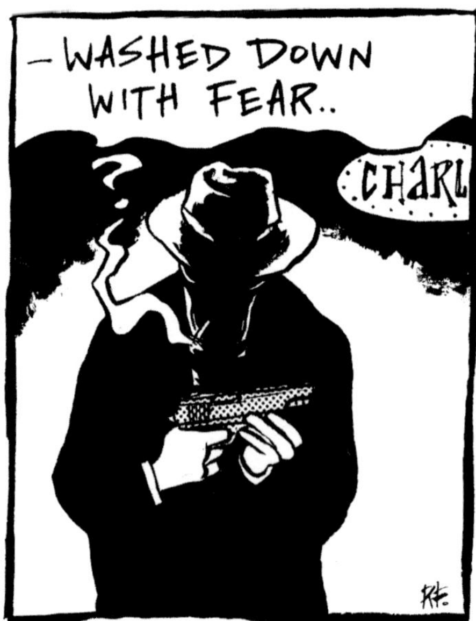

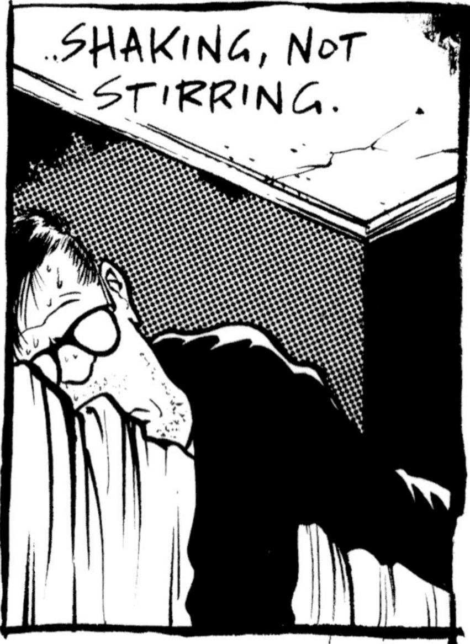

WOMBAT BY R. FILBRANDT

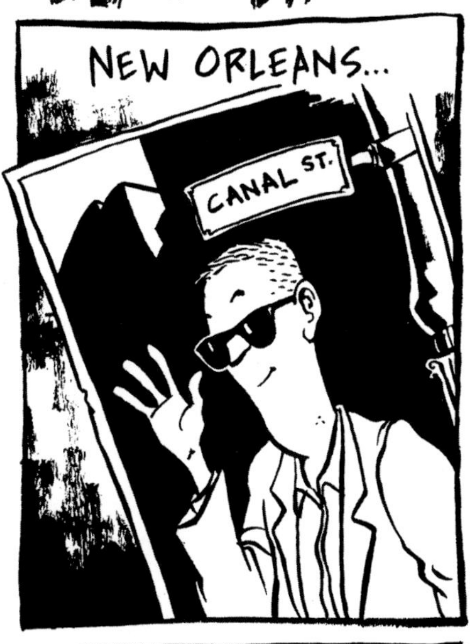

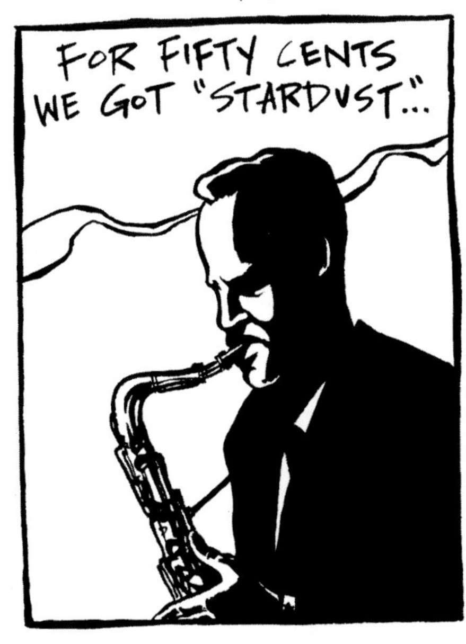

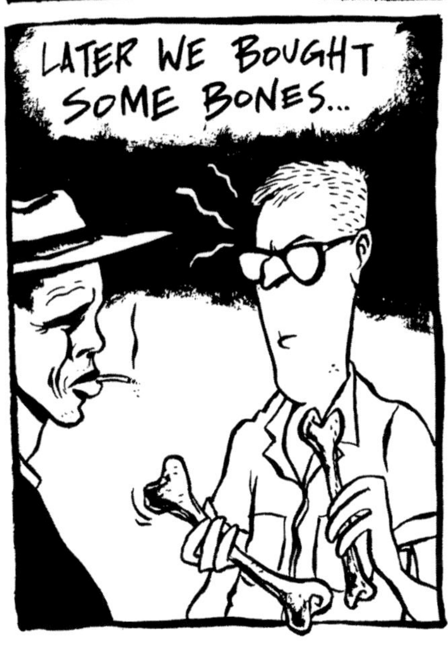

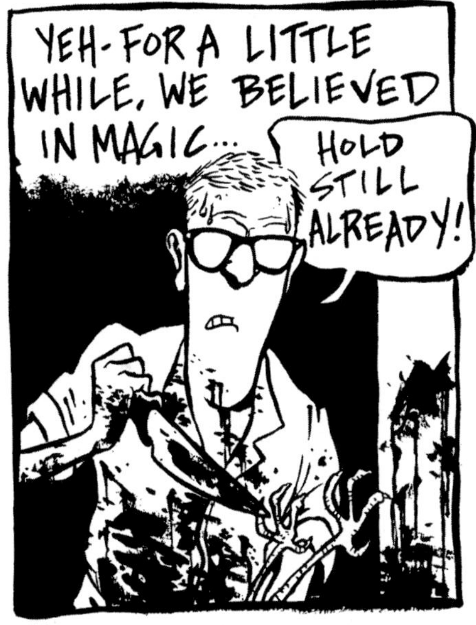

WOMBAT

David Letterman's suit

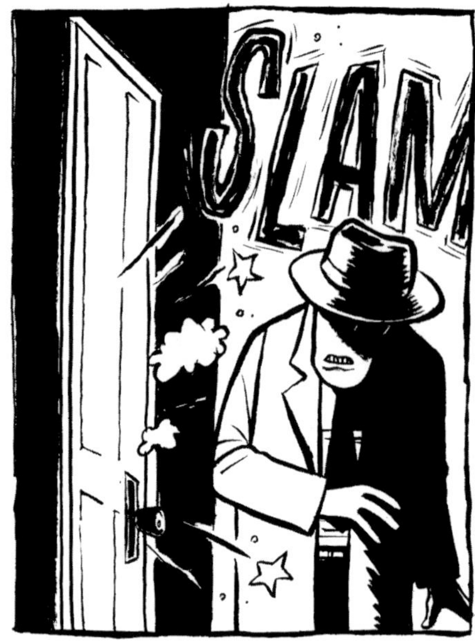

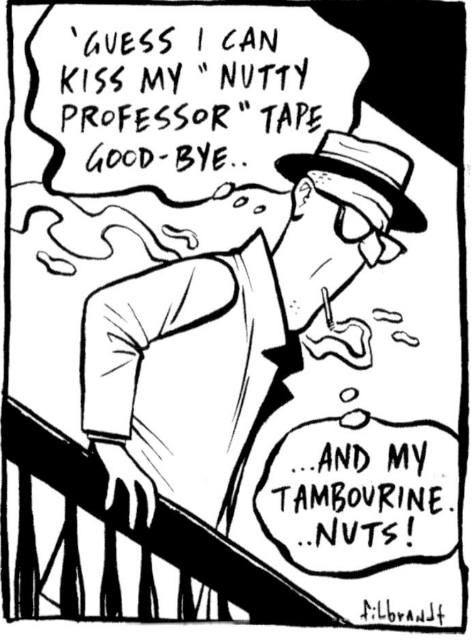

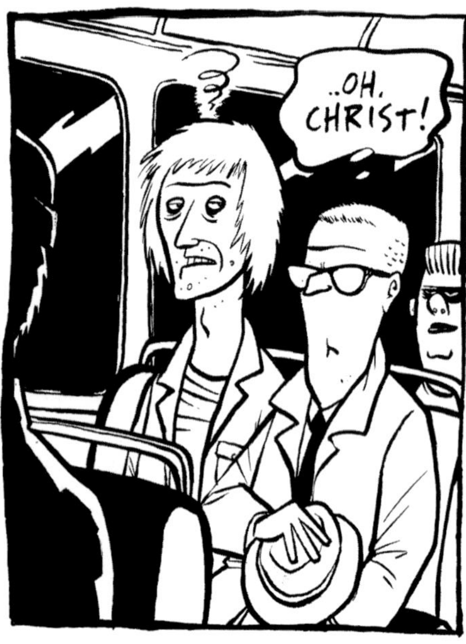

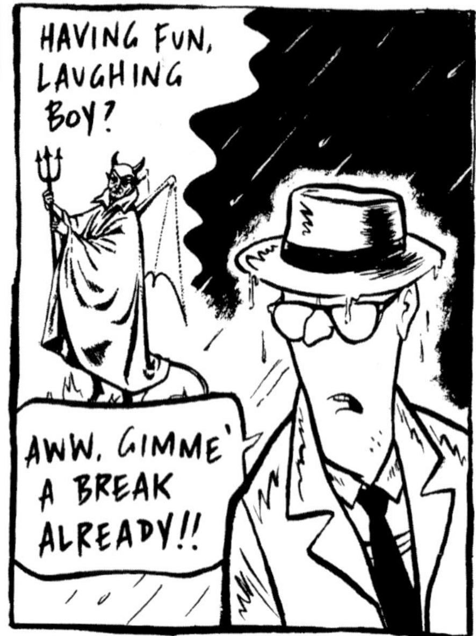

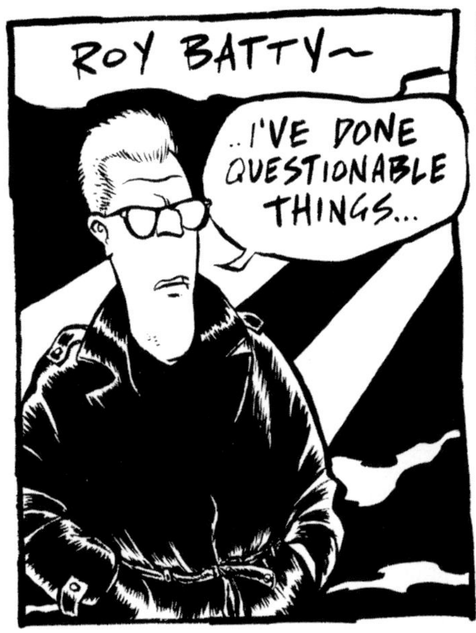
ROY BATTY~
..I'VE DONE QUESTIONABLE THINGS...

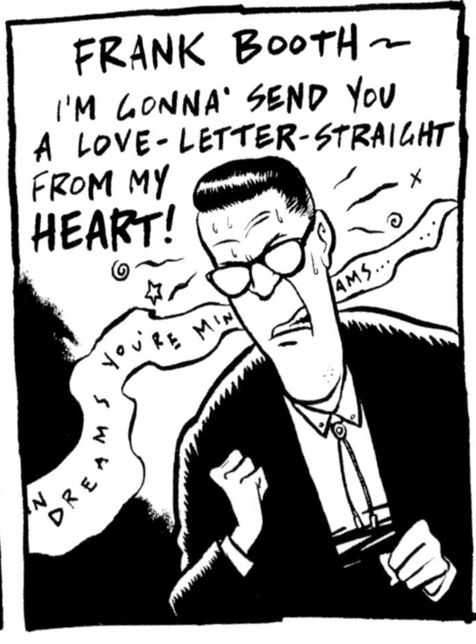
FRANK BOOTH~
I'M GONNA' SEND YOU A LOVE-LETTER-STRAIGHT FROM MY HEART!
DREAMS YOU'RE

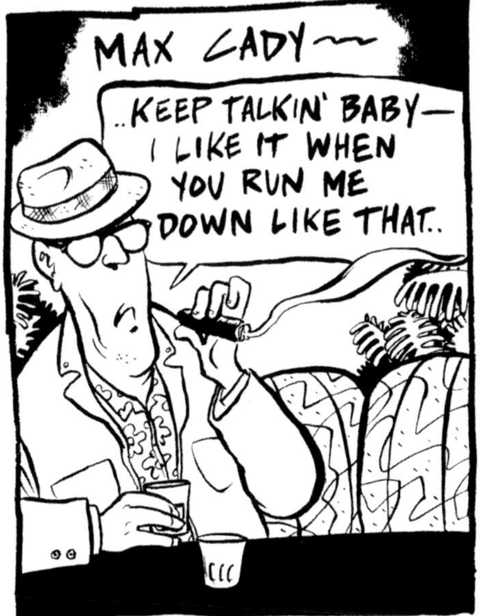
MAX CADY~
..KEEP TALKIN' BABY— I LIKE IT WHEN YOU RUN ME DOWN LIKE THAT..

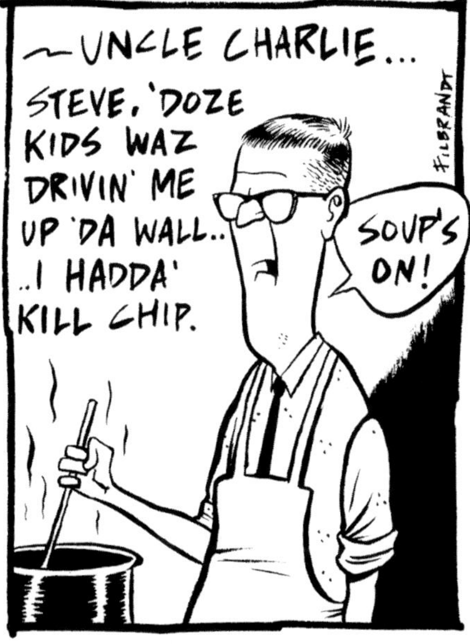
~UNCLE CHARLIE...
STEVE, 'DOZE KIDS WAZ DRIVIN' ME UP 'DA WALL.. ..I HADDA' KILL CHIP.
SOUP'S ON!
FILBRANDT

WomBat ? ? This is Toon #3 ? -wink

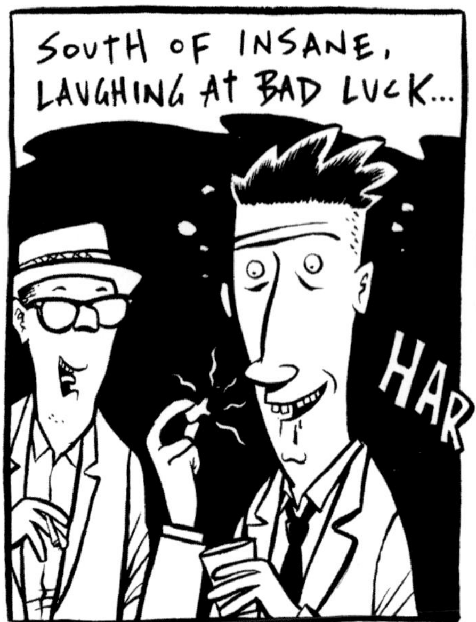

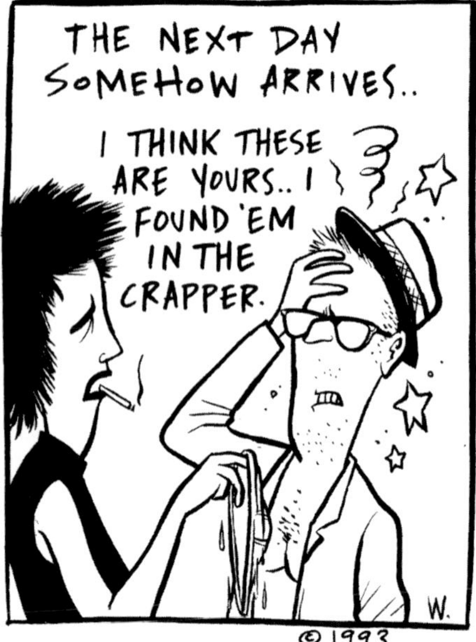

© 1993

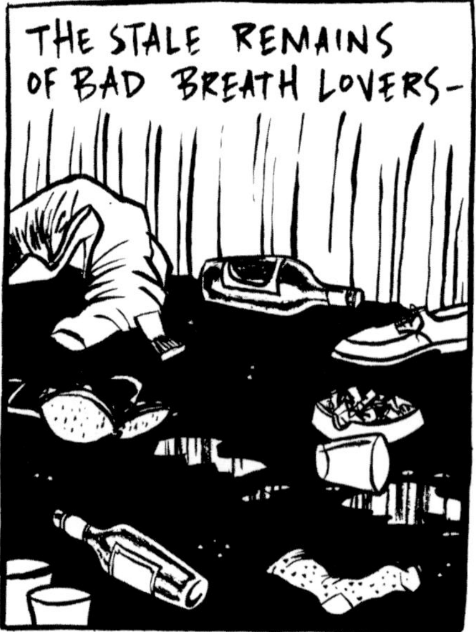

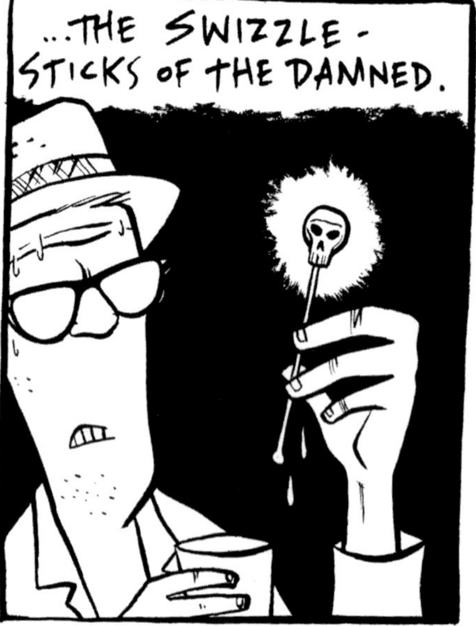

WOMBAT Rogue's of Gallery CONFIRMED ARTISTS

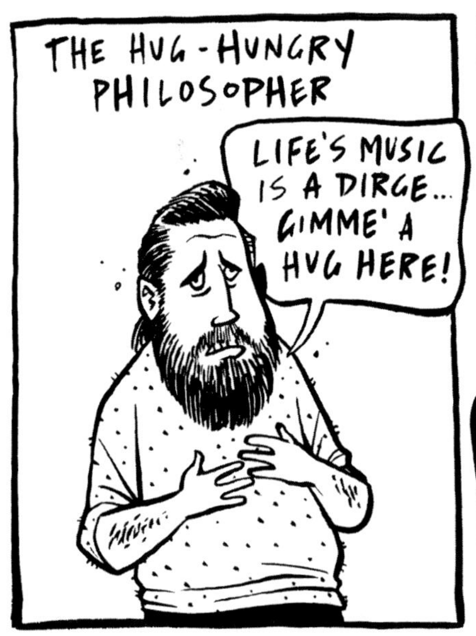

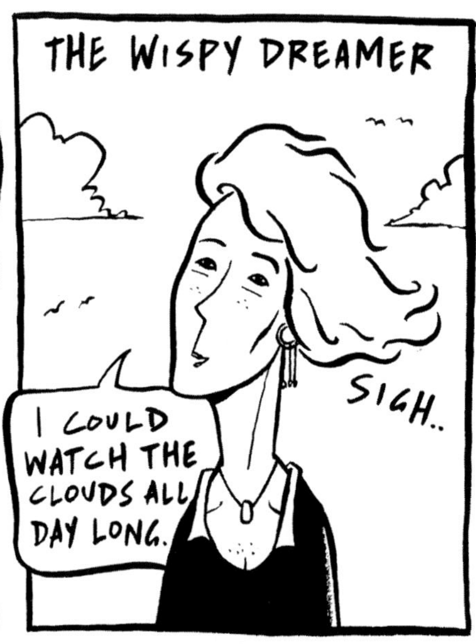

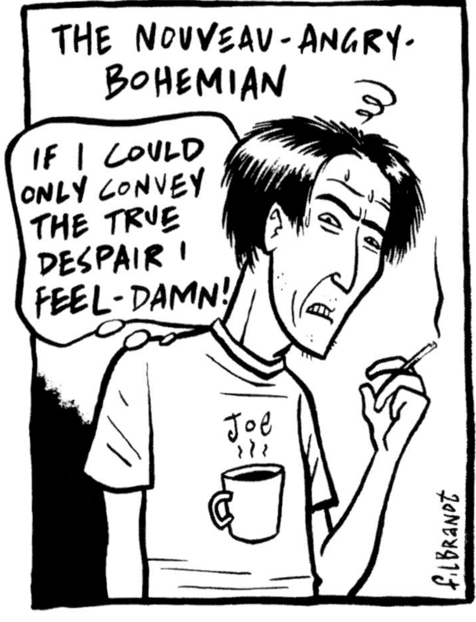

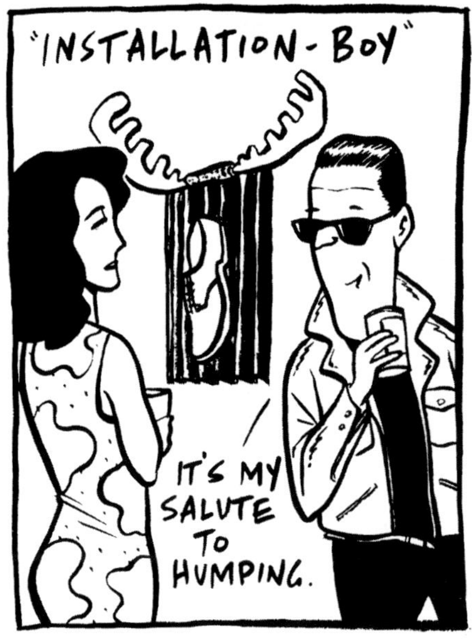

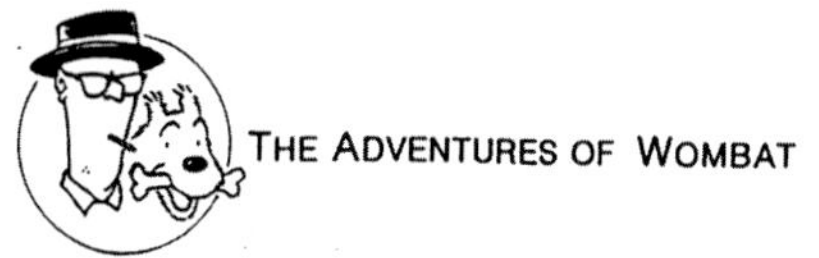
THE ADVENTURES OF WOMBAT
By CORNELIUS BORGNINE

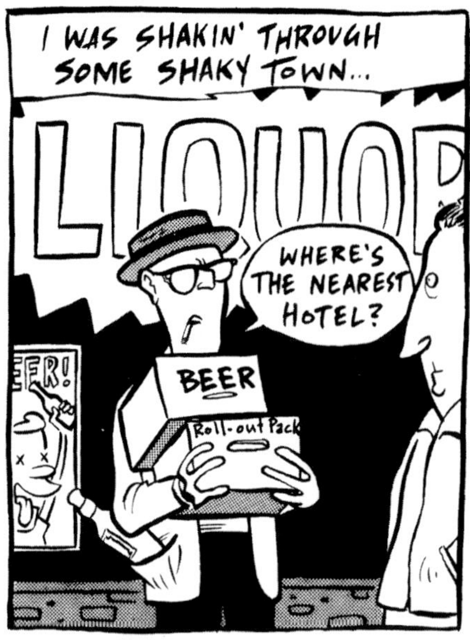
I WAS SHAKIN' THROUGH SOME SHAKY TOWN...
LIQUOR
WHERE'S THE NEAREST HOTEL?
BEER
Roll-out Pack

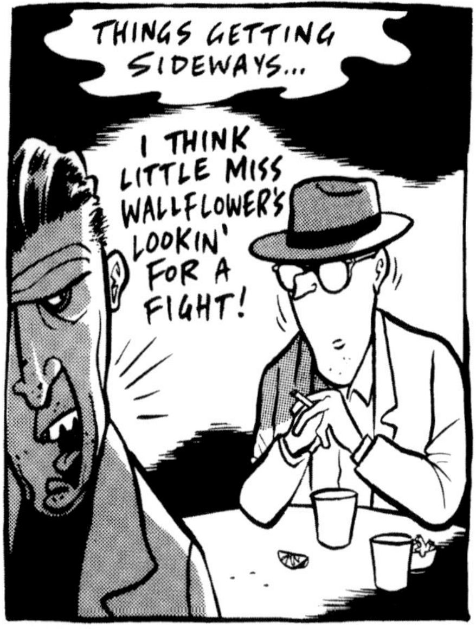
THINGS GETTING SIDEWAYS...
I THINK LITTLE MISS WALLFLOWER'S LOOKIN' FOR A FIGHT!

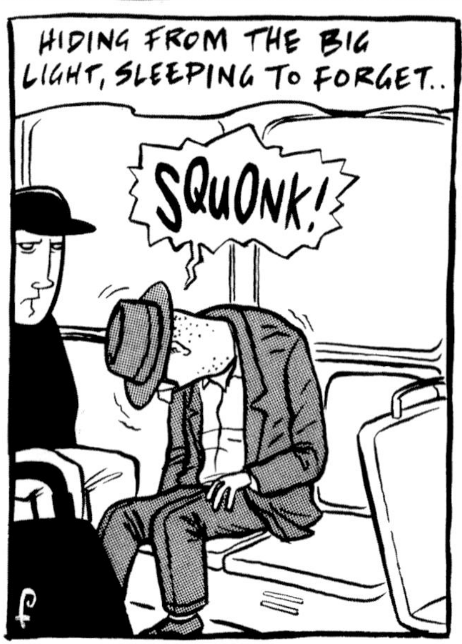
HIDING FROM THE BIG LIGHT, SLEEPING TO FORGET..
SQUONK!

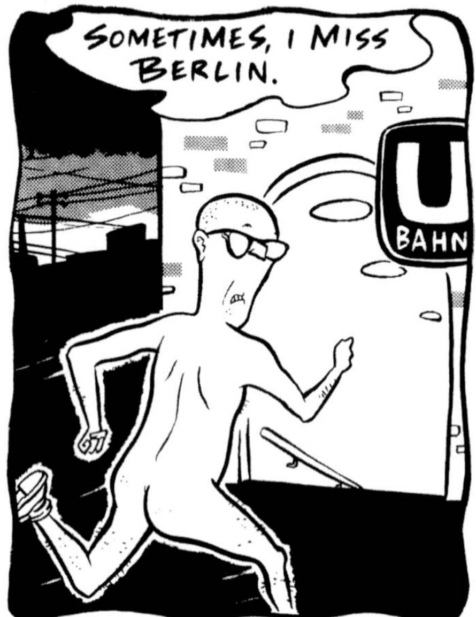
SOMETIMES, I MISS BERLIN.
U
BAHN

WINK :: ©'93

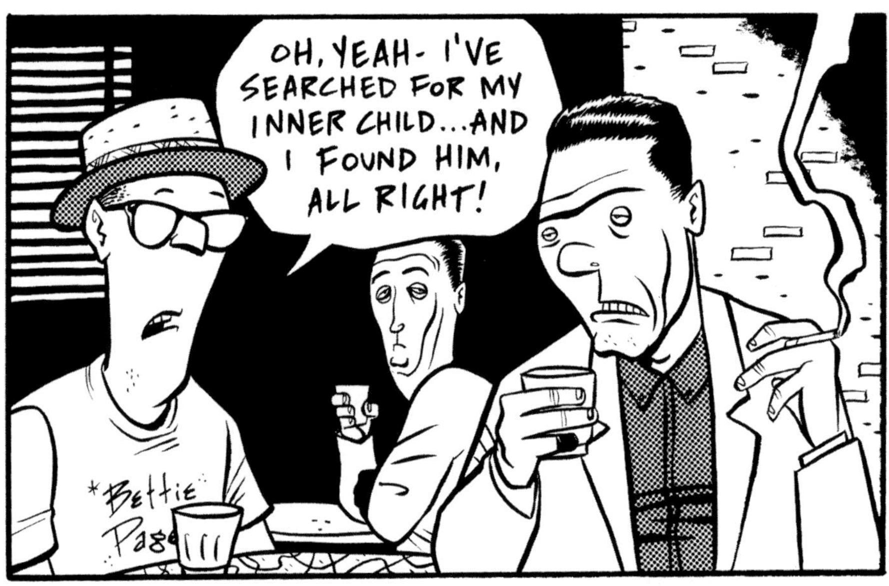
OH, YEAH- I'VE SEARCHED FOR MY INNER CHILD...AND I FOUND HIM, ALL RIGHT!
*Bettie Page

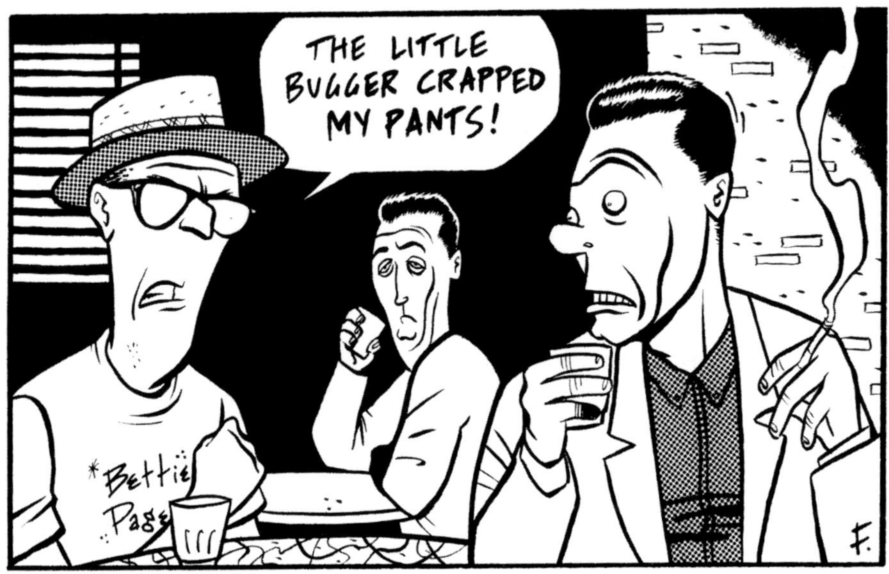
THE LITTLE BUGGER CRAPPED MY PANTS!
*Bettie Page
F.

The Devil's Hangover

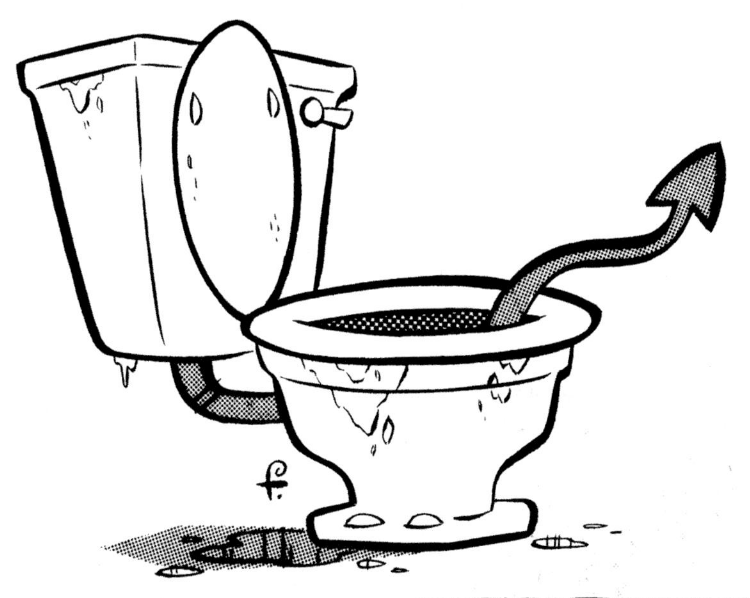

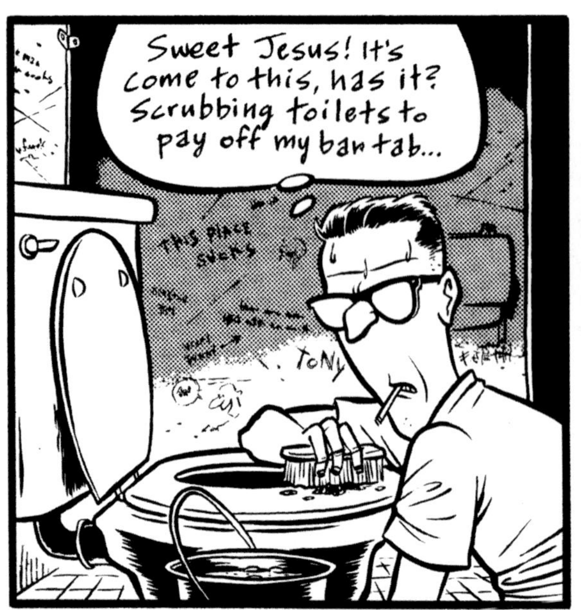
Sweet Jesus! It's come to this, has it? Scrubbing toilets to pay off my bar tab...
THIS PLACE SUCKS
TONY

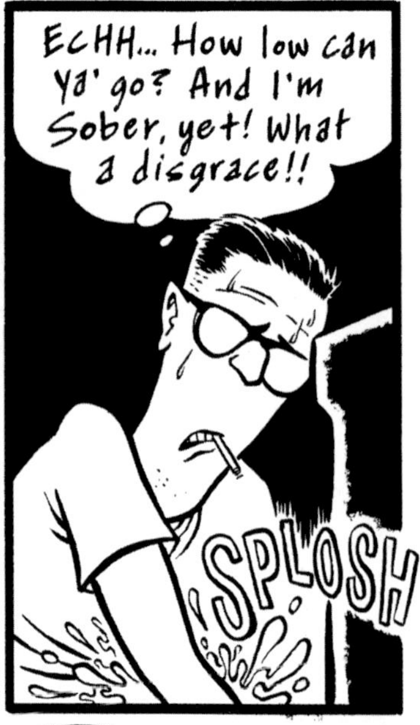
ECHH... How low can ya' go? And I'm Sober, yet! What a disgrace!!
SPLOSH

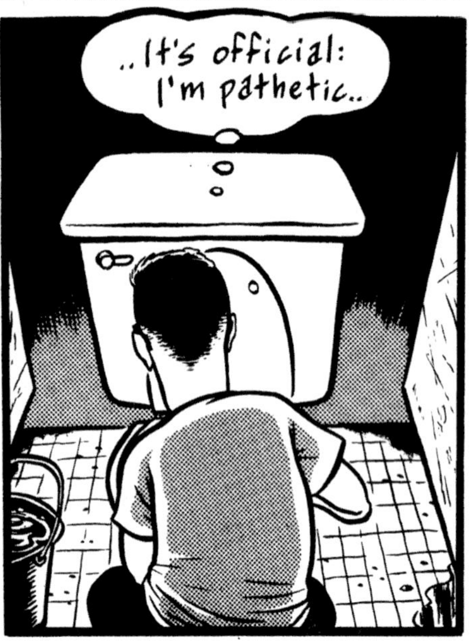
..It's official: I'm pathetic..

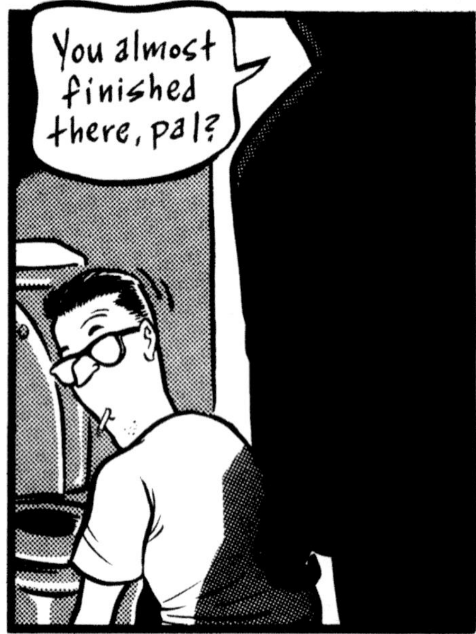
You almost finished there, pal?

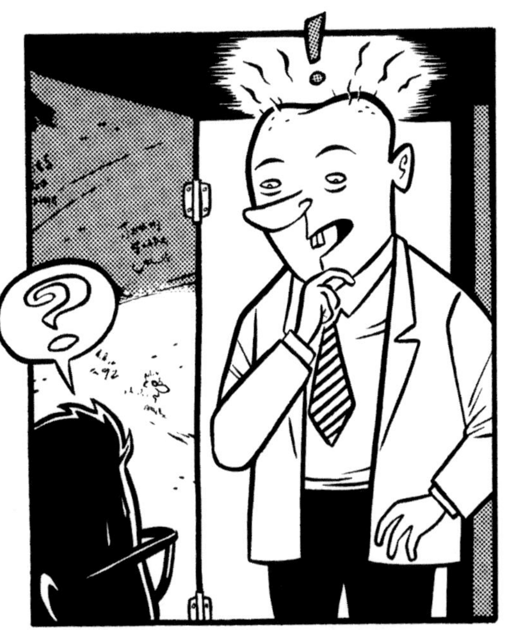
!
?

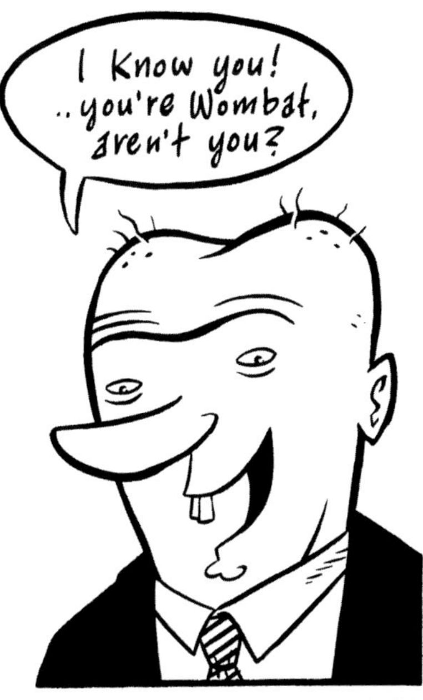
I Know you! ..you're Wombat, aren't you?

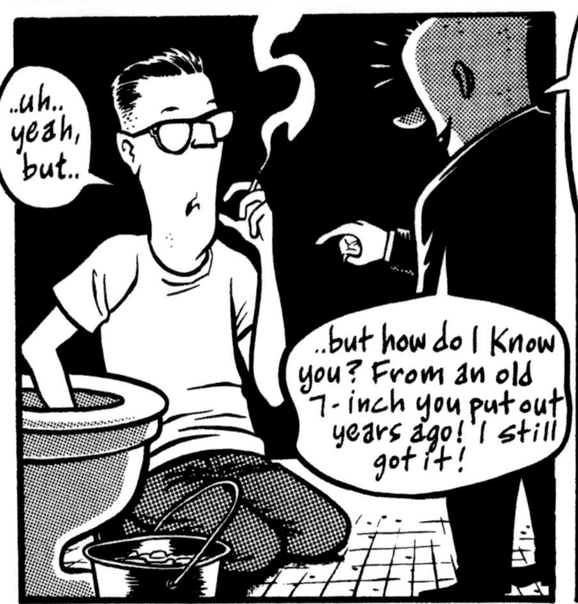
..uh.. yeah, but..
..but how do I Know you? From an old 7-inch you put out years ago! I still got it!

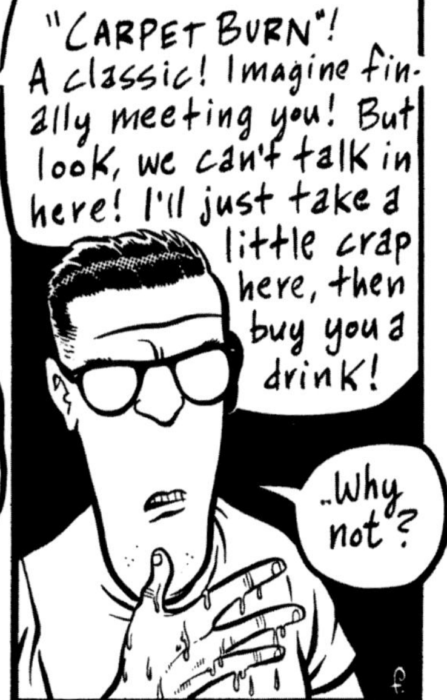
"CARPET BURN"! A classic! Imagine finally meeting you! But look, we can't talk in here! I'll just take a little crap here, then buy you a drink!
..Why not?

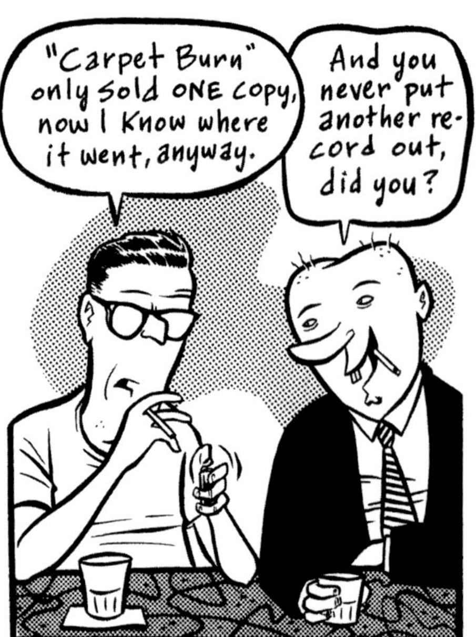
"Carpet Burn" only sold ONE copy, now I know where it went, anyway.
And you never put another record out, did you?

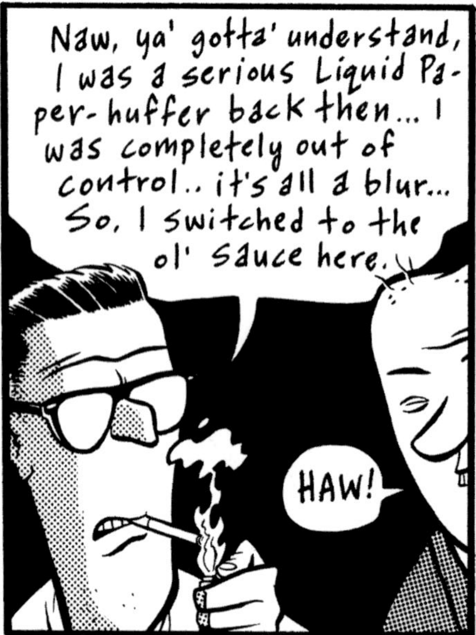
Naw, ya' gotta' understand, I was a serious Liquid Paper-huffer back then... I was completely out of control.. it's all a blur... So, I switched to the ol' sauce here.
HAW!

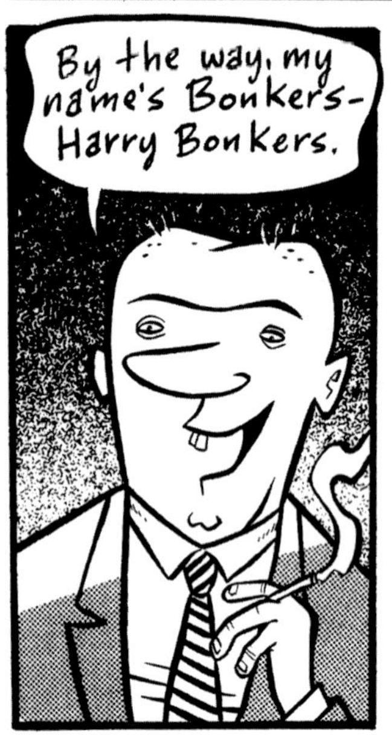
By the way, my name's Bonkers- Harry Bonkers.

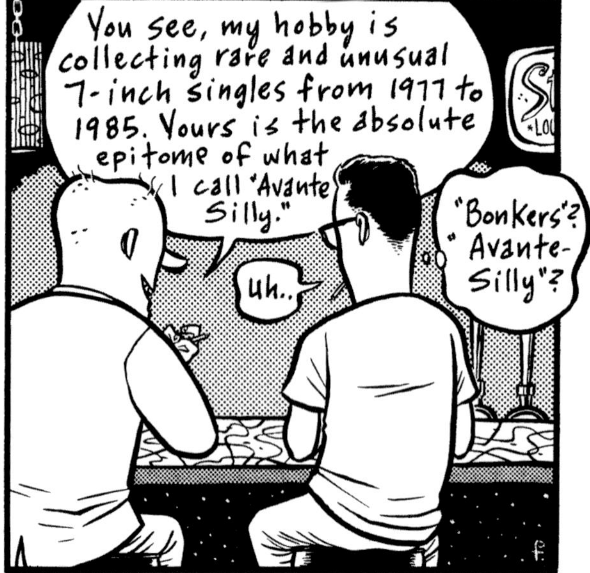
You see, my hobby is collecting rare and unusual 7-inch singles from 1977 to 1985. Yours is the absolute epitome of what I call "Avante Silly."
uh..
"Bonkers"? "Avante-Silly"?

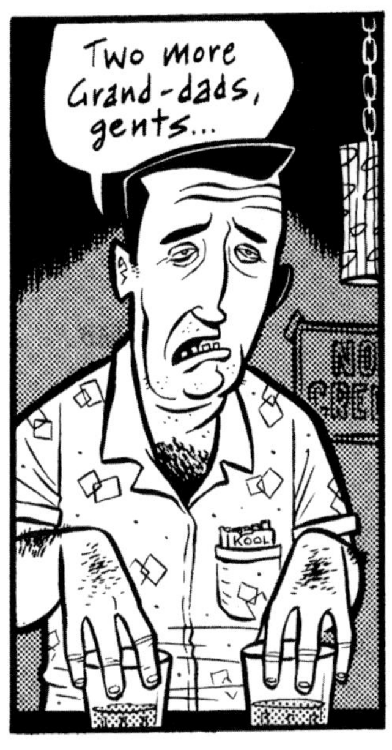

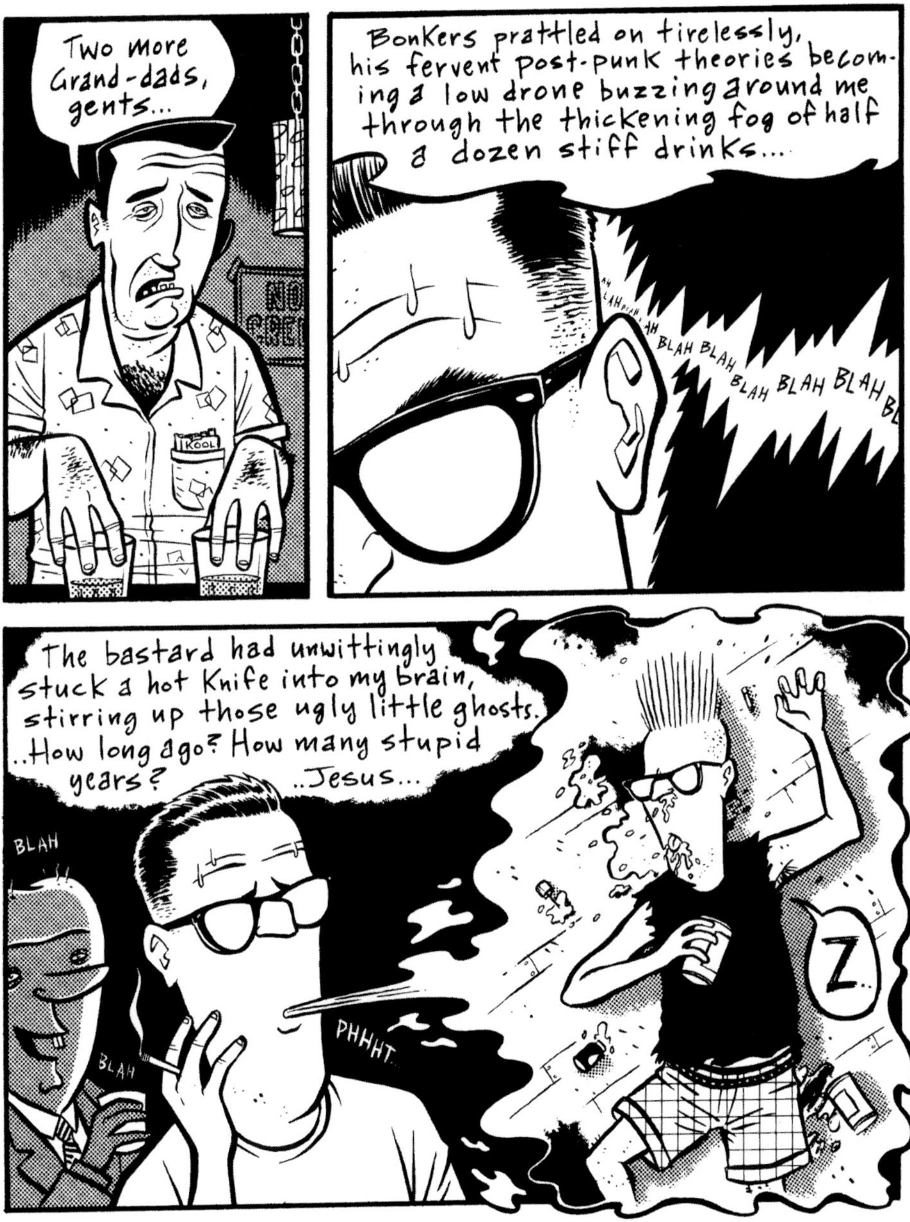

Bonkers prattled on tirelessly, his fervent post-punk theories becoming a low drone buzzing around me through the thickening fog of half a dozen stiff drinks...

BLAH BLAH BLAH BLAH BLAH

The bastard had unwittingly stuck a hot knife into my brain, stirring up those ugly little ghosts. ..How long ago? How many stupid years? ..Jesus...

BLAH

BLAH

PHHHT

Z..

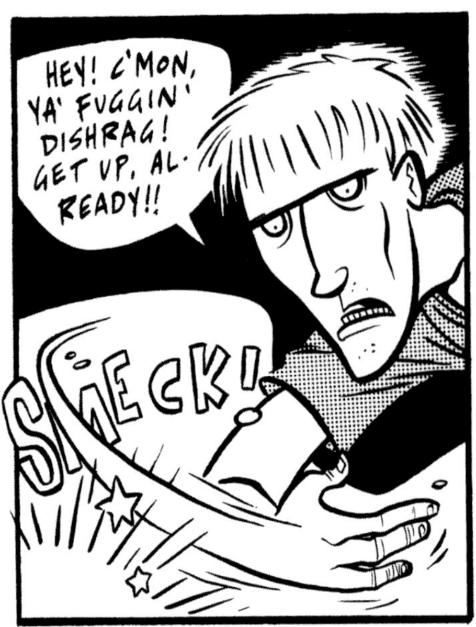
HEY! C'MON, YA' FUGGIN' DISHRAG! GET UP, AL-READY!!
SMECK!

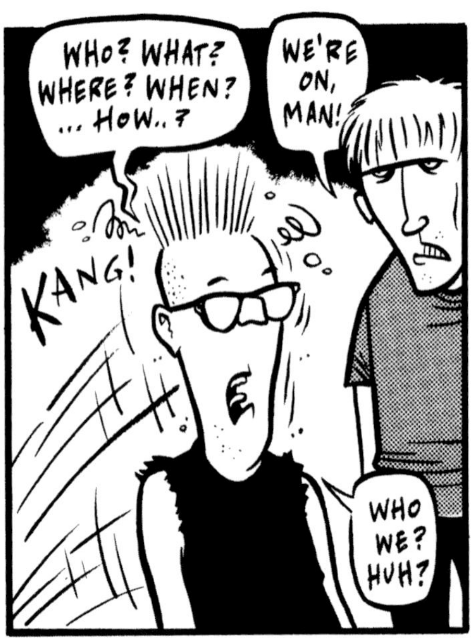
WHO? WHAT? WHERE? WHEN? ... HOW..?
WE'RE ON, MAN!
KANG!
WHO WE? HUH?

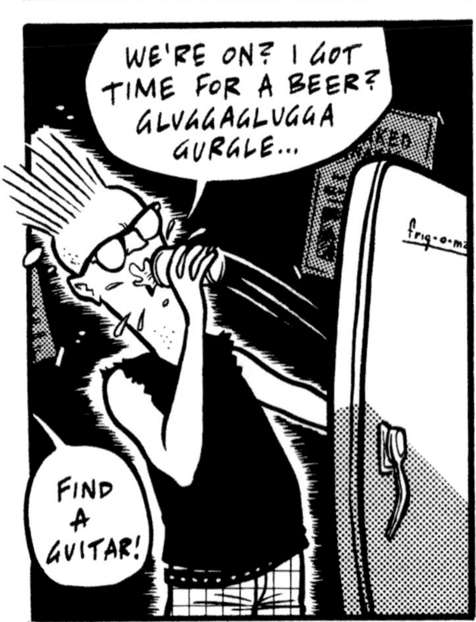
WE'RE ON? I GOT TIME FOR A BEER? GLUGGAGLUGGA GURGLE...
FIND A GUITAR!

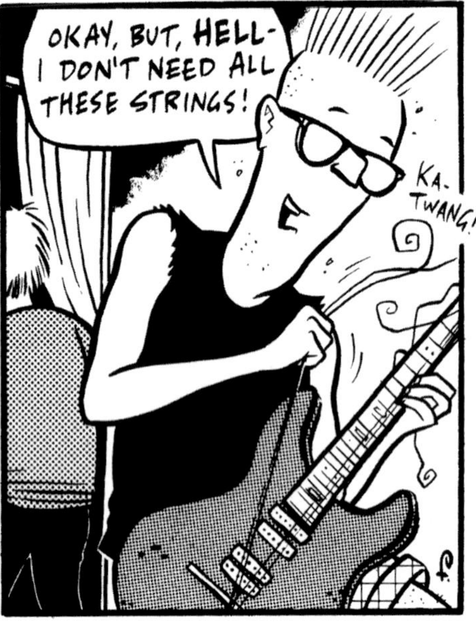
OKAY, BUT, HELL-I DON'T NEED ALL THESE STRINGS!
KA-TWANG!

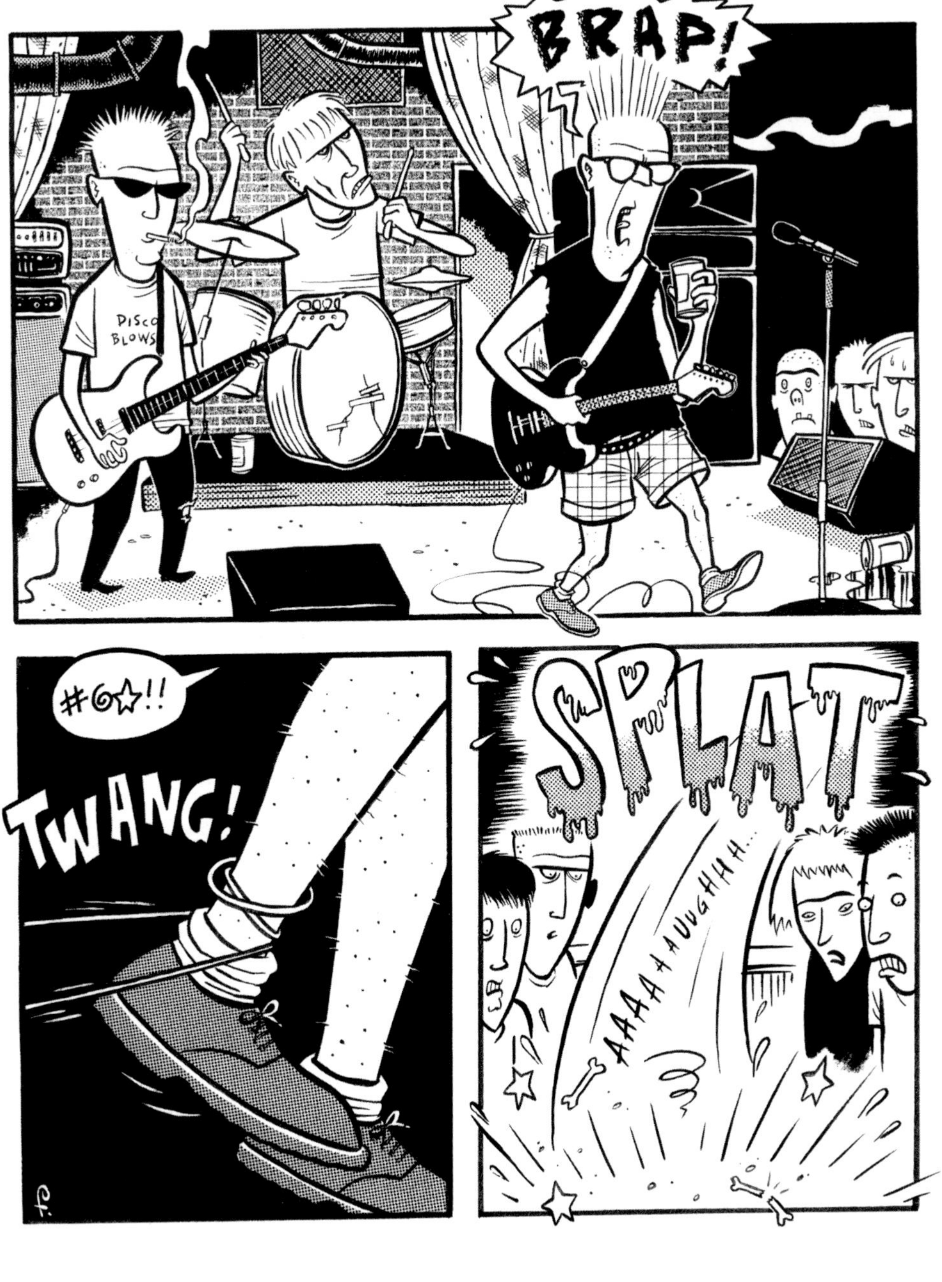

BRAP!
DISCO BLOWS

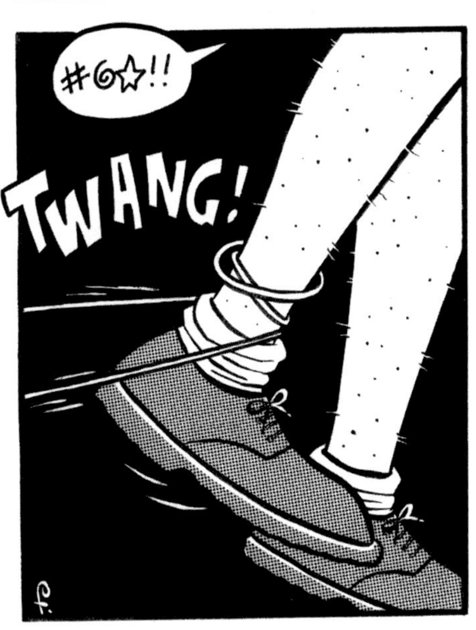
#@☆!!
TWANG!

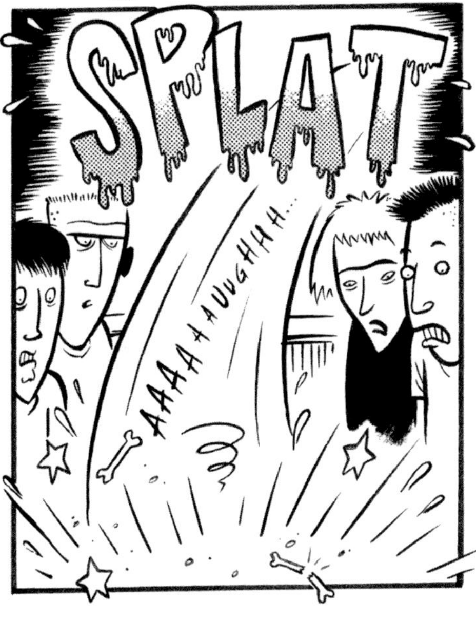
SPLAT
AAAAAAUUGHHH...

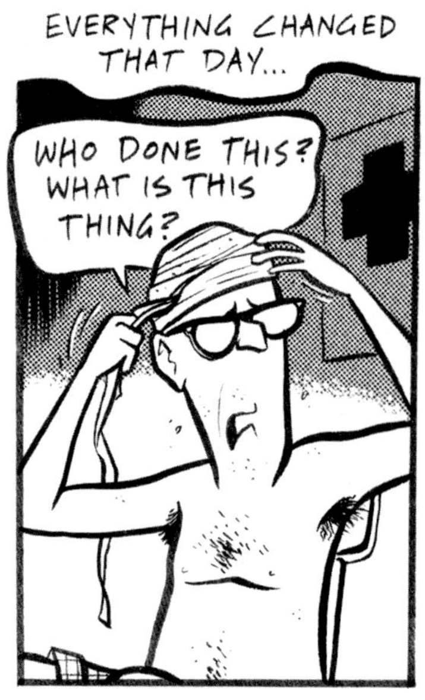
EVERYTHING CHANGED THAT DAY...
WHO DONE THIS? WHAT IS THIS THING?

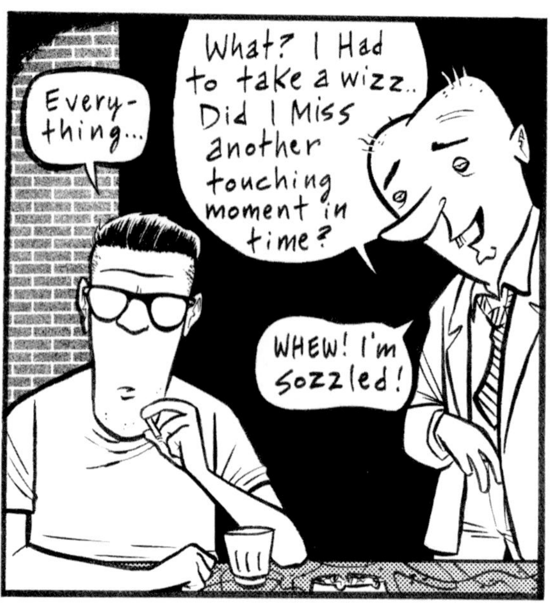
Every-thing...
What? I Had to take a wizz.. Did I Miss another touching moment in time?
WHEW! I'm sozzled!

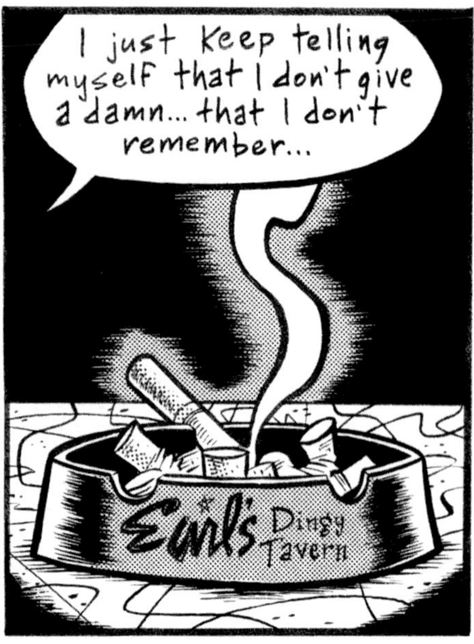
I just keep telling myself that I don't give a damn... that I don't remember...
Earl's Dingy Tavern

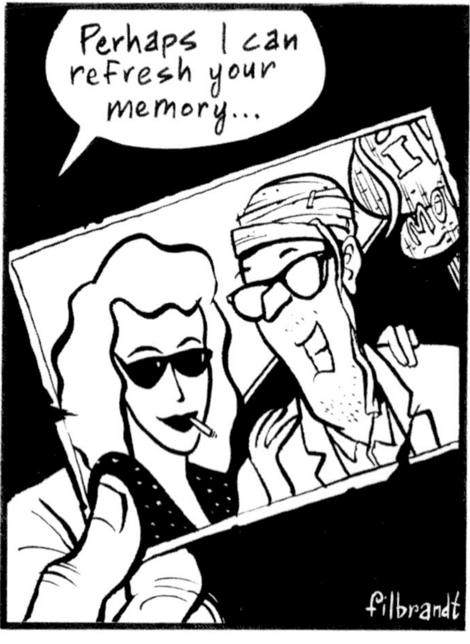
Perhaps I can refresh your memory...
filbrandt

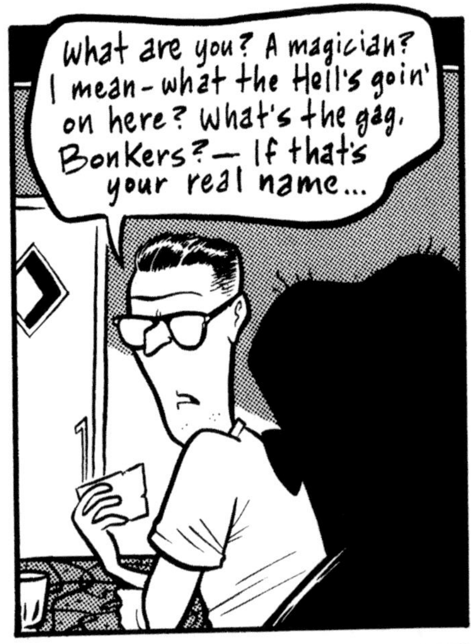
What are you? A magician? I mean-what the Hell's goin' on here? What's the gag, Bonkers?— If that's your real name...

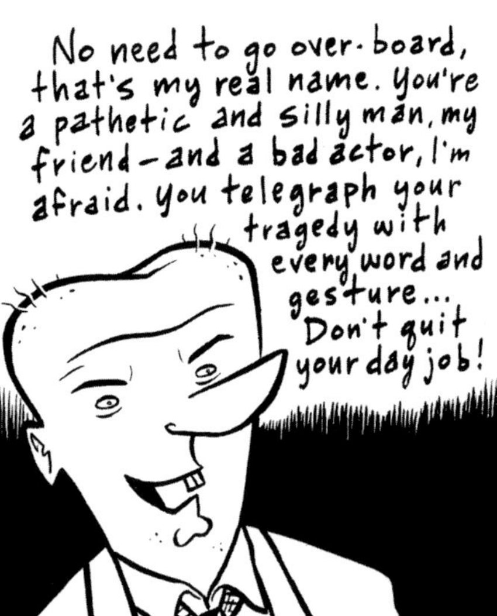
No need to go over-board, that's my real name. You're a pathetic and silly man, my friend-and a bad actor, I'm afraid. You telegraph your tragedy with every word and gesture... Don't quit your day job!
F.

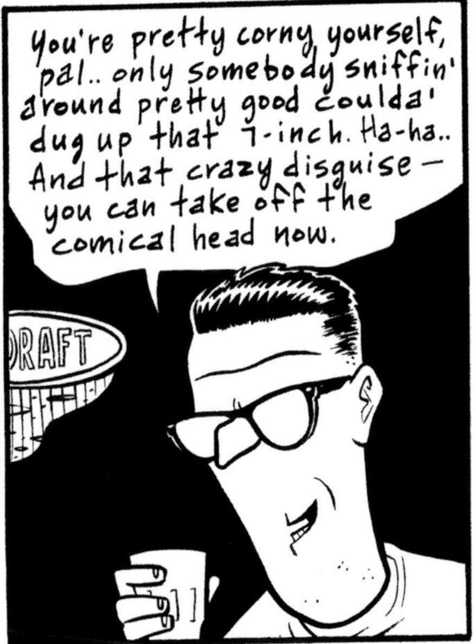
You're pretty corny yourself, pal.. only somebody sniffin' around pretty good coulda' dug up that 7-inch. Ha-ha.. And that crazy disguise— you can take off the comical head now.
DRAFT

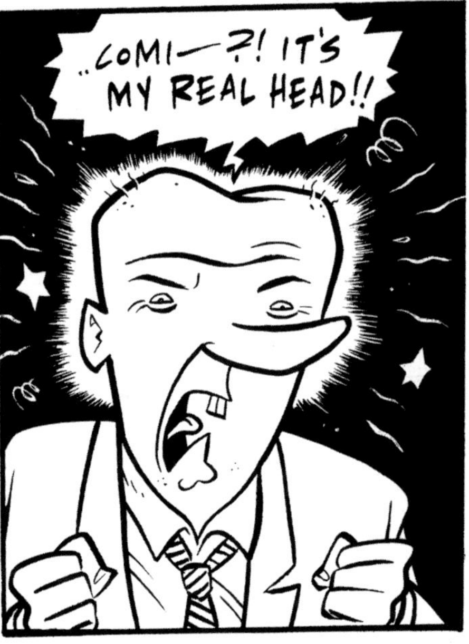
..COMI—?! IT'S MY REAL HEAD!!

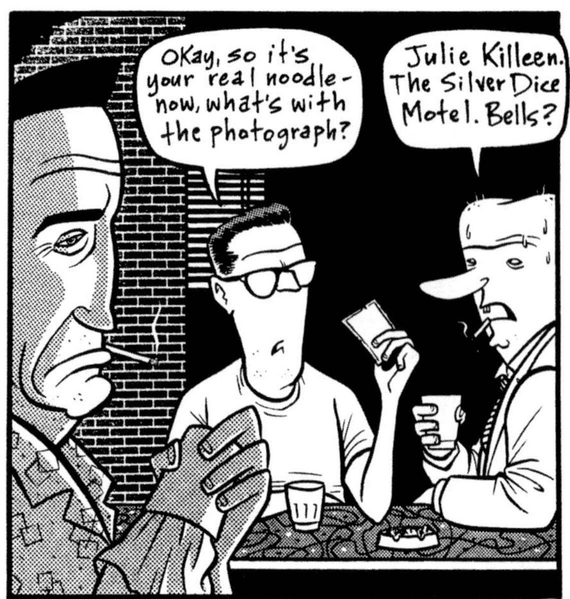
OKay, so it's your real noodle - now, what's with the photograph?
Julie Killeen. The Silver Dice Motel. Bells?

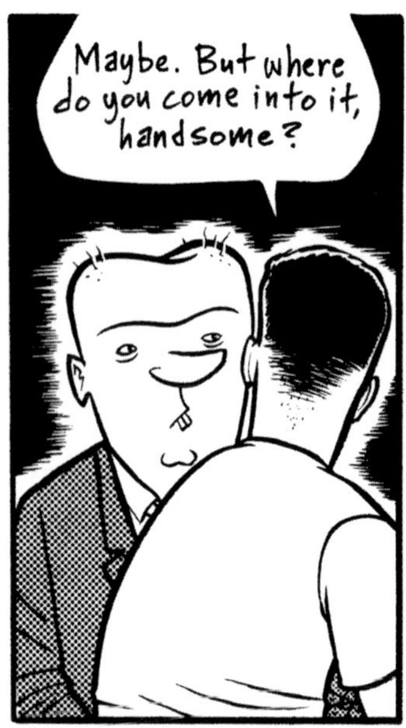
Maybe. But where do you come into it, handsome?

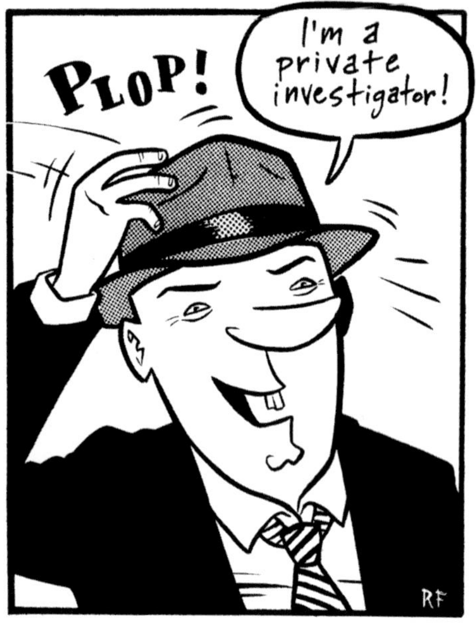
PLOP!
I'm a private investigator!
RF

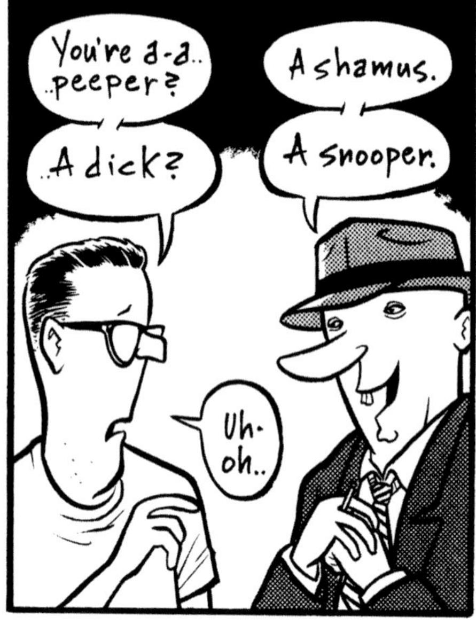
You're a-a.. ..peeper?
..A dick?
A shamus.
A snooper.
Uh. oh..

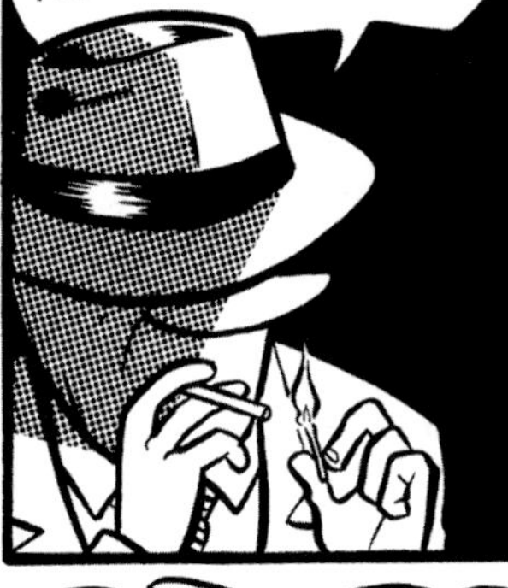
That's right, I'm working for Julie Killeen... you'll find out why in a minute, but getting back to the photo, she told me all about it...

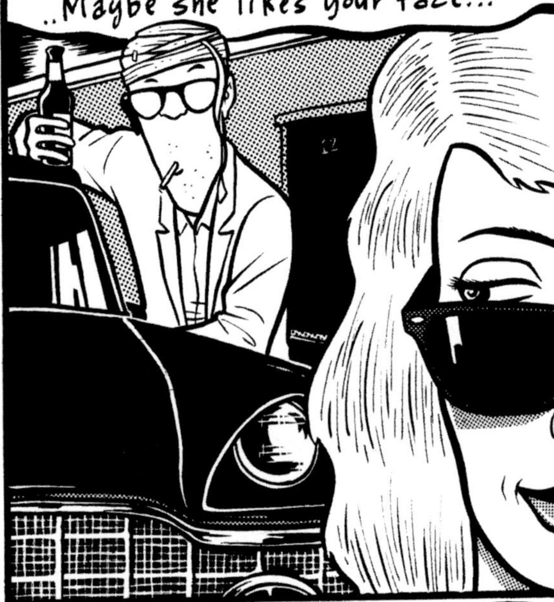
The day you met: in the motel parking lot. She likes the bandage. ..Maybe she likes your face...

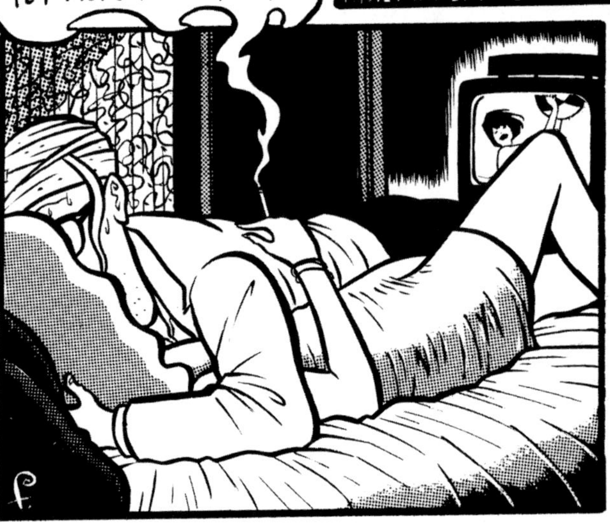
You like a whole lot more than that.

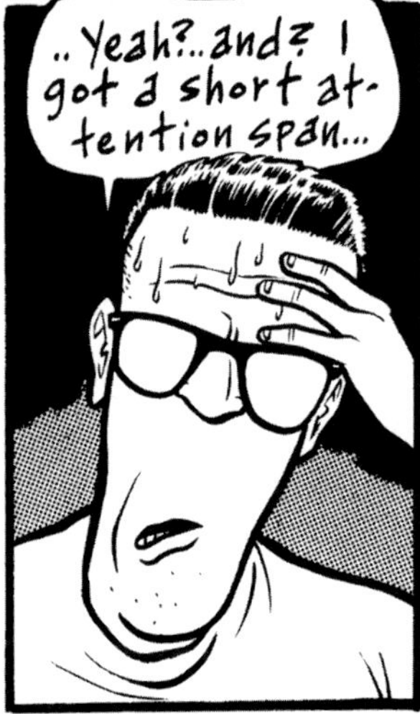
..Yeah?..and? I got a short attention span...

..You spend a few days together, they turn into a few weeks. She buys you a hat in New Orleans...

She's saved you. Saved you from something, maybe yourself. But it's all wrong.

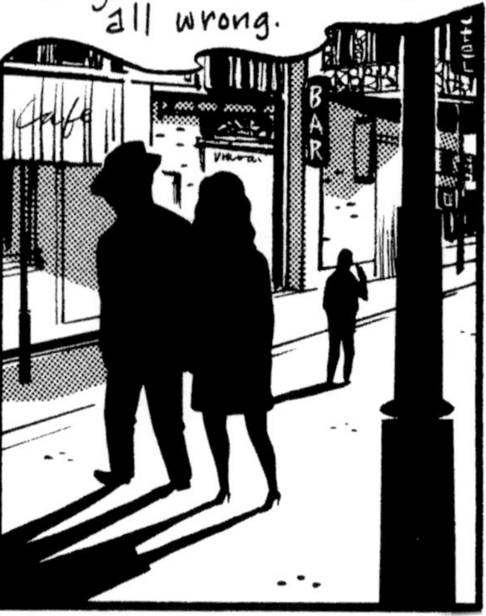

It's like saving a drowning man - they want to be saved so bad, they pull you under...

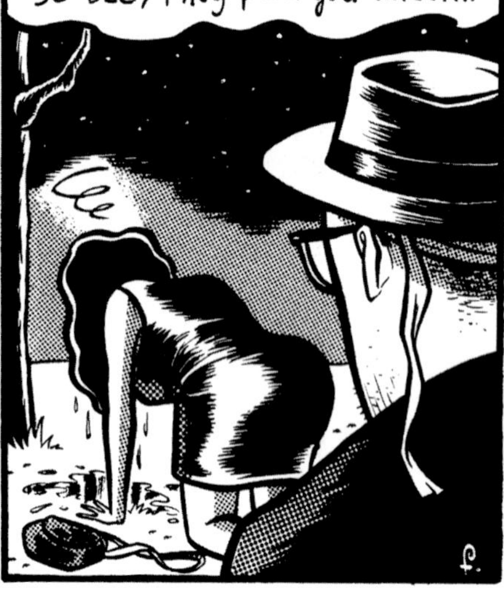

So somewhere in Vegas she takes a powder, leaving you with a wrinkled suit and a whiskey-stained marriage certificate.

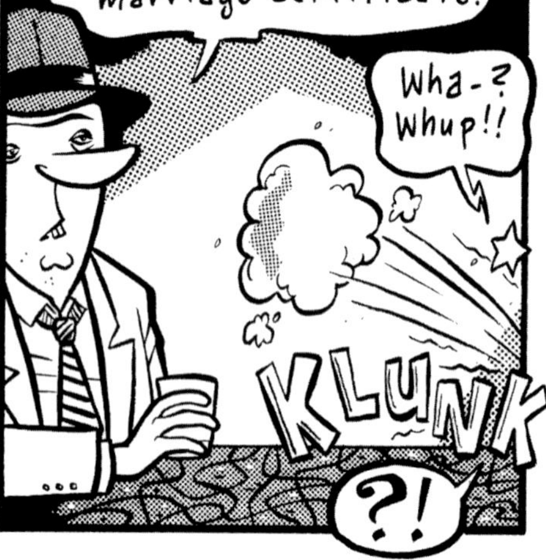

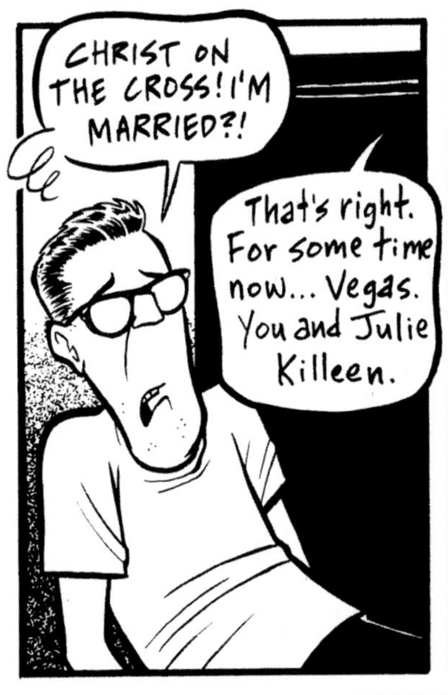
CHRIST ON THE CROSS! I'M MARRIED?!
That's right. For some time now... Vegas. You and Julie Killeen.

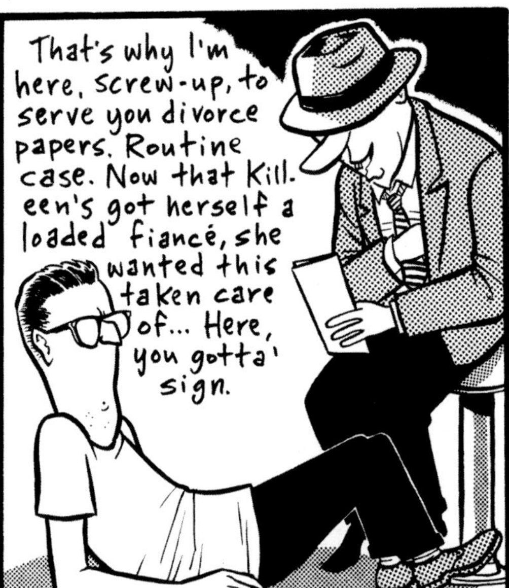
That's why I'm here, screw-up, to serve you divorce papers. Routine case. Now that Killeen's got herself a loaded fiancé, she wanted this taken care of... Here, you gotta' sign.

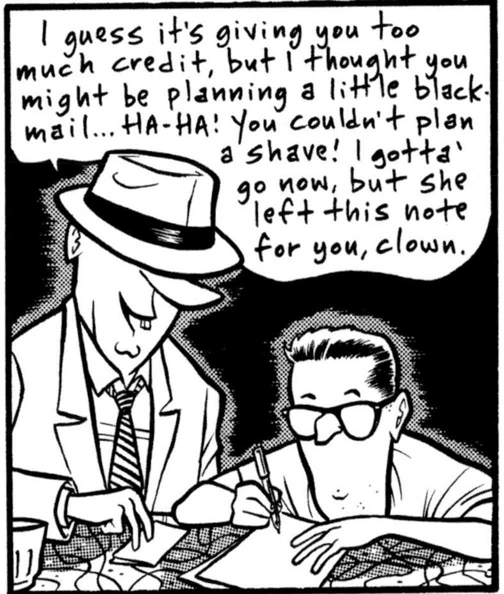
I guess it's giving you too much credit, but I thought you might be planning a little black-mail... HA-HA! You couldn't plan a shave! I gotta' go now, but she left this note for you, clown.

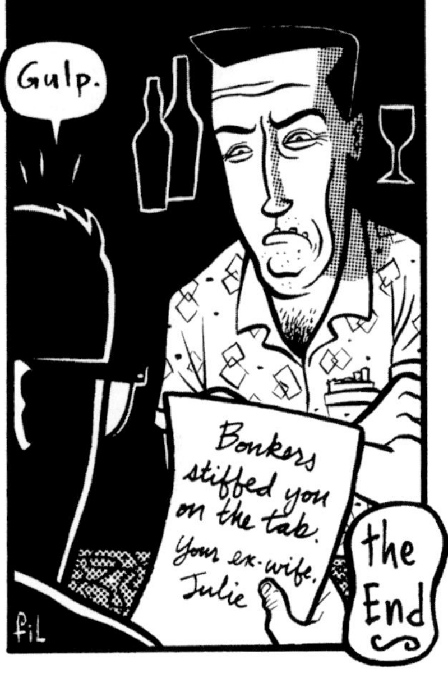
Gulp.
Bonkers stiffed you on the tab. Your ex-wife, Julie
the End
fiL

WOMBAT by R. FILBRANDT

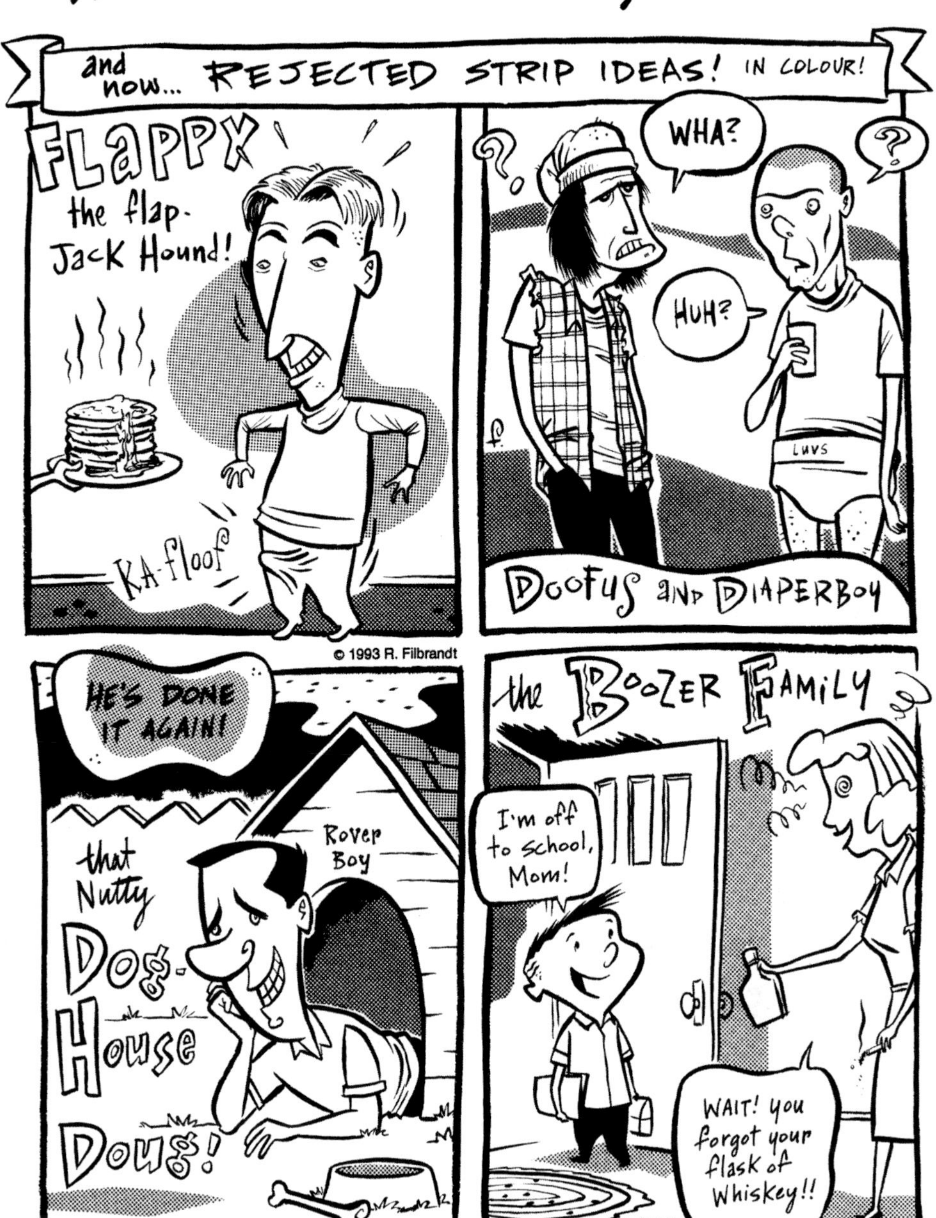

WOMBAT, DAD. "Swing Low, Sweet Cadillac"

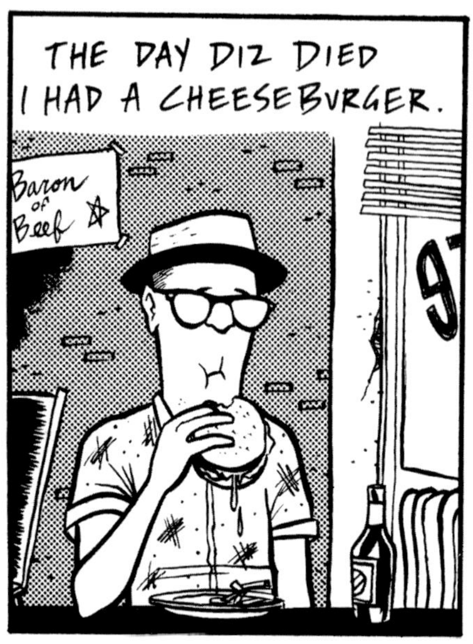

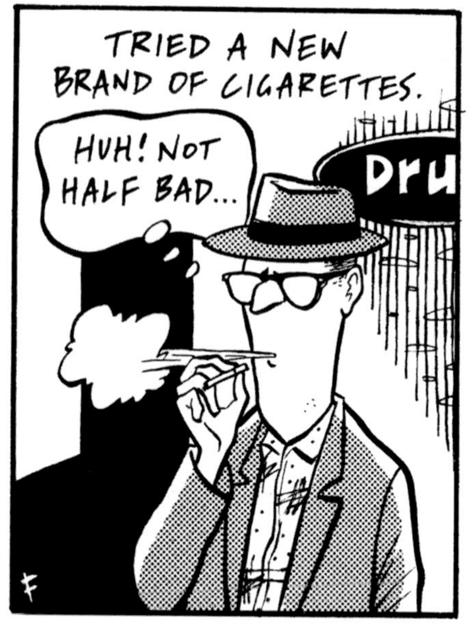

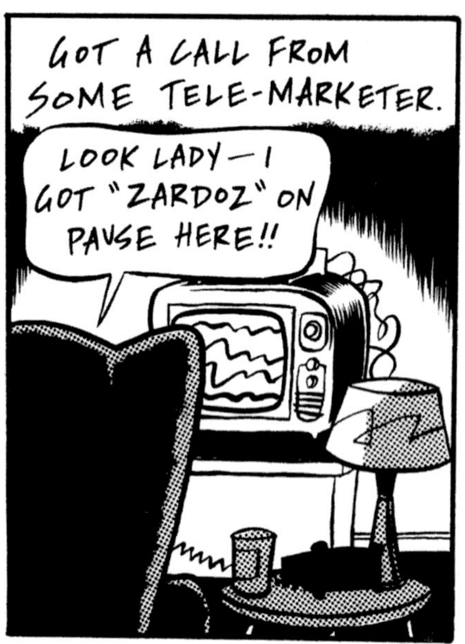

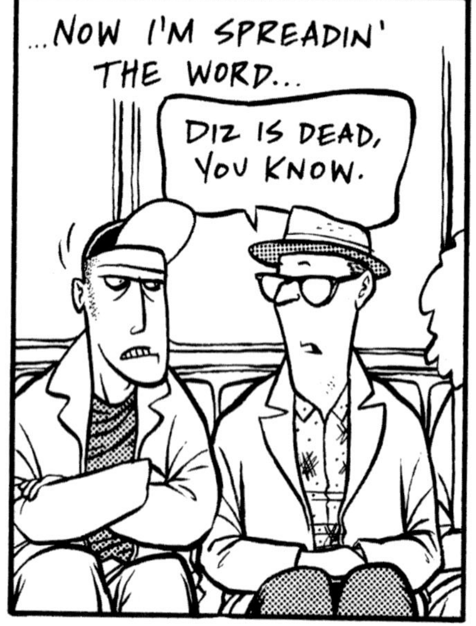

WOMBAT — FILBRANDT

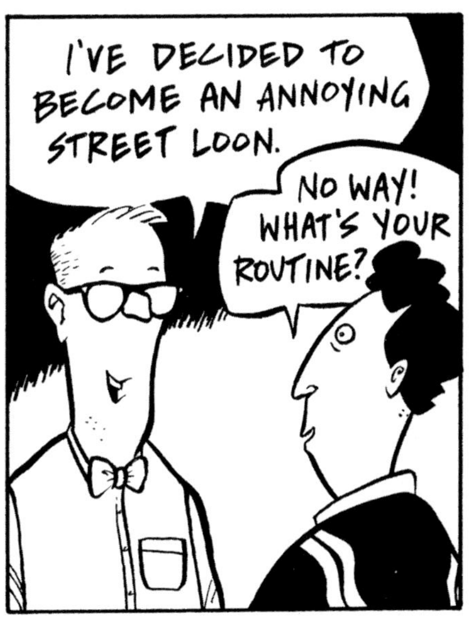

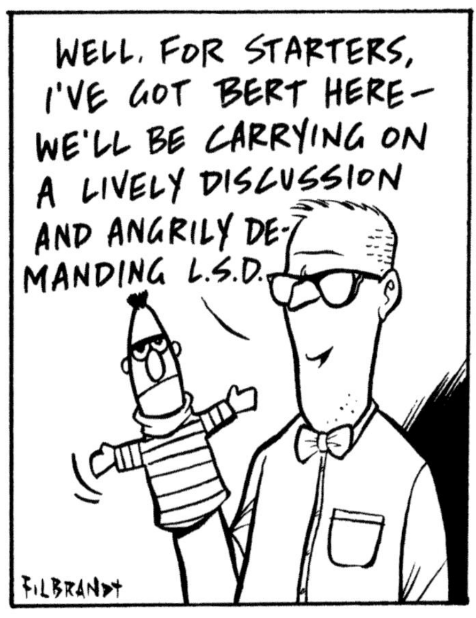

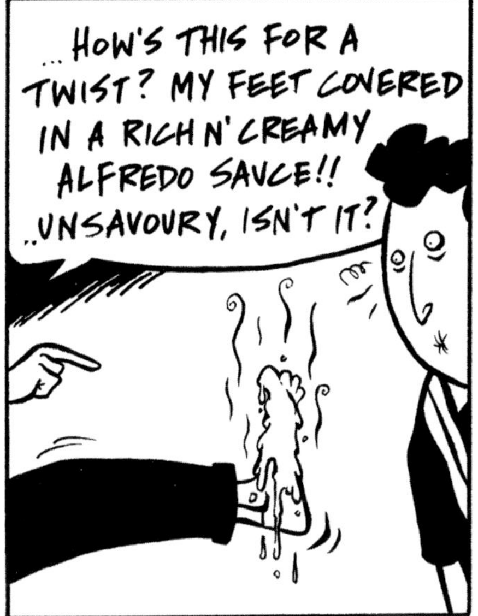

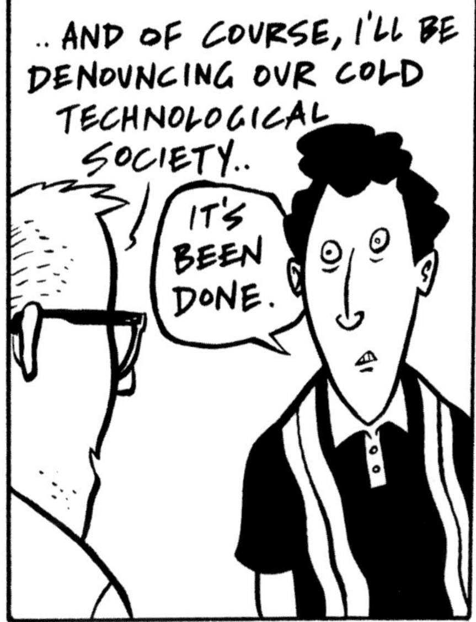

WOMBAT

BY R. FILBRANDT

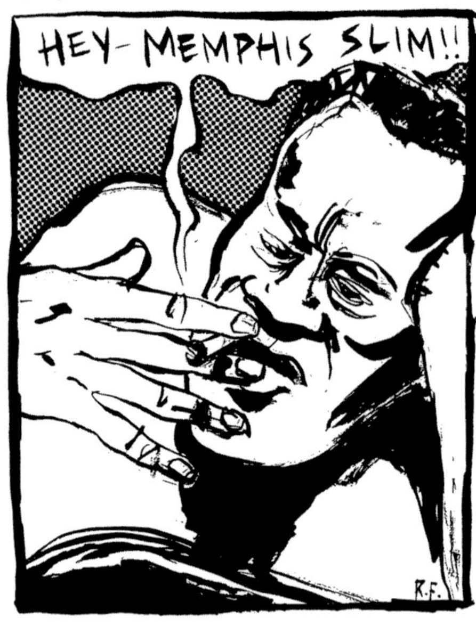

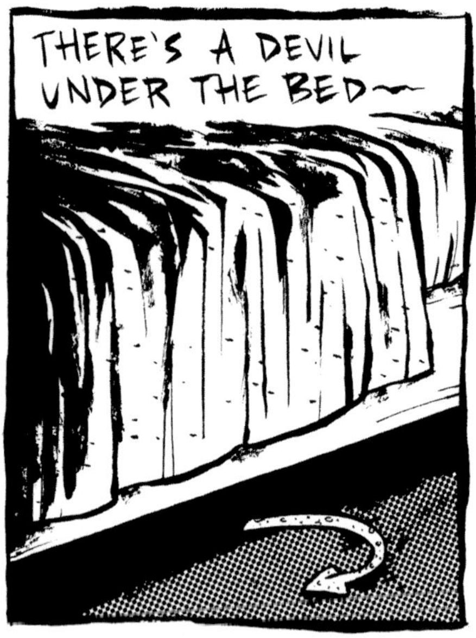

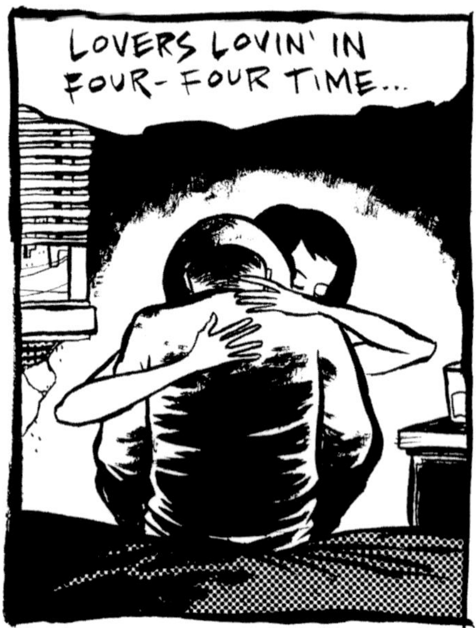

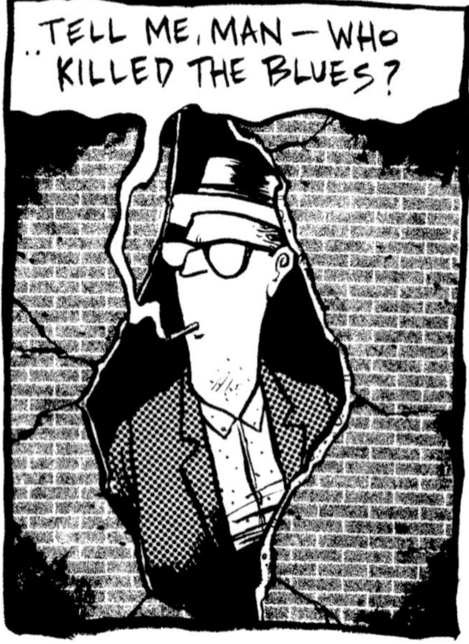

WomBat

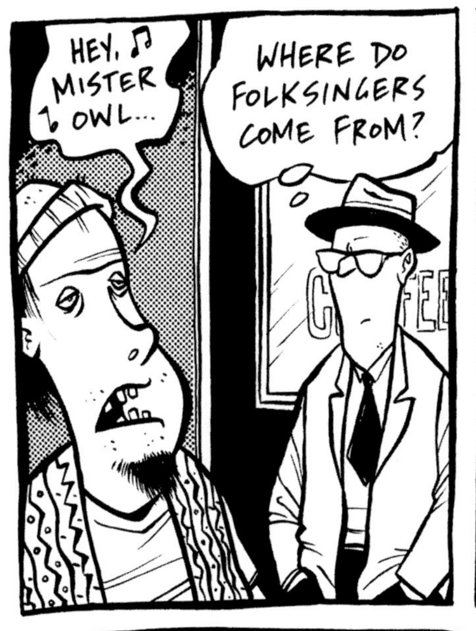
HEY, MISTER OWL...
WHERE DO FOLKSINGERS COME FROM?

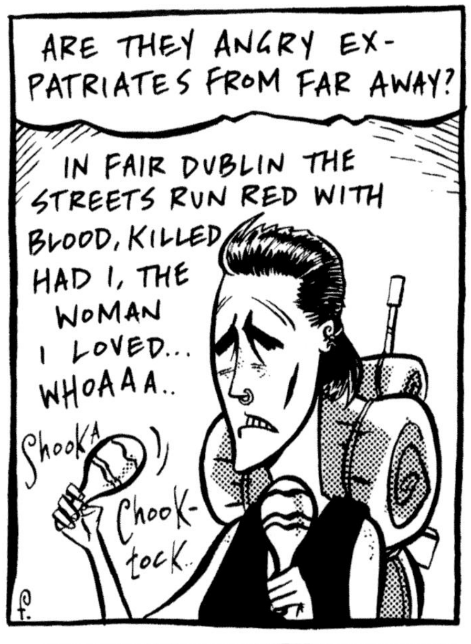
ARE THEY ANGRY EX-PATRIATES FROM FAR AWAY?
IN FAIR DUBLIN THE STREETS RUN RED WITH BLOOD, KILLED HAD I, THE WOMAN I LOVED... WHOAAA..
Shooka
Chook-tock..

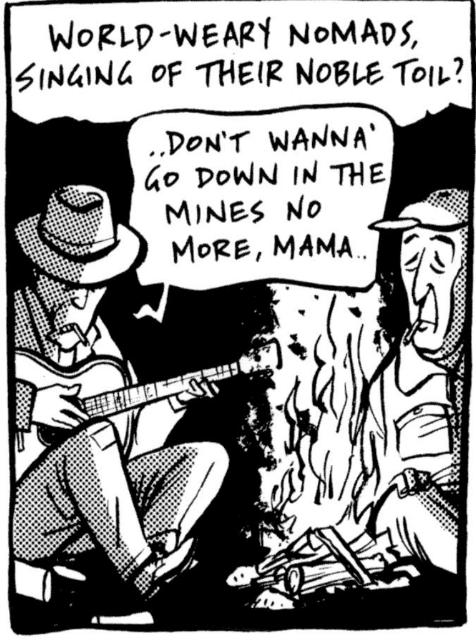
WORLD-WEARY NOMADS, SINGING OF THEIR NOBLE TOIL?
..DON'T WANNA' GO DOWN IN THE MINES NO MORE, MAMA..

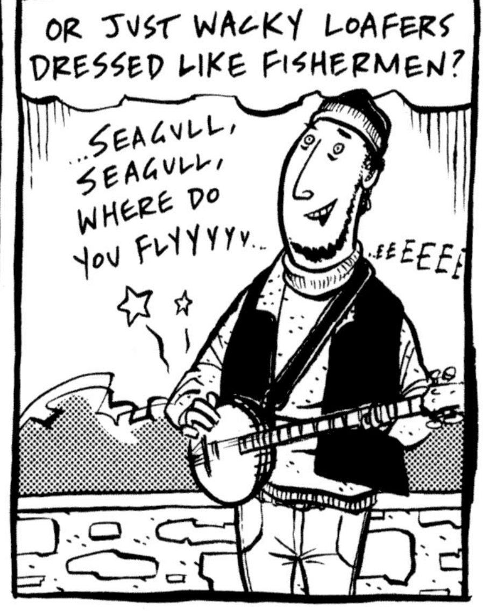
OR JUST WACKY LOAFERS DRESSED LIKE FISHERMEN?
...SEAGULL, SEAGULL, WHERE DO YOU FLYYYYV...
..EEEEE

WOMBAT... "SHIV TROUBLE"

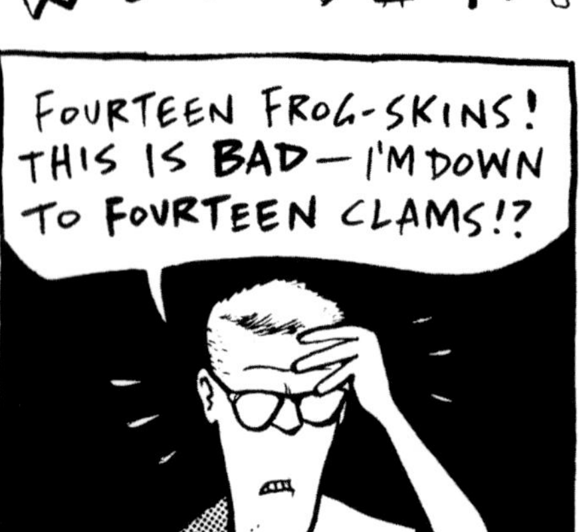

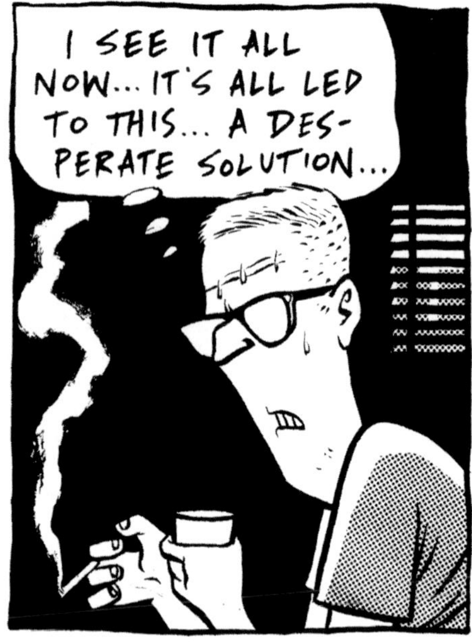

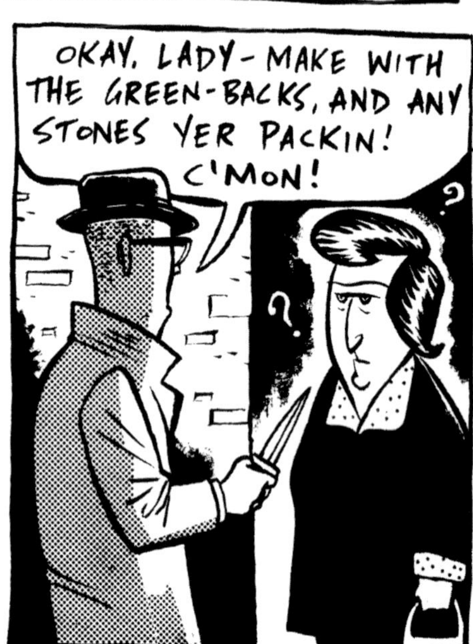

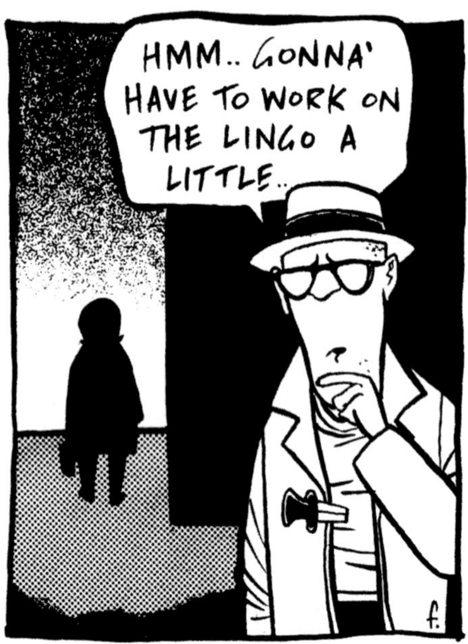

the man who would be WOMBAT

FILBRANDY

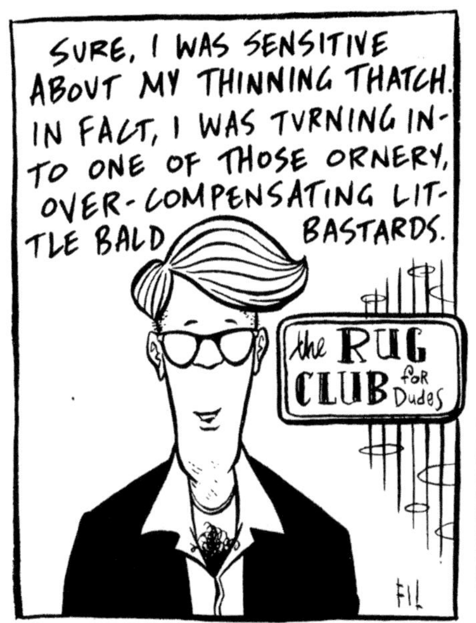

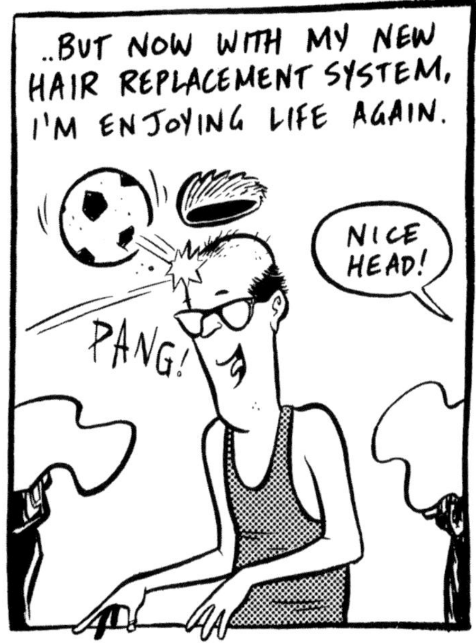

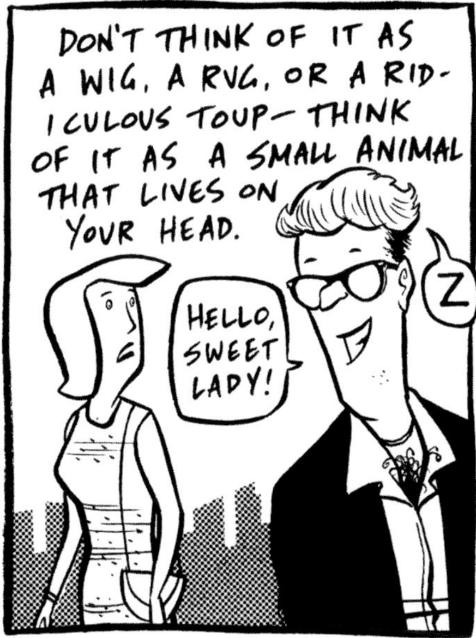

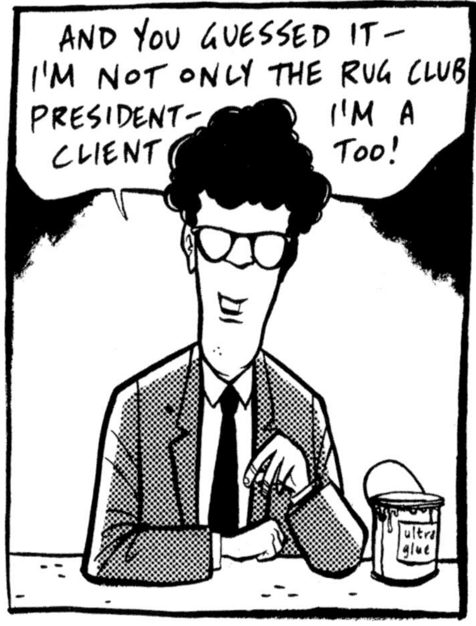

WOMBAT

R. EILBRANDT

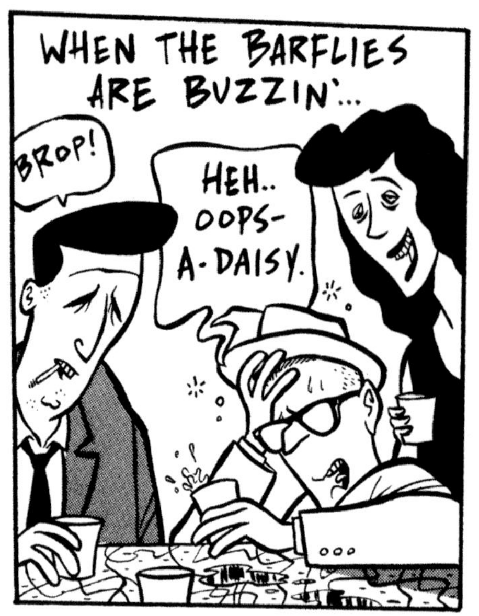

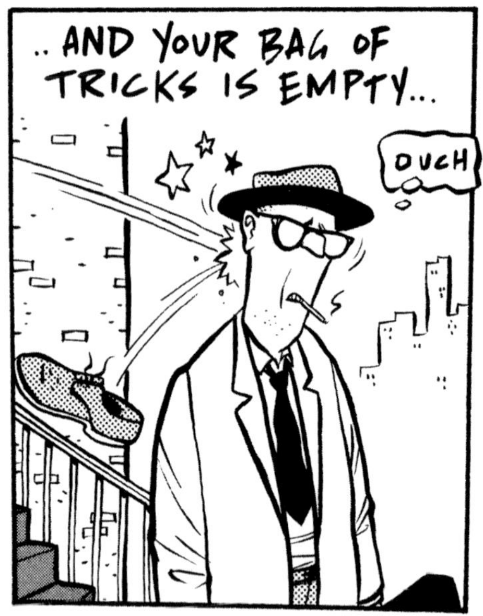

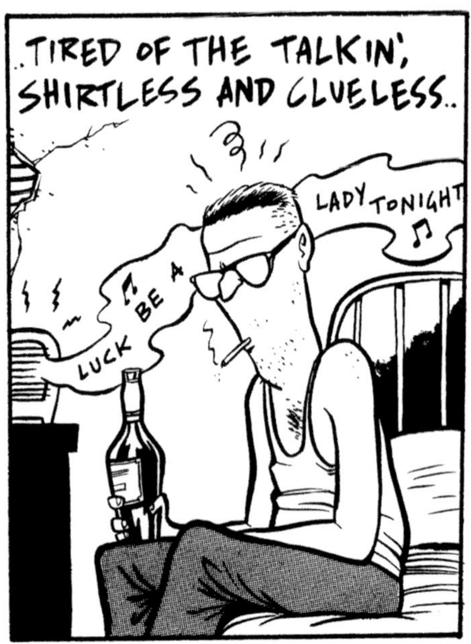

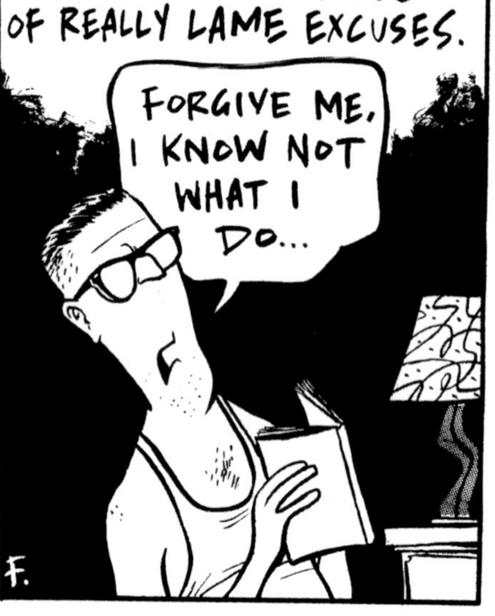

the WOMBAT JUNGLE by FILBRANDT '94

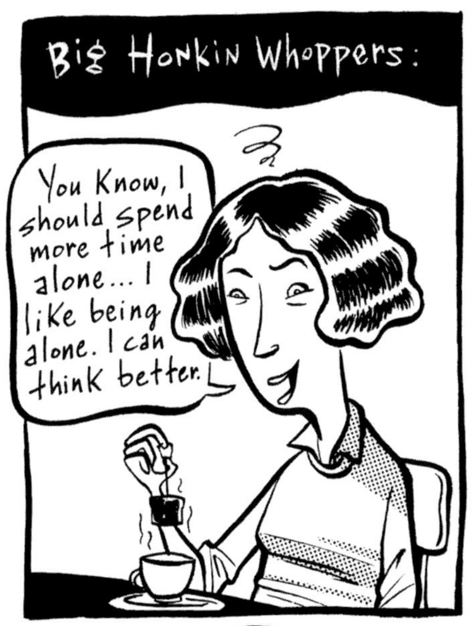

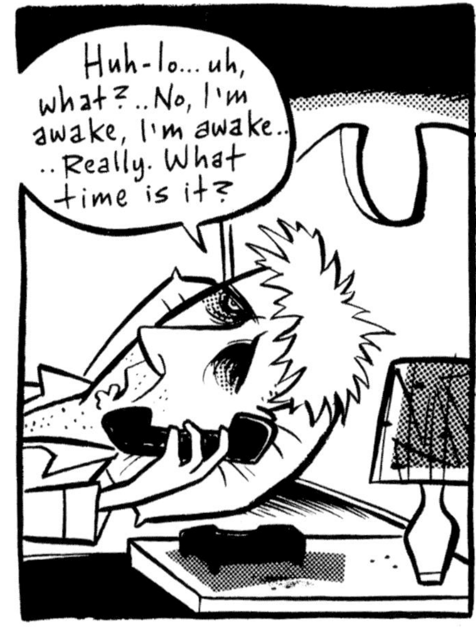

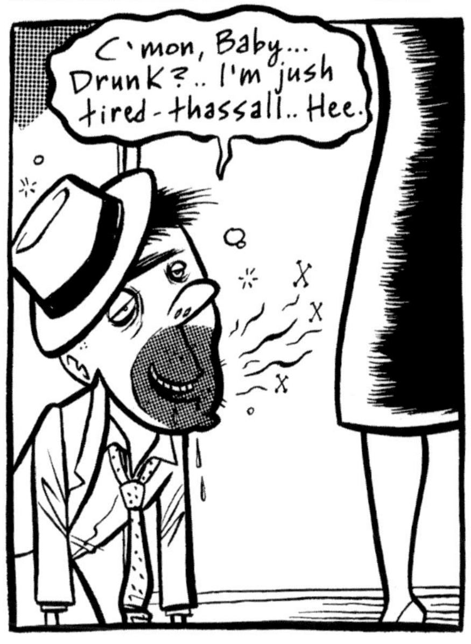

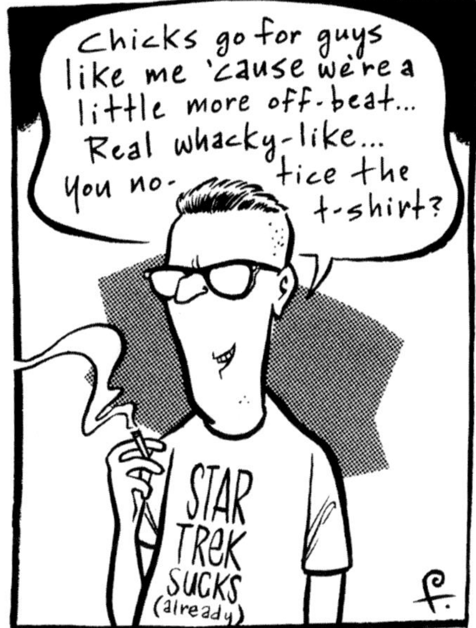

WOMBAT (a Hallmark Presentation)

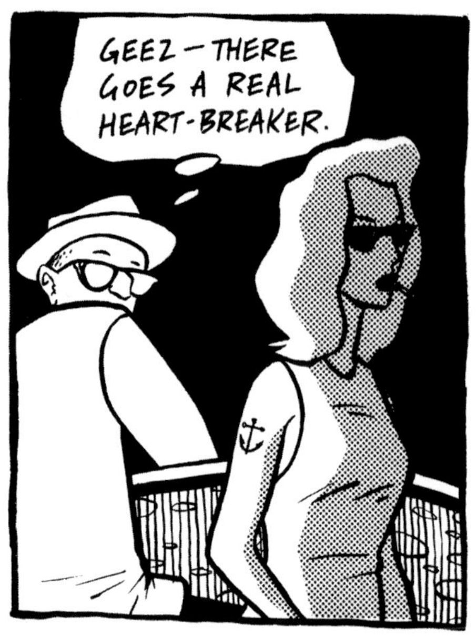

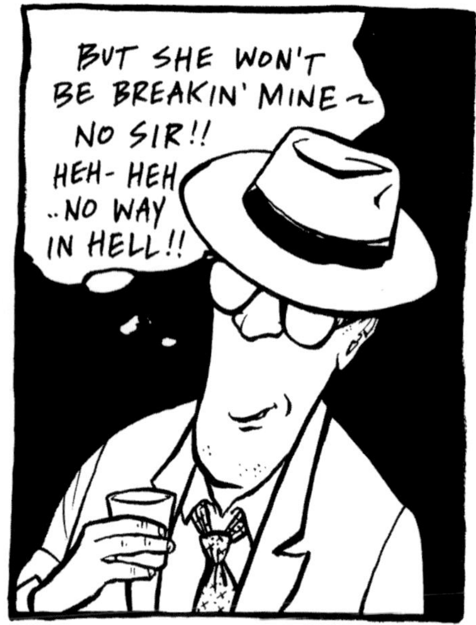

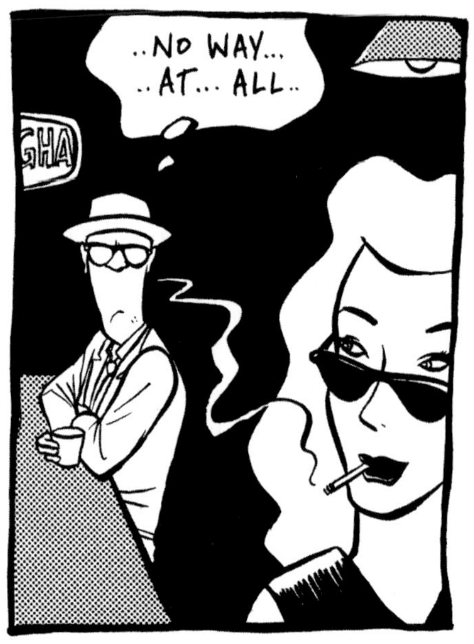

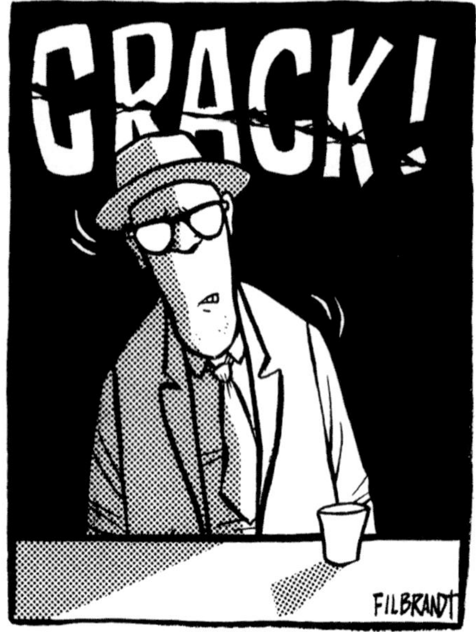

WOMBAT ~ "WE HAD JOY, WE HAD FUN, WE HAD SEASONS IN THE SUN..."

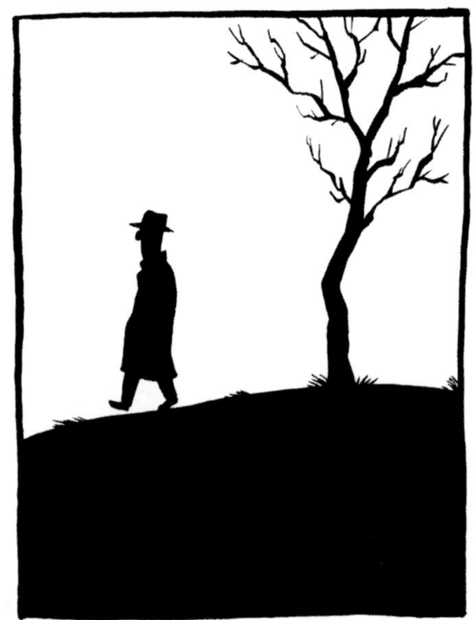

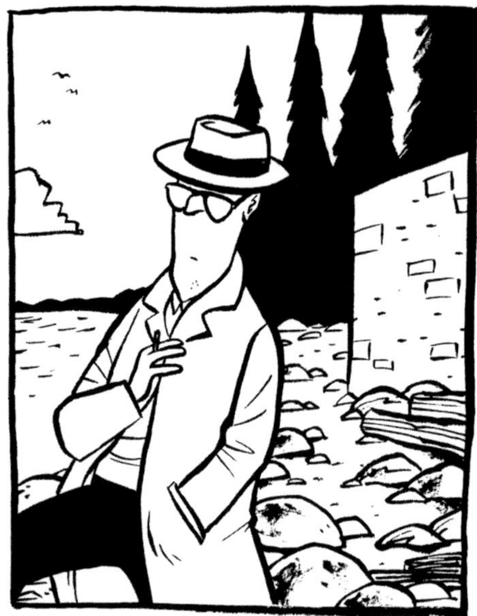

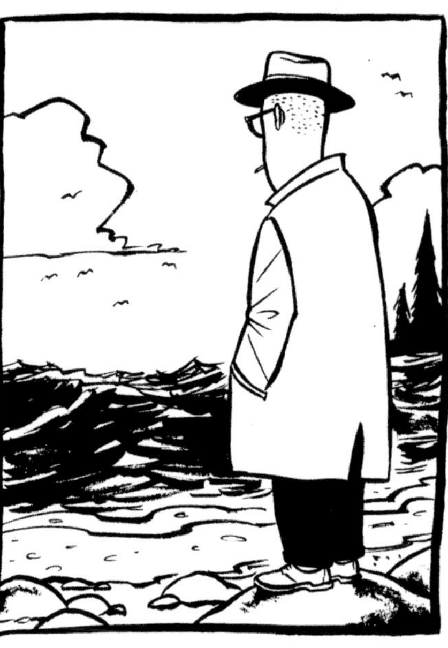

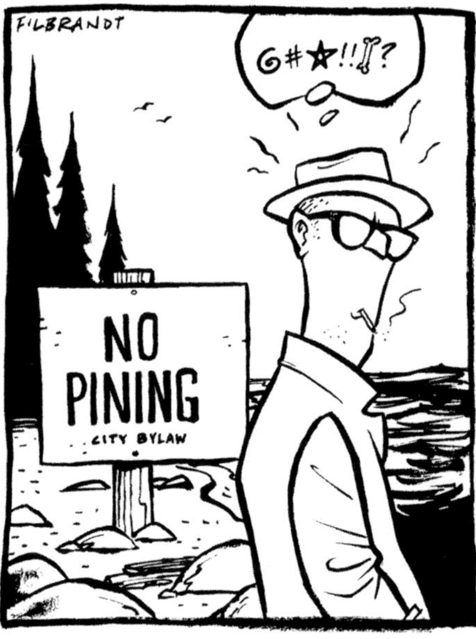

THE WOMBAT JUNGLE ©1994 R. FILBRANDT

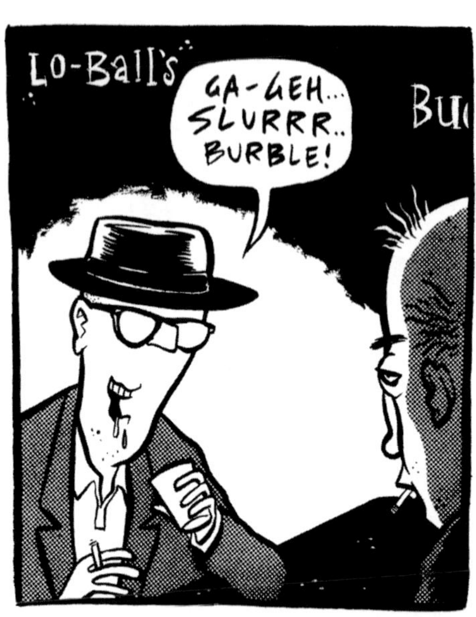

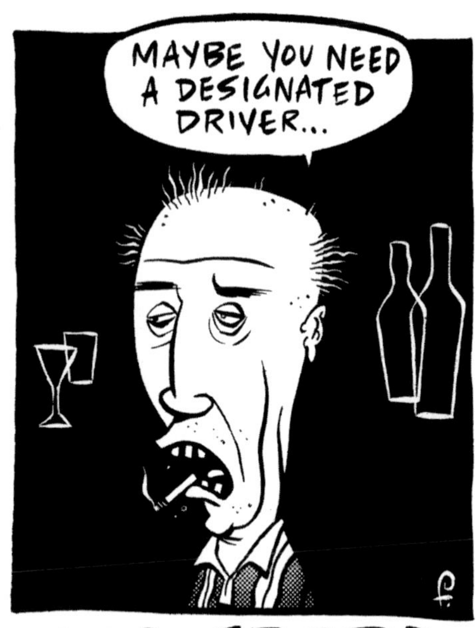

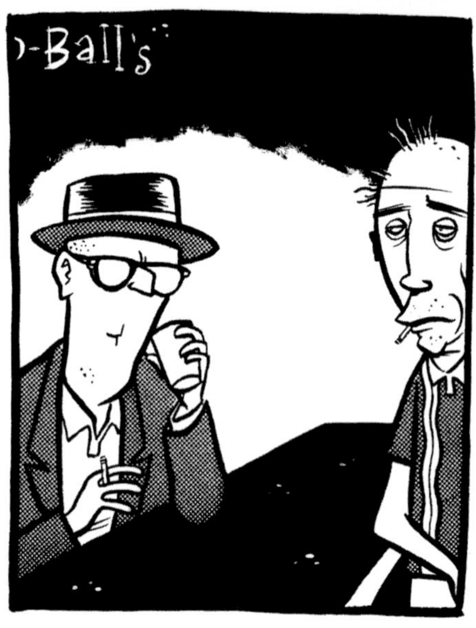

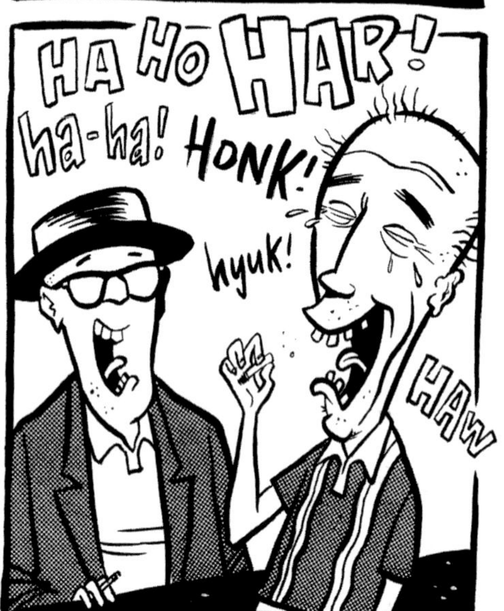

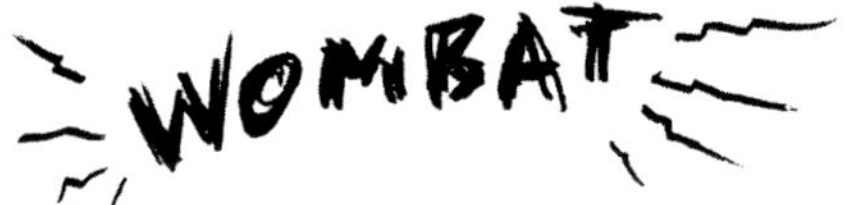
WOMBAT

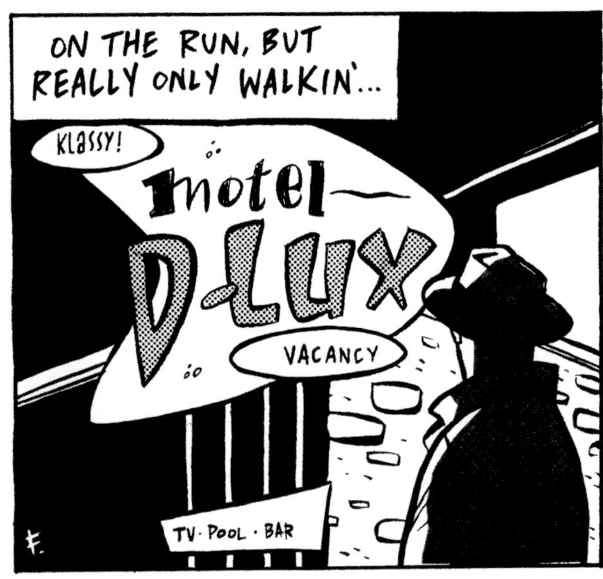
ON THE RUN, BUT REALLY ONLY WALKIN'...
KLASSY!
motel
D-LUX
VACANCY
TV · POOL · BAR

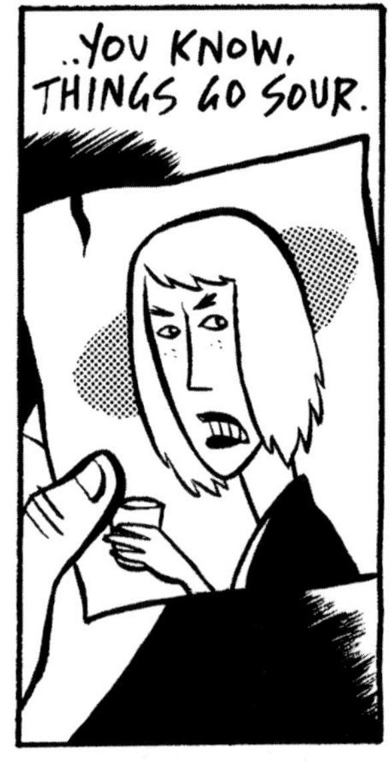
..YOU KNOW, THINGS GO SOUR.

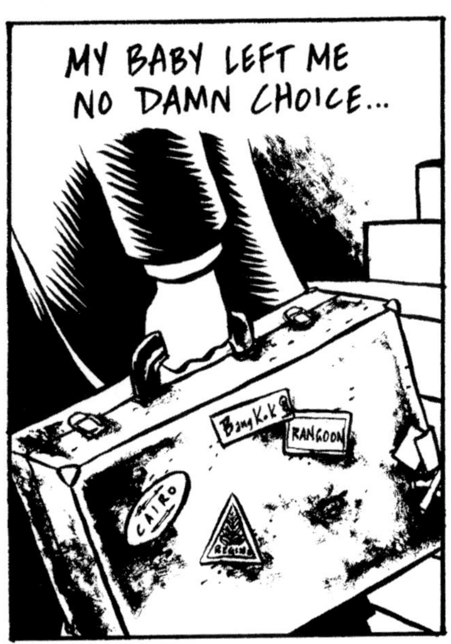
MY BABY LEFT ME NO DAMN CHOICE...
RANGOON
CAIRO

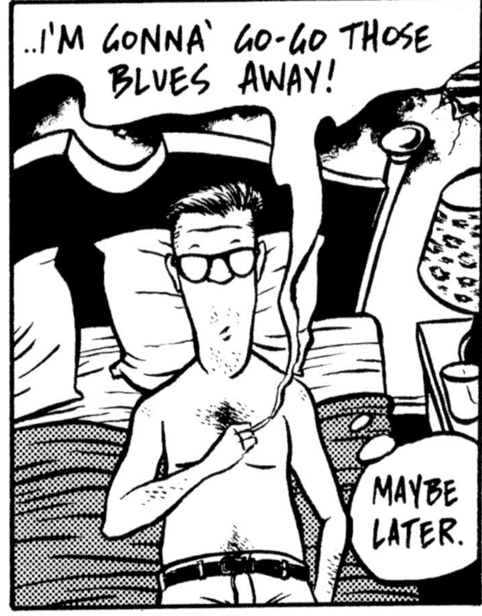
..I'M GONNA' GO-GO THOSE BLUES AWAY!
MAYBE LATER.

WoMBAT a la blue

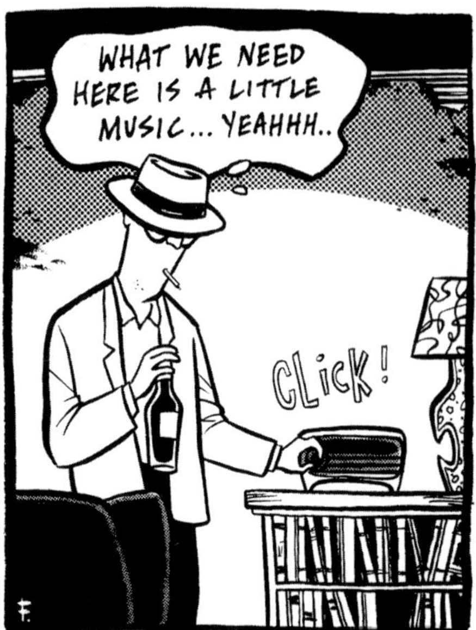

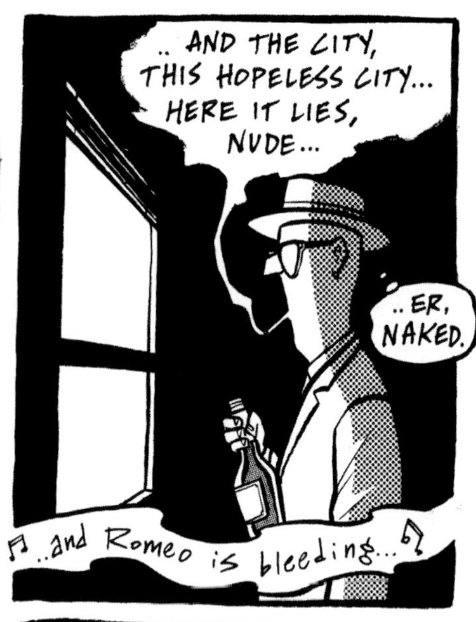

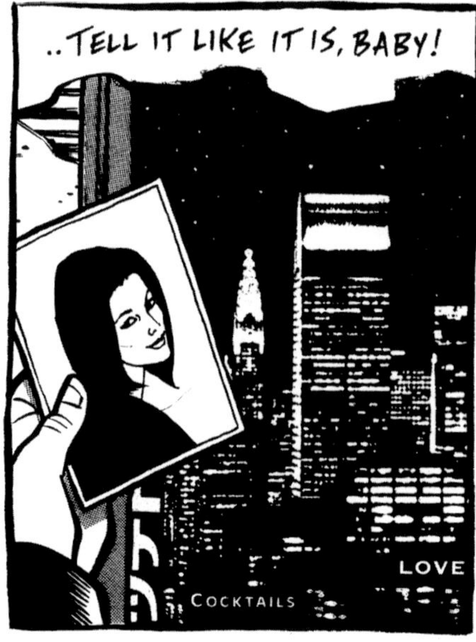

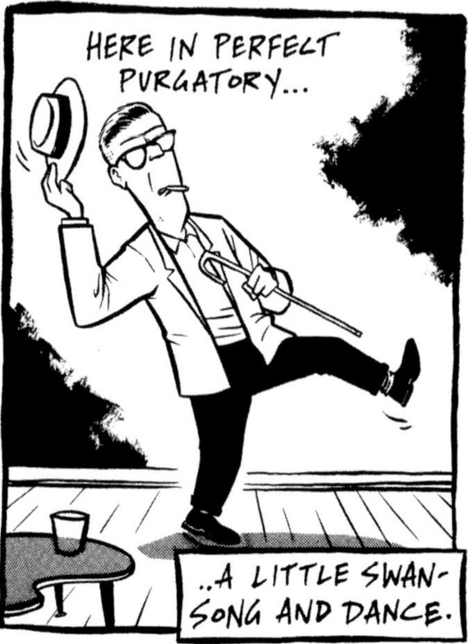

FILBRANDT by WOMBAT

PROBABLY

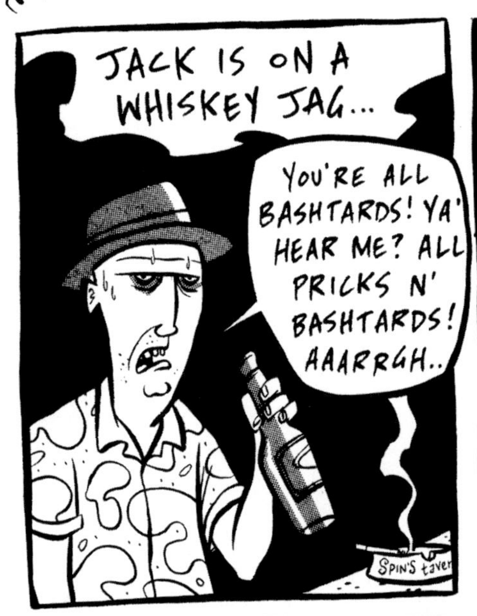

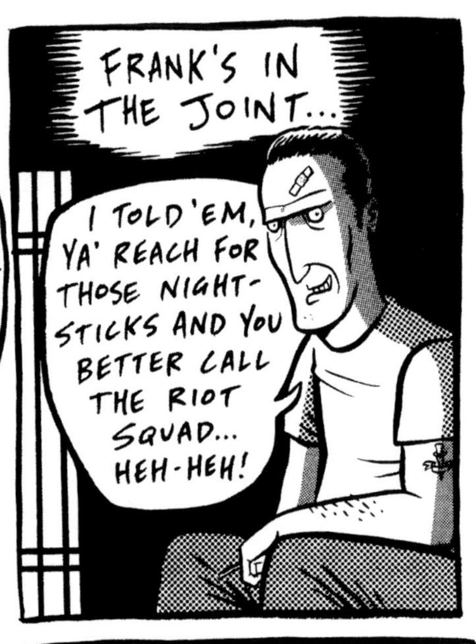

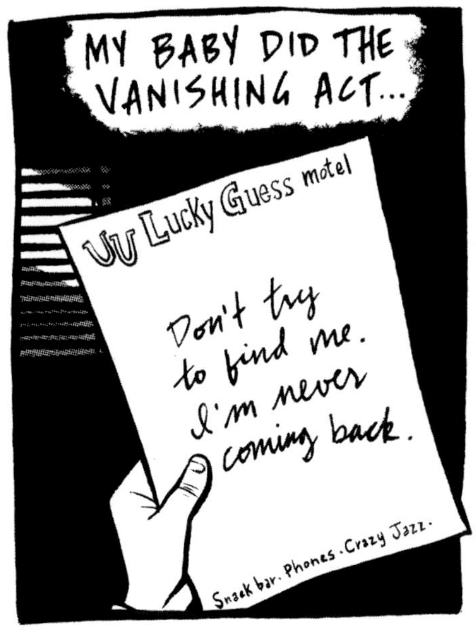

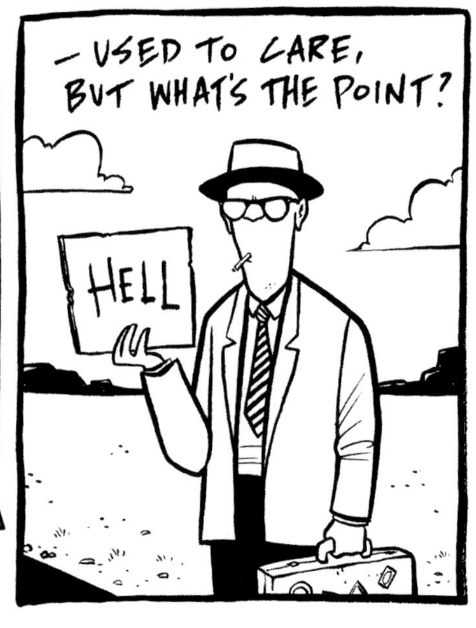